Published by Head Publishing

Copyright © John Nicholson 2019

John Nicholson has asserted his right under the Copyright,
Designs and Patents Act 1988
to be identified as the author of this work.

Edition edit by Robert Marcum

Cover Design by: Dawn Rossiter

Portions of the section "The Gambling Truth" originally appeared in my
book, We Ate All the Pies 2nd ed. (Head Publishing, 2018)

Printed by CMP UK Ltd

ISBN 978-0-9933817-9-9

http://www.johnnicholsonwriter.com

Can We Have Our Football Back?

Can We Have Our Football Back?

JOHN NICHOLSON

HEAD PUBLISHING

ACKNOWLEDGMENTS

Thanks as always go to my patient editor and grammar guru, Robert. A more straight up, rock 'n' roll guy, you couldn't wish to have on your team.

A big hug to Janet for her eagle eyes and her honest, much appreciated support.

A big gin and tonic to Dawn for pulling the whole thing together, designing the cover, laying out the text and for doing a million other things that are totally beyond me, all in between being such a great artist. Where have those 39 years gone?

A big doff of my metaphorical cap to everyone who generously gave me their time, either to chat, or to write about the issues in this book, all of whom were inspirational and thought-provoking. So cheers to Mark Chapman, Chris Sutton, Steve Crossman, Niall Sloane, Simon Jordan, Paddy Barclay, Clive Tyldesley, Jonathan Northcroft, Anthony Vickers, John Roder, Pat Murphy, Pat Nevin and John Murray. Splendid, talented people, one and all.

And then there are all the people who spoke to me on condition of remaining anonymous, for various reasons, usually to do with keeping their jobs! Thank you so much for your often jaw-dropping insights into the world of modern football. You helped cast so much light into the darkness. I massively appreciate all your considerable time and effort.

And finally, I'd like to send love out to all at Football365 both past and present. To Steve and Howard for giving me my break all those years ago, but especially to Sarah who remains the rock upon which so much of my writing is founded.

"Re-examine all that you have been told...dismiss that which insults your soul"

WALT WHITMAN (1819-1982)

CHAPTER	Page

Before We Kick Off   1

Prologue: The Future's In The Past   11

Part One: Myths and Truths   19

The Popularity Myth   21

The Quality and Competitive Myth   39

The History Myth   53

The Cup Isn't Devalued Myth   57

The Money Myth   63

The Generosity Myth   81

The Ecological Truth   91

The Gambling Truth   103

The Abusive Truth   113

The Just Being Here Truth   119

Part Two: A New Country   123

Talking About A Revolution   125

...And In The End   151

Part Three: Maybe I'm A Dreamer, But I'm Not The Only One   155

Other Voices   157

Part Four: The Manifesto   195

BEFORE WE KICK OFF

It can't go on like this, can it? I know it, you know it, we all know it. Things have got to change. We need a revolution and I'm going to explain why and how. Are you up for that? Good. Is everybody in? The ceremony is about to begin.

Hello, it's me. The one that writes for the massively popular website Football365.com. The only football writer that occasionally uses the lyrics of the Doors and Rush to cast light onto football darkness. Aye, him.

Over the best part of the 20 years that I've been paid to write about football, slowly but surely I've come to realise something quite profound about the Premier League and modern football in general. About the nature of it, about the politics of it, about the effect of it on the society it is played in, about the effect of it on the planet it is played on.

The Premier League as we know it is almost done. Its race is run. It is about to reach the finishing line, its jelly legs wobbling like an exhausted marathon runner. There is an excess of supply and not enough demand for football on TV broadcast behind a paywall. Even though coverage of the Premier League has never been better. Even though programmes are in depth, comprehensive and entertaining. Even though it is a great product.

But the trouble is, football isn't a product.

Here's the thing. The whole of what we know modern top-flight football to be, which is essentially a massive amoral money pit into which billions have been thrown in wages and transfer fees, is all predicated on one thing: paywall TV. It is the foundation stone at the core of the footballing skyscraper. And here's another thing. Though we do not realise it deeply or profoundly enough much of the time, you know who the brickies are who laid that stone? No, not Sky, not BT Sport, not the Premier League, not the FA. No. It was you and it was me. We laid those foundations with our money.

So as we take this excursion into the exceptionally weird heart of darkness that is the Premier League, never forget this fact. Never forget that this is an empire we created. Never forget that we keep it going. Never forget that we can come together to stop it. Any. Time. We. Want.

Because we are the people. And we have the power. And y'know what? The time has come to use it.

I must state something from the start which may not be obvious across the coming pages. It is this: I really love football. I wouldn't have spent so many hours writing this book if it wasn't the case. I'm writing this in 2019, in the week of the Liverpool vs Barcelona and the Ajax vs Spurs games. If you want examples of the deep joy and thrills that football can deliver, they are two of the best.

My passion goes back to the late 1960s. As a small boy I was mad about football no matter at what level it was played. I even made up a huge elaborate story (mother called it a lie) that I was so good at football in 4th year of Fairfield Juniors, Stockton, that the school had bought me some white boots which had to be kept in a special cupboard at school but that my parents were never to come and watch me play as it would be bad luck. I maintained this for months as my career as a high-scoring striker flourished, until being finally exposed as living in a dream world and being admonished for such a lengthy deceit. I was unconvinced by the error of my ways, feeling that to invent an alternative reality was something so creative that a child should be praised to the heavens for doing it.

So football was at the beating heart of my childhood until about 1977 when, aged 16, other urges and distractions took me totally away from the game. Indeed, I thought I'd grown out of it. But it was only a temporary divorce and I was reunited in the autumn of 1984 when I realised that I really missed it. Once again, the beautiful ebb and flow of the rhythms of a season became a comforting and all-consuming story; a constant in the flux of life. A skeleton upon which to hang the flesh of existence. That season Everton won the league just as they had done in 1969, my first season of consciously following football and keeping league table ladders on my bedroom wall. It all felt like a full circle and I was back home. For me, like rock 'n' roll, football is a sort of family. Always there: a constant. Often annoying and frustrating. Sometimes making you weep in despair. Sometimes making you happy. But mostly just there.

And ever since, it has been giving shape and form to my life. Throughout, my primary input of football media has been via the radio - on Radio 2 on medium wave, back in the day and from the early 1990s Radio 5 and then 5live, occasionally peppered with local radio broadcasts. And it's through radio that I developed a love, not just of the kicky kicky, but of talking about the kicky kicky and of the psychology, philosophy, history, community and culture behind it. In fact, for a long time now, I've enjoyed discussions about football every bit as much, if not a lot more than the actual football. Where football fits into other human lives seems to me to be at least as interesting as the football itself.

As we take this journey into radical football thinking, don't forget this lifelong commitment. At times over my football writing career (I say career, which is to totally overstate it, but it'll do for now) I have been accused of not even liking the game when I have refused to buy into or have resisted the latest fad or fashion that has preoccupied the more impressionable, even when it was being passed off as a new orthodoxy, when in reality it was little but the latest temporary trend, like zigzag stitching on loon pants in the 1970s, huge shoulder pads in 1980s jackets or Joe Bloggs jeans in the 1990s. And it is this long-lived passion from which much of the river of thinking you are about to swim in derives.

As I approach age 60 nervously, glimpsing it only out of the corner of my eye, the way one does a wild animal in a woodland, I am not someone who thinks being older innately deserves respect or that it confers wisdom per se. Lord knows there are enough stupid old people to disprove that notion. What it does give you though, at least in theory, is a wider screen on which to view how now fits into history. You see where we've been, where we are and where we might be going with a greater clarity than is possible if you're 16 or 26. This is important when we live in an era for which there is only ever The Now. I would also speculate that we oldies are less impressionable and prone to fashions than when younger. But there are downsides. As you get older you can get stuck in your ways, be overly and inaccurately nostalgic, you can stop understanding how the world is for much younger people and become joylessly cynical.

I hope I'm none of these things, and I try to be vigilant about not being old mannish by implicitly understanding that change is innate, that nothing stays the same, and that other people come to issues from different perspectives because they have entered life through a different door. Nothing is absolute. We come and go in a blink of the cosmic eye. All we have is right here, right now. So let's make it as good as possible for the many, not the few, that's my feeling. This book isn't just one long moan-up about now not being then; it is based in deeper, heavier notions such as morality, mental health, community, ecology and non-materialism. There are jokes too, mind. Honest.

OK, so what's this book about? Simple.

That one word: Revolution.

No, not the sort of revolution that involves growing a beard, running through the streets with burning torches while shooting guns. Not the sort that involves making molotov cocktails or having to wear a beret. I look terrible in a beret and believe unless you're a French existentialist, all men do, though I've always found the beret-wearing woman to be enticing and possibly dangerous.

This book aims to deconstruct the orthodoxies that have been imposed upon us all, as though they are innate and natural. It is an overturning of all the cultural assumptions and political drivers behind the game at the highest level.

Put simply, I want to see an end to the Premier League, an end to the financial model upon which it is founded, an end to paywall TV, and an end to astronomical wages, transfer fees and agents fees. Replacing the current, fetid, bloated corpse of top flight football will be a more sane, less abusive, more competitive, more fun and less venal competition which puts fans at the centre of everything and works for the advantage of everyone, not just a tiny elite.

This will be a revolution that replaces extremism with modest reason. And in order to light the fires of this revolution, as I will explain, all we need to do is perform one small act, en masse.

But before we get started, all I ask you to do is give the keys to your old consciousness to my cosmic valet parkers. They'll keep them safe for you, but you may find that once you've read this book you won't need them anymore.

My aim with these 80,000+ words is to entertain, amuse and inform, but far, far more than those things, it is to inspire thought. No change can happen without change in how we think about, in this case, football, but in general about life; about who and how we are, what we feel and believe, how we go about living our lives.

So, just as so often is the case in my Football365.com writings, there isn't a lot of football in this book. There's no discussion of players or referees nor of teams or tactics. In short, if you don't like football, I hope this will still stimulate and entertain you. It is as much about philosophy, politics and spirituality as sport. But if you do like football, then don't worry, the whole book is predicated on it one way or another.

Some of my thinking may seem very odd. I ask you not to dismiss it because of its unfamiliarity or because you've not heard anyone talk about football in this way before. I am a self-confessed overthinker. It is what I do. And it's a useful sort of madness to have if you're a writer. But this book isn't an exercise in dogma, or branded politics, it doesn't provide solutions to everything, and perforce it is a simplification of things that would need detailed negotiation and planning over time. What I'm about here is concepts, notions and ideas. As I say, I'm about revolutionary thinking in order to make football more fun, less abusive, more competitive and more unpredictable. And I want to consider how football fits and works in society and what it can do to help improve the future prospects of our planet.

That's all pretty ambitious, I know, but that's where I'm coming from when I say I have a massive problem with the Premier League. With the culture, politics and economics. It is a very troubling construct. I've long felt it has aggrandised itself on the back of our passion for football and made itself and its participants rich in the process by imposing an economic orthodoxy that benefits them but not us. The consequent toxins it has released into the cultural, political, ecological and sporting water table of English football have poisoned us all in many and varied ways. On an economic, sporting and even moral level it has become a destructive, pernicious force in our lives and on the planet too, but because we love football per se, we have been co-opted into the league's peculiar worldview to such a degree that its masterminds now pretend they did all this in our name. They didn't. We let it happen. But it was never about us, it was always about them.

For the last few years in particular, the volume of negativity towards the English top-flight money binge has gotten louder and louder and is now at Hawkwind levels. If you don't know how loud that is, Hawkwind would play at such a volume and at such a specific pitch that they could destabilize the sanity of their audiences in what was little more than a sonic attack. Indeed, they had a song titled "Sonic Attack" and it absolutely was. It made you feel dizzy, then sick and sometimes even pass out. Their strobes famously induced epileptic episodes, and while the Premier League doesn't do that, it certainly often makes many of us feel quite nauseous.

More typically I think it is best described as a general feeling that something is wrong; an existential despair at how things are that many of us share. A third-eye sense that regardless of the quality of the football on offer, which can be great, though mostly isn't, that regardless of the game itself, things feel sick, feel askew, feel out of whack with reality. It is often hard to focus on exactly what this malady is, or where it has come from because it's become such a normal aspect to our football lives. There is an empty gnawing void in the pit of our stomachs which we never used to have but now is with us always. A restless worry, a feeling that we are living in a house that is not ours, that we are on our own, lost and with no direction home.

This manifests itself all the time in one way or another, whether it is over ticket prices, transfer fees, wages or advertising sponsors. I've heard and met fans who are very discontented and annoyed by the top-flight game but just don't really know why, can't really put a finger on it, but feel it strongly all the same. I have felt exactly the same way for years and I finally had to find out exactly why.

Right now, there is a palpable shift of mood against sports being available only behind paywalls. The Women's World Cup has been a huge TV success this summer, pulling 11.7 million people in to watch England's semi-final on the BBC. With talk turning to how the women's game is going to develop in the future, many have expressed fear that it will be bought by Sky. Once, this would have been seen as a positive confirmation of success and popularity, but now, the opposite is true. Now, it is seen very much as a negative which will shrivel and shrink the audience, starving the game of interest and enthusiasm, denying the roots of the game the nourishing water of publicity and exposure, whilst simultaneously inducing addiction to its money.

This is perhaps a strange season to write this in that recently both Liverpool and Manchester City have been playing some of the most thrilling, breathtaking football we've seen for many a long year. What can be wrong with a league which features two sides that are so magnificent? However, this book is not a critique of football, the game. Football itself remains remarkably resilient and whatever level you watch it at, still delivers its timeless joys. This book isn't about that. The Premier League loves to conflate our love of football with love of itself. Anything good that happens, it's happy to own, anything bad and like Macavity, it's not there.

For years I've felt a cognitive dissonance about the Premier League - between what I'm told I'm seeing and should feel, and what I am actually seeing and feeling. So I felt it was time to open up my mind and drag this beast out of me once and for all, time to confront the alien infection and deal with it. I wanted to give voice to all these emotions, to identify the roots of problems and find a pathway to some solutions.

What I didn't fully understand as I began this journey was just how many people felt likewise and were asking themselves some of the same questions both inside the game and the media, as well as on the terraces. You are about to read some bonkers stuff, so don't say I didn't warn you. Except it's not bonkers, it's just sensible. But sensible seeming to be bonkers is a very Premier League thing. It is, in fact, a very modern thing in general. We live in a time of extremes passed off as normality, of sense portrayed as nonsense. We have all had the Premier League software uploaded to our synapses, and as a result we react in the way it wants us to react. We have stopped questioning and become accepting.

Throughout the 27 years of its existence it has constantly been hailed - most often by itself - as a huge success, hailed as incredibly popular and as The Best League In the World. I now believe all of this is just propaganda. I believe that it has had a negative impact on the game and on society, a negative effect on all of our lives, a negative effect even on our mental health and sense of contentment. And not least, a negative effect on the earth.

But this is not a dry research book. It is not packed full of facts and figures beyond a few basic illustrations of issues. There are plenty of other people out there who are experts in that sort of thing. You will know them already. The likes of David Conn, Danny Taylor, Daniel Storey (of our F365 parish) and Michael Cox are just four amongst many. I admire people who are across statistics. I like to read them, but I have always worried that facts get in the way of truth, just as much as they can expose lies. I see life as a Pointillist painting like those of Georges-Pierre Seurat; a picture made up of a billion small dots.

While you need to change each dot to change the picture, too much focus on each dot prevents you from seeing how the picture is altering.

So I don't plan to look at too many dots too closely for too long. What I hope to do is put forward some thinking that might help shape and articulate what many feel about the Premier League and suggest ways we can come together to effect serious and profound change.

I come from a long tradition of blue-sky dreamers and struggle to accept anything sold to me as normality. It is just how I'm made. And maybe I am a dreamer, but I'm not the only one. I also firmly feel that any revolution of the mind needs sparking by people who do not think along the usual straight lines and maybe that's why I'm here.

I'm not naïve. I know this sounds like the sort of sensationalist hyperbole a publisher tries to sell a book on. But trust me, it really isn't. Indeed, as I shall explain, it is only the normalisation of the current extreme situation that might even make anything I'm about to say seem in any way radical or crazy. And behind it all, all I want to do is make a better world, a world that is more fair and generous, peaceful and green.

But even so, I guarantee that some of you reading this will think I have lost my hippie mind. All I ask from you, as we embark on this journey into the heart of football darkness, is that you bear in mind that everything we know to be reality is but a construct of billionaires and global corporations; a matrix they built from our money which they sell to us as an immutable, unchangeable reality, every second, of every minute, of every hour, of every day, of every week, of every month, of every year.

The comedian Bill Hicks used to end his show on this theme and while Hicks has more recently been subjected to some much-needed modern day revisionism (the whole Goat Boy thing was never any good) its profound truth still holds true. And it went like this:

"The world is like a ride in an amusement park, and when you choose to go on it you think it's real because that's how powerful our minds are. The ride goes up and down, around and around, it has thrills and chills, and it's very brightly coloured, and it's very loud, and it's fun for a while. Many people have been on the ride a long time, and they begin to wonder, 'Hey, is this real, or is this just a ride?' And other people have remembered, and they come back to us and say, 'Hey, don't worry; don't be afraid, ever, because this is just a ride.' And we...kill those people. 'Shut him up! I've got a lot invested in this ride, shut him up! Look at my furrows of worry, look at my big bank account, and my family. This has to be real.' It's just a ride. But we always kill the good guys who try and tell us that, you ever notice that? And let the demons run amok....But it doesn't matter, because it's just a ride. And we can change it anytime we want. It's only a choice. No effort, no work, no job, no savings and money. Just a simple choice, right now, between fear and love. The eyes of fear want you to put bigger locks on your doors, buy guns, close yourself off. The eyes of love instead see all of us as one. Here's what we can do to change the world, right now, to a better ride. Take all that money we spend on weapons and defenses each year and instead spend it feeding and clothing and educating the poor of the world, which it would pay for many times over, not one human being excluded, and we could explore space, together, both inner and outer, forever, in peace."

That is still one of the most beautiful, stirring and inspiring pieces of work that I have ever seen, heard or read. It stands the test of time and, yes, it pulls back the curtain on the Premier League. No, don't worry, it's OK, I've not been eating peyote buttons. It really does. The Premier League isn't real, it's just a ride. And we can change it anytime we want. It's only a choice. The Premier League is an amusement park. A ride that goes up and down, around and around, it has thrills and chills, and it's very brightly coloured, and it's very loud, and it's fun for a while. That is all absolutely true.

It's 27 years old now, so many of us have been on the ride a long time, and we begin to wonder, "Hey, is this real, or is this just a ride?" And other people have remembered, and they come back to us and say, "Hey, don't worry; don't be afraid, ever, because this is just a ride."

And it is. It's not real. It's just a ride. It's an invention. A construct that has become embedded into our synapses that feels like the only way things can be or have ever been. But it's just a ride. And when some, as they inevitably will, read this and shout, "Shut him up! I've got a lot invested in this ride, shut him up! Look at my furrows of worry, look at my big bank account, and my family. This has to be real," it doesn't matter, because it's just a ride and we can change it anytime we want.

Well, the time has come to change it. Time to change the world to a better ride. Are you up for that? I hope so because we're going to need each other.

I know this is a lot to absorb and it all sounds mad right now, but I hope by the end of this trip to the centre of our minds, you will look back and realise that actually we're the sane ones around here.

The beating dark heart of the Premier League is the sulphurous devil that is money. The love of which, as we know, is the root of all evil, at least according to the Bible: Timothy 6:10. Have you heard of Timothy? Me neither. The Gospel According to Tim? Tim Sherwood, perhaps. Now that's a pwoper gospel, my son.

In some ways this book is a celebration of football, of why it is so wonderful as a sport and what is so good about the role it does or can play in the civic life of the country. Indeed, without that sense of joy and importance, I wouldn't feel so strongly that the Premier League has taken so much from us, has taken hold of the game we loved, a game that was ours, was in the common embrace and has sold a shiny plastic version back to us. Oh, it's got the glamour of money, but I come from the philosophical and spiritual viewpoint that we should take love over gold every single time and that only doing so will make us happy and content.

I can still recall watching England win the World Cup in 1966. Yes, I am that old. But this anti-Premier League polemical evisceration is not an exercise in nostalgia in the slightest. It is not advocating a return to the past. I know what was wrong with how things were, with every bit the same certainty that I feel I know what is wrong now. This is about a wholly new future. A more fair, sensible and progressive future. A model which delivers for all of us and not just a few of them. But I am not naïve, I realise one book is not going to change anything on its own; however, it can be a colourful brush stroke in a new painting of a new world. It can inspire and enlighten. I am an idealist and optimistic that change is always possible and feel that we helped bring the Premier League and football to where they are now and we can take them somewhere else if we so wish.

If this book helps articulate and coalesce that nameless, troubling, uncomfortable and multi-faceted discontented feeling which so many of us have all the time when we see or hear about the Premier League, then it will have done its job. What we do afterwards is up to us. If we want radical change, we can have radical change. We just need to come together.

I don't pretend to have all the answers to the many and complex issues, or that this is some sort of hardline manifesto. The whole purpose of me writing this is to first try and articulate why we feel as we do, because without understanding what we don't like, we can't create something we do.

So come with me. This book may only be one step on the road to a new future, but all the greatest journeys start with one step, so let's make that step together now. We'll need to act collectively in order to make this revolution happen. But it is a revolution that we can win because ultimately football is ours, it's always been ours, but they took it from us. And one day soon, you know what? You and me, we should take it back.

JOHNNY, JUNE 2019

PROLOGUE: THE FUTURE'S IN THE PAST

It was a freezing cold Tuesday night in Middlesbrough, 7th December 1976. Frost and fog were rolling down off the Cleveland Hills across the lands that surround the River Tees, lands known to everyone who lives there, and everyone who is from there, as Teesside, even though Teesside, like a mythical land that lives only in the imagination, is not to be found on any map, no matter how hard you look.

But Teessiders all know where it starts and we all know where it ends. And if you don't know, we're not about to tell you. Teesside lives in our hearts, in our souls and in the elongated vowels that it has blessed our unique accent with. Not quite Yorkshire, not quite Geordie; a hybrid of both, totally unique and, we like to think, superior in some unknowable way.

That cold night, as the fog and frost hit the yellow smoke belching from the steel and chemical industries, with orange and yellow spumes of burning gas firing high into the night sky, it created, as it did more days than it didn't, that most Teesside of words, a portmanteau word that is even now, even though the air is clean and salmon swim in the Tees and you can take a deep breath without a strange burning sensation attacking your lungs, a word the area is still synonymous with: smog.

The smog was ours. It made us. It was an industrial fragrance that we all wore. And as odd as it might sound to people from cleaner, less industrial places, I think it's safe to say, in many ways, many of us Teessiders miss the smog or at least feel nostalgic about it. The smog was the product of industry, so the smog was wages, the smog was money, the smog was security, the smog was respect, self-worth, labour and noble self-identity. But there's no smog any more. The smog has gone and taken much with it. No wonder it is missed.

Forged out of the sweat and the snot, the laughter and tears of Teesside's industrial workforce came Middlesbrough FC - known locally as the Boro - who played at Ayresome Park. If you doubt the role heavy industry played in formation of football clubs, the town's first professional club was called Middlesbrough Ironopolis FC. Yes, Ironopolis!! While it sounds like something out of Brave New World, in the five years of their existence between 1889 and 1894 they won the Northern League Division One three years consecutively, won two cups, got into the second division and reached the quarter-finals of the FA Cup. And they had a 32,000-capacity Paradise Ground right next door to Ayresome Park. It was Ayresome that I was making my way towards in order to watch the Boro play in the First Division against Manchester City. I was on my own, as I often was in those days, not having many friends who were interested in going to the game and even fewer who were prepared or even interested in having a few pre-match pints in one of the many pubs in the area that would serve alcohol to 15 ½ year-old boys who were sporting a 'my first moustache'. In my case, this was a wispy thing which somehow made me look not older, as I hoped, but younger. Not that I need have worried about not getting served. I always got served. Only once in my three years of underage drinking was I refused drink, and that was at Newcastle City Hall during a Uriah Heep gig when I and approximately 1,500 others nipped to the bar during Lee Kerslake's interminable drum solo.

Most pubs around Ayresome Park, and indeed pretty much throughout the region, would sell you pints of lager and lime in the full knowledge that you were not 18, on the unspoken condition that you sit in a corner, sup your pint, keep quiet and don't upset the regulars. So that's what I did. It made me feel good. It gave me an identity at a time in life when you are searching for who you really are; for who you might grow up to be. And I knew as I sat in the Masham Hotel, a now closed mid-Victorian pub with a wonderful Art Deco green-tiled frontage, opposite the Cleveland Centre, an hour before the game, that I was a Boro fan, a drinker and a rock 'n' roll kid. Some things never change.

As someone about to spend an hour and a half in the company of MFC, it always helped to have two or three pints in your bloodstream before kick off, just to mildly anesthetize your synapses so as to better tolerate what was quite likely to be an hour and a half of quite average, even boring football.

When, a few years ago, a chap was thrown out of Riverside Stadium - Boro's post-1996 home - for being so intoxicated that he fell asleep during the game, it was treated locally as a sort of human rights crime. Even if you'd never been drunk at the Boro, you knew someone who had been, or someone who wished they had been. And we all knew it was a perfectly understandable response to the sort of entertainment he surely knew would be on offer from the football club that day. For the club itself not to appreciate this was one of their rare misjudgements of their paying customers. After the outcry and outrage at this decision, the club backed down and accepted that being sleepy and drunk was a harmless enough activity and one which many Teessiders consider to be an entirely sane response to both football and indeed, the modern world itself.

What the club had failed to understand is something which many football observers, executives and officials often fail to understand. And they fail to understand it because they've all drunk too deeply from the cup marked Premier League. It is a strong, plentiful and intoxicating brew which eventually makes many go blind.

And that thing they failed to understand was that just being there, even if full of drink and taking a nap, is the whole point. We are not there to see great football played by the elite of the game, even though we're constantly told we are. No. Going is the whole point. The joy is in being present. Only idiots who don't understand football, idiots who think it is part of show business - and these are all too influential, powerful and wealthy these days - will expect to have anything more than an occasional few seconds of excitement per game and if you miss those moments whilst in the arms of morpheus then fine. You were still there. But because being drunk and asleep suggests to the modern-day football executive that your elite product is boring (and Boro played some deathly football that season) they took it as an insult, or as bad behaviour, or disrespectful to their brand. They'd definitely use the word brand. But before the Premier League came into existence, no-one inside the ground or at the club would ever have thought someone getting some kip in during a game was worthy even of comment, much less a banning order. There's your trouble. Right there.

Back in 1976 at Ayresome Park, I stood in the Holgate behind the goal. I loved the Holgate, even though a rational consideration of the place would only see a concrete, wood and metal stand. A typical Archibald Leach creation, not unlike many dozens of other grounds, architecturally it was never going to rival the great buildings of the world, but even so, it was ours and somehow it seemed to personally welcome me every time I went. This may have been the drink kicking in, of course.

It was a typically smoggy, bitter and cold night, the sort of penetrating cold that you can feel eating at your bone marrow like cancer, even though the Bovril sold in thin white plastic cups is hotter than 100 degrees and needs handling with the sort of leather gauntlets that you might wear in a foundry to protect your hands against the molten pig iron. I took my usual position on the Holgate; halfway up and slightly to the left of the goal. Soon, an old fella arrived with a young boy in tow.

I say he was old, he was probably 40, but everyone over 20 seems ancient when you're 15, don't they? He lit up and pulled on a fag, the tip glowing orange against the black velvet night sky. I always liked how cigarettes smelled in a football ground. I can't really explain this. I was brought up in a house where smoking was an everyday, in fact, an every-30-minute thing. Mother got through 40 or more in her waking hours and would've smoked when asleep if it was possible without setting the bed alight. The living room was thick with it most of the time, meaning that we always had to have 'the little window' open to offer the chance of actually seeing the TV through the fug. If my grandma was staying, the whole house became like a gas attack at the battle of Ypres. I sat there eyes streaming as the tobacco conflagration took hold and I vowed never to smoke. Exposure to it in extremis put me right off. And although I've ended up doing most of the things I previously said I would never, ever do (except voting Tory), I've never smoked. I couldn't do it. I still can't. I tried but it always felt like I was drowning. And although I was fond of altered states, the ciggies didn't do that for me. As the years have gone on, I've got more and more sensitive to it and can't stand the slightest smell now, but when at the Boro in the 70s on a cold smoggy night, it was somehow perfect and comforting.

So the auld fella sucked down on the Embassy No. 5 and blew out smoke as his young son, about eight years old, looked out at the beautiful expanse of green. And Ayresome Park under the lights really was stunning, to the point of being almost fluorescent. It had been good enough to host World Cup games played by North Korea 10 years earlier. Teessiders took the NK to their hearts, possibly feeling an affinity for people who are oppressed by the dead hand of a cruel state that neither knows nor cares about who you are and what sort of ambition you might have in life.

A night game, illuminated by the huge floodlights, was an otherworldly experience closer to science fiction, to an impressionable youngster, than to everyday life. So the boy had the same wide eyes I had when I first went to a night game. I knew how he felt. Night games are still my favourite games. If all the games were played after dark, I would not object. It just adds something. Something metaphysical and hard to grasp or explain, but which many of us feel.

"Dad!" said the young chap, tugging at his dad's hand excitedly.

"What, son?"

"Dad. The grass is dead green. How come the grass is so green?"

The colour was intense under the floodlights.

The man paused, took a last drag on the smoke, tossed it to the terrace floor and ground it down with his foot, then looked to his boy, smiled and said,

"That's because there's been so much shite on it over the years, son."

Let that comment sink in.

And 'that's because there's been so much shite on it over the years, son' is what this book is really about.

OK, this was Middlesbrough, but it could have been anywhere in the country and at any football club, any club rooted in its local community, in its local industry, in its local people. Any club that has been around for decades and decades as a focal point for the people. Any club that provides hope to kids and occasionally some entertainment for all. My experience that cold December night in 1976 was far from unique. You've probably experienced something very similar. Football clubs are a sort of secular holy place. Few if any other places can claim to have had so much hope invested in them, nor have shattered so many dreams. Few can claim to draw generations of the same family to them to worship at the same altar. These are not normal places and they belong to the people in a way that little else in our society does. To mistake these places, large or small, for mere repositories of our leisure activity spending, is to bring wholly the wrong cultural, social and political mindset to the issue. They are invested with something beyond our mere purchasing power. The affection, the bonds, the joy and loathing they can engender are, in so many ways, the same as our relationships with our extended family. Even when you fall out with them, you're stuck with them. They're family. So when someone says, "That's because there's been so much shite on it over the years," that is part of the love. It is like taking the piss out of your best mate. And it is why that statement is the wellspring from which all our love of football comes from. You can't brand it, you can't sponsor it, you can't fake it, you can't sell broadcasting rights in it, you can't package it, you can't redesign it so it can be trademarked, you can't put it in an executive box and sell canapes to it, and you can't drum up an audience in China or India on a mobile phone for it. I believe everything in that poetic comment is everything that the people who stole football from us do not understand, either literally, metaphorically, existentially and for all I know, meta-bloody-physically. It is our soul and our roots. For me at the Boro, for you wherever you are, we are all as one in this. It is very much not a corporate thing. It is a comment which cares a lot but doesn't show it. It is modest; it is, in short, of the people and by the people. It is, in short, everything top flight football has largely had stolen from it by the Premier League.

Keep his comment on that cold night in 1976 in mind throughout the whole of this book, as we talk about money and power and television and official coconut water partners. Never forget it. It is where our soul lies. It has the whiff of the real, a whiff that big money and big marketing have tried to bleach away. It is the real counterpoint to the illusion we've been sold. It doesn't fit with corporate branding. It glories in an appreciation of failure. It is ornery and it doesn't take any of the charade too seriously, whilst knowing it is part of both an individual and collective local identity. In short, it is an expression of the lives we live, of us and ours, of you and yours. It is the warmth of togetherness and community.

And my god, Big Money doesn't want that. Oh no no no. This is a serious global product. You will get on your knees and genuflect in front of their investments in managers, players, and stadia and especially in front of the huge piles of cash. Yeah, just worship the money. Worship it. Believe in it. Embrace it. You can't have it but you want it, you crave it and we've got it. It is first, it is foremost and it is everything now. Forget what you were, forget what you are, shut up, pipe down and start consuming, kid. Get your hand in your pocket and be a good little customer. You are ours now. We have bought you. You are our asset to exploit and exploit you and everything that is in your soul, we most assuredly will.

No. No. No. That's not for me, pal. Not for many of us.

Football belongs to you and me, to us and ours. Back then and still now. It was birthed by the working-class industrial communities of this country, in places like the Ironopolis of Middlesbrough. It is our culture. It is our civic pride and it is part of our collective identity wherever we may roam on this infinitely idyllic, profoundly cosmic blue and green marble floating in space.

But the top flight of the game in England was captured from the Football League and the Football Association - or more correctly, surrendered - put behind a paywall and force-fed on rich, fatty cash in order to make a kind of football foie-gras, cruel, wrong and yet delicious. In doing so they transformed it from the game we had known and enjoyed into a bloated something else. It was stolen from the common embrace and made an elitist product called the Premier League. The effect on the whole game, on our whole lives, on the planet, even, has been profound.

Since 1992, those who run the Premier League have tried to sell something to us that we were once the most important part of, to the point where we are now bit part players in their drama. They have taken television from being a guest at football to football being a guest on television. They have warped our minds with ceaseless propaganda and a profound redrawing of both what football is and what it should be, with the aim of making it a global franchise and just another branch on the entertainment industry money tree. And their evil plan has worked.

But this book exists to stand against all that, because I can't take this any more. I can't take the simpering acquiescence so many have towards the league, nor how it has become a plaything of people who use the words 'market forces' and 'supply and demand'. I can't bear the way people supplicate at the feet of the rich. It makes me sick that they're forever telling us how bloody great the league is when, like all football at any level in any country, it sometimes is, sometimes isn't. I keep trying to just look at Premier League games as a mere spectacle. I've tried to disengage from the negativity, I keep trying to see only the good football played, as just that: good football. And from time to time, I can almost manage it, but the nagging feeling that in doing so I'm ignoring the massive, sulphurous shitting elephant in the room, which just won't ever go completely away. And no-one wants a huge, sulphurous shitting elephant in their living room, do they? You'd never get the stains out of the carpet.

I can't not think about the sort of people that own the clubs. I can't not think about the roots and sources of their wealth and the implications that uncritically endorsing what they've done have had on our national game. I can't not think of how we can only watch it on TV if we pay someone money to specifically do so. I can't not think of the huge income from the sales of those broadcast rights and what the consequences of that have been. I can't not think about the vast amount of money that players earn and where that comes from and why. I can't not think about the transfer fees swollen now like gargantuan buboes on the plague-ridden body of our once-healthy game. I can't divorce football's wealth from the deprivation and poverty so many endure. I find it morally objectionable to the point of outrage that such disparity of wealth exists and still more that its existence is celebrated, vaunted and encouraged as a positive thing, as if there's a human right to earn whatever the hell you want to earn no matter how vast, or what the consequences might be. And lastly, I can't not think that the promulgation of such an economic philosophy and the notions behind it are destroying the planet, its resources and ourselves via rampant, destructive consumerism.

This not because I am holy or a killjoy, but how can anyone just ignore all of this and keep paying money to broadcasters in order to perpetuate it? How can we just go along with it like it isn't what it really is? There are clubs owned by companies with connections to the dodgy end of the financial industry, with connections to oppressive regimes, with connections to businesses that have been admonished for terrible working practices. There have been owners accused of human rights crimes by organisations such as Amnesty International. Are we just supposed to think this is all OK? Should we turn a blind eye to all these sins? Should we just stick our fingers in our ears? Should we just pretend it isn't even happening? Do we let ourselves get sucked into its amoral vacuum?

Critics will say this is a paean to a time that has gone. That it is living in the past, that I am an old man shouting at clouds. And if you expound the same views, they will accuse you of the same things too. But they are wrong. This is all about creating a manifesto for a new future, not a plan for a museum to the past. It is about being progressive, empathetic, thoughtful and anti-establishment. It's about taking the best of the past and present and moulding a better future. It's about knowing exactly why you would tell your kid that the grass is so green because there's been so much shite on it.

Because it is time to choose sides. Time to take a stand. Time to use the power innate to us as consumers. Time to say, in the words of that great heavy metal philosopher, Dee Snider, "We're not going to take it, no, we're not gonna take it, we're not gonna take it anymore."

PART ONE:
MYTHS AND TRUTHS

THE POPULARITY MYTH

The Premier League: it's really popular, isn't it? Go anywhere in the world and it's on the TV. It is a global phenomenon. The grounds are full. The rights to broadcast the game cost a fortune precisely because the league is so popular. That's all correct, isn't it? Turns out, Yes, sort of, but mostly No, actually.

The Premier League began in 1992 and had been in the planning by then for a couple of years. Did anyone ask us if we'd like the Premier League to be created? Of course not, we're just the punters. Remember us? The people who support football clubs so that they can exist; only the most important people in the whole equation. But the clubs and the FA and the newly formed corporation called the Premier League Ltd just did what they wanted regardless without consulting with us. It had been brewing for a few years, with various threats from 'top' clubs to break away. The history of how the league came to be formed is well documented and I shall leave it to you to read up on it. But the important takeaway point from this ignominious period in our football history is that supporters and football fans more broadly were not considered in the whole process, except as cash cows. It's a bit like the publishing industry where the author gets a far smaller cut of the sale than the bookshop and publisher, even though neither can't exist without the author.

What it would do to the game to deny the possibility of seeing top-flight league football on TV without paying subscription money to do so was not considered.

Someone relatively close to events talked to me about how it all went down:

"I don't think it is unreasonable to say the whole thing, from day one, from before day one, in fact, was all about money and nothing but money. The big five - which included Everton back then, funnily enough - had been pushing for years to get more TV money. The 1988 deal with ITV to broadcast First Division games on Sundays gave them four years to get their shit together to break away. When push came to shove, there was all these big TV executives like Greg Dyke, club chairmen like David Dein and Martin Edwards all hustling for the creation of the Premier League. They'd even got in someone from Saatchi and Saatchi to devise the new structure of the league and all these hard-nosed money men turned up at Lancaster Gate, [the FA HQ]. The old FA boys, bless 'em, were all out of their depth in that sort of company. The FA chairman was a decent chap, Bert Millichip, who I always thought was like

Young Mr Grace in Are You Being Served? If you remember that. He was in his late 70s by then. You've got to remember that there had been some bad blood between the FA and the Football League and I think that was one reason the FA sided with the idea of the Premier League. They wanted to slap down the Football League. They also bought the PR that a new league of 18 clubs (which never happened) would be good for England's national team because it would avoid fixture congestion. No-one believed that but cleverly it gave the FA something to justify their decision with. The Premier League knew that they needed some meat to throw to the wolves and improving the national team was it. It just gave Bert and the rest something to say to the press as he handed them the keys to the toy cupboard. Even though the Premier League needed the approval of the FA to be created, and so the FA in theory held all the cards, it's my view that they had no idea how to negotiate a deal. How could they? No-one had done a deal like this before. They'd never had to do anything like this in the past, never had any experience of such a thing. Brian Glanville used to call Millichip Bert the Inert! He just waved the whole thing through and he even gave them all a room in Lancaster Gate to thrash out the founding agreement and to use as offices for the new league. I bet they couldn't believe their luck. It was such a fundamental change in English football but it was in the hands of these amateurish if mostly well-meaning people."

When I cast my mind back to 1992, I can barely remember the process of transforming the First Division into the Premier League. It did not really even register with me at the time and when it did, it felt like it was more of a name change, than anything more profound or long term. I wasn't up in arms the way I should've been and I certainly don't recall any widespread protests. I doubt we could have imagined that no live top-flight football would ever be seen on free-to-air TV ever again. Also, we need to remember that league football was on TV much less than we have got used to ever since - usually just one game on a Sunday afternoon by 1992. So it didn't feel as profound a change. As a radio listener, nothing much was different anyway. It was still on at the same time and in the same amount. So the hiving off of the top division from the Football League by a private corporation didn't seem to me, as a punter who got most of his football from the radio, that big a thing. Oh, but how wrong I was.

Sky outbid ITV for the rights to broadcast the new league's games and the BBC won the highlights package. The satellite broadcaster set about inventing this brave new world with adverts for the coming extravaganza sold on the tagline 'It's a whole new ball game' which, in a way, was prescient for many reasons in that it absolutely wasn't and yet at the same time, absolutely was.

It wasn't in that it still looked like football, it was still the same game with the same rules (apart from the newly introduced back-pass law), unchanged from the year before on terrestrial TV when Leeds United had won the title. But it was new because now you had to subscribe to Sky to watch it. Premier League football was not premier in any other way. It was still just the First Division and it still is.

Looking back on it now, using Simple Minds' music for the inaugural ad was an odd choice. By 1992 the song 'Alive and Kicking' very much sounded like the music of the mid-1980s. It had been a #7 hit in the UK in 1985 and #3 in the USA. So by the law which says things that have just been fashionable are now the least fashionable things, it sounded really dated in the 1992 era of Nirvana, Pearl Jam and Soundgarden. It was all very shell suit, very Lynx, very stone-washed jeans. Compared to the BBC's genre-defining big hit using Pavarotti at the 1990 World Cup, it did seem a bit lager and fag ash; a bit behind the times, perhaps even intentionally so. I spoke to someone who was in advertising at the time:

"As far as I can recall, the brief was to aim primarily at the C1s and C2s: basically working class but with a bit of money. A self-employed builder or someone skilled who worked in a garage, maybe. They were sure that was where the market was and that's why it looked as it did and why they used pop music, not opera or classical. Looking back with the benefit of hindsight, my opinion is that they were off the mark. They didn't factor in how much it would alienate some people, or at least not as much as they should have. A1 and A2s were not catered to at all and that's a lot of people. Again, with hindsight, the roots of the failure to attract a majority of the audience for football on Sky were established back then. They got off on the wrong foot. It lacked a bit of class and polish. The BBC had done Italia 90 like it was art. That was the new standard. In my view, ever since, Sky in particular failed to realise the nature of their potential audience and that people wanted something a little more upmarket and intelligent. I'm still not sure that is a lesson they've fully yet learned, though their coverage has never, ever been better than it is now. At last they've embraced some meaningful diversity, but it hasn't half taken a long time."

The first Super Sunday was Nottingham Forest vs Liverpool, which Forest won with a single Teddy Sheringham goal. If you watched it, it simply wasn't that Super and for the first time we felt that cognitive dissonance between what we were being marketed and what we were seeing. This cognitive dissonance has remained a constant over the last 27 years and that's because from day one it was all about money and not about football. They couldn't have cared less about the actual game and they still don't. It is still all about making as much money as possible for all concerned. So it is still all about selling this as a superior product that we'd be happy to pay for, in the same way that we might pay for an upmarket designer brand. But it never was and it still isn't that. Now, I know what defenders of the faith will say, they will point to some of the great football played in the league. And I enjoy that as much as anyone, of course I do. But that isn't because it is the Premier League, that is because it is football. The league has managed to conflate people's enjoyment of football with enjoyment of the Premier League per se, as though football did not and does not exist without it. But of course, we enjoy football at many different levels.

It was as though it would no longer be normal football but some rarified version of the game and that's why we'd have to pay to watch it live on TV. Do you remember being told that we'd never, ever, ever be able to watch the Premier League on TV without paying a broadcaster to do so? I don't. I'm fairly sure that wasn't trumpeted loudly. It all seemed like a temporary situation, somehow. It didn't seem serious that this was now The Best League In The World.

It may be hard to remember what it was like to have a satellite dish in 1992 as it became such a normal part of life. It's now rather clunky and is being superseded by the internet and any number of connected devices. Sometimes it seems as if everything is a television now, up to and including your underwear. The oblong screen and box that I call the TV, but which isn't really, or at least not in the sense it once was, is now so complicated that I don't know where the pictures even come from. It takes two boxes with a total of 128 buttons on them to operate. It takes ages finding programmes, much longer than used to be the case and it regularly presents things to me that I can't believe even exist let alone might attract viewers. Even with Freeview I have so much choice that it makes the whole process ugly and clunky. If ever there was an example of more choice being a worse thing, then it is multi-channel TV. It ensures I watch almost no TV at all, in fact. I don't have the time or inclination to wade through the sea of crap to find something that won't sicken, enrage or disturb me. From time to time things happen on the screen which I will have to go to the internet to try and find out how to correct. The other day an audio commentary began apropos of nothing, describing what was happening in the programme. Nothing I pressed would make it stop. So what did I do? I did what any sane person does in such situations: I put up with it. And not just for a day or two but for three long weeks. Then one day, the cat walked across one of the boxes and the commentary stopped. Cats know more than we do about operating a television. That, my friends, is where we are at.

The only thing I do know about my television is that it no longer shows Sky. That's because I ended the contract when we moved last year, after over 20 years. I do have BT Sport but only because the contract has not yet expired. I shall let it wither on the digital vine; or at least I will unless the cat decides otherwise, as he is clearly in charge.

But for those first few years the whole satellite dish thing was very divisive. To put this broadly and somewhat crudely, to some it was a sign of vulgarity, of being 'common'. To others it was new and exciting and a sign that you had a bob or two. To be honest, I didn't care either way. I'm not snooty about such things, it seems such a waste of emotion and intellect to take against circles of metal fixed to walls. By all means hide them in roof gullies on top of blocks of Georgian apartments if you wish but don't put people down for which technology they opt for; I mean, there are bigger issues in life, like getting annoyed at people who begin every sentence with the word 'So...'

We signed up for the whole Sky Package in 1996; sports, movies, everything. By the time we cancelled it over 20 years later, we had yet to actually watch a movie on the movie channels. We don't really watch TV much, an hour here or there, we don't seem to have the time spare or rather are not inclined to make the time. I'm busy writing books and feeding the cat, Dawn is an artist and is usually to be found covered from head to toe in ink or paint or messing with a gelli plate. The idea of sitting in front of the telly for three or four hours feels like it'd be such a waste of valuable production time. But I realise we're probably unusual in this. For 20 years we paid a sub for hundreds of channels that we never watched, not even once, and for years I watched football and literally nothing else that wasn't on BBC or ITV or C4.

'Sky Sports Shown Here' was a real attraction when you saw the banners outside of pubs because most of us didn't have Sky and the only way to now see the football was in a pub.

This actually brought a communal aspect to football on TV and pubs could be packed out with people keen to see this new phenomenon. By putting it behind the paywall which most people couldn't afford or didn't want to pay, it did make it more social in those early years, simply by virtue of exclusivity. The fact you had to be in the Duck and Vomit to see it, and that it was the centrepiece of the entertainment in the pub, sometimes projected onto big screens, definitely made it more of an event. There's no point in denying that getting drunk with your pals while watching football was living H on the H for many. Interesting then, that in recent years it has been on the wane and no longer has the pull it once did for anything other than the biggest games.

But as far as subscribers at home went, football on Sky was not at all popular when it started. Indeed, it stood a very good chance of failing altogether and was only really kept afloat by Sky's profits from elsewhere in the company. It's also been suggested that the BBC's opting to keep on showing Match of the Day highlights was a relief to Sky. Niall Sloane, now head of Sport at ITV, told me that "without the big numbers that Match of the Day delivered on the BBC, Sky's football coverage could easily have failed. It was effectively an advertising tool for the league. If they'd had the highlights as well, no-one would have seen any Premier League football at all."

If you liked what you saw in the highlights, you could pick up the phone and get Sky to install a massive dish on your house to the opprobrium of some and admiration of others. And if you think about it, Niall's absolutely right. There was now no live top-flight football on TV so we'd have had no idea if it was any good or not if Sky had also bought the highlights package. The fact it was picked up by the BBC saved their bacon because then, as now, nearly 30 years later, the only place to get a large share of the available audience is on terrestrial TV. In 1992 Sky may have thought it was only a matter of time before we all woke up and realised what we were missing and that we really should take out a subscription to watch their football. However, while more punters, like me, got on board as the years went by, still only a small minority of the people of these lands who love football, who watch it live in person, or watch it on TV when it's on BBC or ITV, have ever bought it from Sky or anyone else. The concept has now totally hit a brick wall. We all think it is massively popular. It isn't. Paywall football on TV has small or smallish audiences, never big audiences. The Premier League is high profile. Almost everyone has heard of it, even if they do not care for football. And that is a form of popularity I guess, but in terms of people watching broadcasts, it's much, much less impressive.

I'm writing this in 2019, the day after the Fulham vs Liverpool game was shown on Sky. It was watched by at peak 1.5 million people. At the same time, BBC One was showing Millwall vs Brighton in the FA Cup and it was watched by a peak of 4.4 million people. This degree of out-performance is typical. If that FA Cup game had featured any of the most supported clubs it'd have been bigger still. Their broadcast of Wolves vs Manchester United on a Saturday night in the FA Cup peaked at just under 6 million. Manchester United's FA Cup 4th Round win over Arsenal attracted a peak audience of 7.6 million on BBC One. The Women's World Cup numbers for England games have risen from 6.1 million to 7.4 million for their quarter-final vs Norway, and 11.7 million for the semi-final vs U.S.A. These are stunning numbers for what is still a developing sport and the sort of numbers that paywall TV simply will never, ever achieve. If size of TV audience matters - and we'll discuss why it does - football needs to bin off paywall TV. Simple as that. Get rid. It will never provide them. That much is abundantly clear.

I'm told Sky have always been very, very coy about their subscription numbers. Now, I think a company like Sky would only be coy when the numbers are not what they think people will expect them to be. If they're sure everyone will swoon, mop their brows and with wide eyes and dilated pupils gasp, "How many?! That's amazing!," you can bet your bottom dollar that they'd be all over the media trumpeting the fact with as a big and loud a trumpet as has ever been blown.

Even if the numbers are good enough for the company's needs, maybe they fear if they are thought to be low, the company will be seen as a flop. So they've kept them very close to their chest. Niall Sloane again: "It's hard to know exactly but it seems to me that the vast majority of homes in the UK do not have a Sky subscription. Some may have just the sports, some have other packages but not sports. Twenty-five per cent would be my best guess. It may be much less."

And if we look at viewing figures both now and historically, they at the very least bear this fact out. Even now, all these years later when digital viewing is well established and you don't have to have a big circle of steel on your wall to indicate that you have satellite TV and thus may well be watching the naked channels late at night, even now Sky typically get between one and two million viewers for a Premier League game. It can go lower to 750,000 or less, if the game is between two smaller clubs, both of whom are notorious for draining the blood out of your face with an hour and a half of tedious, uneventful, grindcore football.

It has gone as high as three to four million on very odd occasions, but this is very much an outlier. Manchester United played Liverpool in February 2018 in a rather dull 0-0 draw. It peaked at approximately 2.1 million on Sky. There are 66 million people living in this country. So at best that is about 1 in 32 people, or about 4 per cent of the population, watching a game between two of the most supported teams in the UK. Now obviously there will be some who have a subscription but didn't watch that game, and others who have Sky but not the sport, but Niall's 25 per cent estimate looks, to me, to be quite high. But we know from the numbers who watch live games on terrestrial TV that there is a far, far bigger audience available for games who are not watching. And we know football is really popular as a sport with millions playing and going to games every week.

So where are they all?

Why were they not watching United vs Liverpool in big numbers? There can only be one overarching reason; they didn't want to pay to do so. I know people say the cost is too high and maybe it is. As I write it seems to cost £24 per month for one HD Sky Sports Channel, £28 for two, though I may have got that wrong as there seems to be so many package permutations and, like many, I really can't be arsed to sift through them all. (Maybe that is also part of the problem. When subscription deals are opaque you always fear getting ripped off or buying something you'll never need.) But that fee would pretty much allow you to see most of the Premier League games they broadcast but probably not absolutely everything. That's £288 per year and you can now dip in and out with your subscription, cancelling it for a month or two in the close season. I don't have the figures on this but I suspect that is as cheap in real terms as it has ever been. And the reason most things are cheap is because they either cost little to produce - not the case with Sky - or they just can't sell it for more. It isn't as though they're competing against a huge market. Just BT. That's all. Of course, most people have some sports channels built into a wider digital subscription, so costing it all out can be as muddy as Sky's subscription numbers.

Whether you think the cost is too high or not I'd suggest, though it is very hard to prove, that the last 27 years have reared an audience who simply on principle won't pay Sky or anyone else to watch football. And that's it. It's not to do with the football, with the game, with the 'product' or even sometimes with the cost. It is simply a resistance to the very concept.

However, it's been said that for the 2019-20 season if you're in the UK and want access to 100 per cent of all televised HD football it will cost you £1,026.64: Sky Sports - £420, BT Sport - £335.88, Premier Sports - £119.88, Eleven Sports - £71.88, Amazon - £79. Now that really is a hefty chunk of change, especially if you add in going to actual football for 19 home games, which for two people might cost you a minimum of another £1,000 plus travel costs.

Of course, a lot of people hoover up a dodgy feed to watch the game. We will never know how many. Piracy is rife and has created an audience that is beyond monetising. You can't get a fee from them, or advertise to them. They are beyond the control of the broadcasters. This is a reason why the Sky model of paying the Premier League a stink load of cash for broadcast rights must be in its end game. What mug keeps paying over the odds for something that they then, in effect, give away free to illegal streamers and which the vast majority of potential customers have no intention of ever paying you to see?

Just to reinforce this point, let's compare this performance to the biggest games on ITV or BBC. Sweden vs England in the 2018 World Cup, for example, got 18-20 million watching it on BBC. OK, it's England and it is a World Cup quarter-final, but again, that is a number Sky or any other pay-TV company would never be able to come anywhere near achieving. England's semi-final against Croatia on ITV attracted the biggest audience for any single game ever broadcast on one channel, topping out at 26.6 million with another 4.3 million watching it on ITV's Hub online. That's a total of 30.9 million and as I say, it is a broadcasting record for football in the UK broadcast on a single channel. Not only that, it is the record audience for anything at all broadcast on a single channel. Only the 1966 World Cup Final (32.3 million) and Princess Diana's funeral (32.1 million) were watched by more people but both of those went out on BBC and ITV simultaneously.

You know what is so great about that?: the fact that nearly 50 per cent of the country saw it, probably a majority of people who live in England. Us being all together at a moment in time is not an insignificant thing. We came together to watch that. It meant we all had something in common, something we could relate to, not just at the time or the next day but also into the future. Had that been on Sky or BT Sport it would've had maybe 1.5 million to 3 million viewers. Still niche. Still elite. Not of, or by, the people. And there's your trouble.

I know that was a huge game and a one-off, but it shows all too well just what the level of interest can be in football matches.

But back to the weedy world of paywall telly. Currently BT Sport also show the Premier League and they are excellent at it. Their programmes are lovely to watch. They're full of arty clips and interviews. They have excellent presenters and pundits. If you like watching football on TV, you won't see anything better.

But. But. But. They are much less popular than Sky. Much less. So unpopular in fact that a game between unfashionable smaller sides won't even get 300,000 watching it at the peak. Yes, they can get up to a million for bigger games; they got 1.5 million for the League Cup Final between Chelsea and Manchester City - two of the most followed clubs in the country - but to only have so few for a Cup Final would shock many. I bet, like me, you thought these broadcasters were far more popular than they actually are. For Liverpool vs Barcelona, which the Reds won 4-0, 1.6-2.6 million watched one of the most remarkable games of this or any other season. Hard not to believe it'd have gotten 8-10 million on terrestrial. Even many more, perhaps.

The Premier League's website boasts that in the 2017/18 season, nine games attracted an audience of 2 million, and the Manchester Derby 3.24 million. Interestingly, while in the same section it states that 28 overseas 'broadcast partners' attended that game, the league does not state what the global audience was for that, its biggest of big games. Wouldn't you think the league would if it was in the high millions or billions? I would. The fact that the website does not state even a ballpark figure is oddly shy.

NBC Sports Group's presentation of Manchester United's 3-2 victory over Manchester City in the Manchester Derby on Saturday, 7th April 2018 averaged a Total Audience Delivery of 1.72 million viewers across all platforms. More typically the average audience is 449,000. This in a country of 350 million people. Oh. That's, well, that's OK, I guess but this is The Best League In The World. At this point I should insert a raised-eyebrow emoji.

In the 2018/19 season, 16 games got over 2 million viewers but Sky broadcast 128. So that 112 games under 2 million. I wonder how many were under 500,000? It just doesn't sound very good, does it? There are 66 million people living in this country. Almost no-one is watching. But even this has been trumpeted by league and broadcaster as proof of their growing popularity. The Premier League website says "The titanic title race helped to deliver a 12 per cent growth for Sky Sports' audiences in the UK this season."

But as ever with this mob, the words look crafted to give maximum impression from as little actual information as possible. Does "12 per cent growth" means the total audience for live football on Sky was 12 per cent up? Why use "growth" and not the more plain "up"? When they say "Sky Sports' audiences" do they mean for Sky Sports overall across all channels and for all sports, or only for their football coverage? It could've been written more clearly, but they love things to be opaque, it seems. They also boast that BT got its highest ever audience of 1.7 million for Liverpool v Arsenal. But that does feel a little like trying to pretend a small thing is a big thing, doesn't it?

Breezily, the Premier League in its ongoing attempt to pretend everything is fine assert this on their website. "In total, about 70 per cent of the UK population watched the Premier League this season, either through Sky, BT or the BBC."

Hold on, son. Hold on. 70 per cent of the UK population is 46.2 million people! 46.2 million people have not watched the Premier League. I do not believe that. We know it couldn't even get 2 million (3% of the population) for 112 games on Sky. We know the BTSport has an absolute peak of 1.7 million, but more usually in the hundreds of thousands. We know Match of the Day gets around 3 to 4 million (5% of the population) for its highlights.

We also know that this is a pretty fixed audience. Sky doesn't get 500,000 one game and 10 million another. The BBC don't get 1 million one week and 15 million the next. The numbers are constant within a bracket. Thus it can be reasonably assumed to be largely drawn from the same pool of people watching each time which at best would suggest a core audience of maybe about 8 - 10 million people which is about 15 per cent of the population, not 70 per cent.

So I wrote to the Premier League to ask them how they'd got this figure. Their reply was very revealing.

"We follow the industry standard BARB measurement for our audience figures. In terms of the 70% figure, that was from research done by Nielsen. They used BARB data to measure the number of unique viewers who watched at least three consecutive minutes of Premier League football on Sky, BT or BBC during the 2018/19 season. The total number was just over 41m which accounts for 70% (68.95% to be precise, but it was rounded up in the web article you read) of the UK TV viewing public. The three minutes measurement is industry standard as defined by BARB."

I think we would not normally think of someone who watches three consecutive minutes of a football match in one whole season as a viewer. Indeed, Dawn, who cares nothing for football and knows even less about it, has probably watched three minutes in the last nine months just accidently. They state this number baldly but obviously want us to be impressed by the size of it. It does show how exposed we all are to the Premier League, I guess. But I wanted to drill deeper so I wrote back asking for a breakdown of these viewers between Sky, BT and the BBC and also for the numbers of viewers watching an hour of football or more - as I'd say that represented the actual interest more accurately. As we go to press, I've not had a reply.

One thing is for sure, nearly all of those 3-minute views will have been of the BBC's Match of the Day highlights, simply because of the low viewership numbers on the paywall channels. It also accidentally reveals how small what we might call their interested audience is. That is, those who are watching a majority of the action and are really engaged. Some BTSport games might only have 50,000 who are actually glued to the game, some Sky games less than 200,000. See? We think Premier League football is really popular on television. But it isn't.

I know within the broadcast industry viewing figures in general are widely mistrusted and given a cynical eye for being the sort of thing which can be manipulated by management to prove whatever they want to prove. Researching this has made that all too clear to me.

The irony of all this song and dance is that both Sky and BT Sport now make excellent programmes and employ some top people. They are really, really enjoyable to watch. Sky's Monday Night Football analysis with Gary Neville and Jamie Carragher absolutely revolutionised punditry and forced all broadcasters to insist on more and better from their pundits and contributors. They employ Kelly Cates, one of the best, most erudite, warm and popular people in the business, a woman is who is brilliant at her job and whose woody purr of a laugh warms many a cold heart in this cold world. No-one doesn't love Kelly's work. She brings light into the grey fog of ordinariness, gold cast upon darkness. But even so, her broadcasts just are not getting the big audiences. A terrestrial TV audience would fall in love en masse with who Ian Wright calls Kells. People would tune in to see her present football. They'd make an effort to do so. But when it comes to paywall, no. Sorry. In a way, I think this is emblematic of where we are. That we have such a warm, inclusive, informed broadcaster with an everywoman common touch, whose smile makes all of our lives better, who has been pushed out into the paywall TV margins and despite these obvious qualities still can't pull a crowd, well, that shows how strong the will to resist paywall TV is.

BT Sport's Saturday Night Football with Jake Humphrey, a last hour of conversation and discussion mixed with fan reaction and input was, in its own way, a new departure and very enjoyable. They employ Gary Lineker to do Champions League football and brilliant broadcasters such as Jake, Lynsey Hipgrave and James Richardson. All these are top professionals; the absolute best in the business. I seriously doubt that the quality of broadcasting of football could ever get any better than it currently is on Sky and BT Sport. They do it brilliantly. There is absolutely nothing wrong with the product at all. It is top notch. That's why it shocks me just how few people as a percentage of those interested in football want to pay to see it. Shocks me. This is the apex of football broadcasting - warm, informed, informal, intelligent, amusing, attractive and brilliant. But it is still not enough to be popular. What more can these broadcasters do?

BT Sport and Sky have even taken to putting goals on Twitter as little clips, which I presume they use to boost some sort of 'engagement' numbers but is really giving football's money shot away for free.

The stone-cold truth of this is a majority of the football public simply reject the very concept of paying to watch football on TV. It doesn't matter how much it costs, it doesn't matter who is on, or how great the programmes are. It seems to me that we have a whole generation of people who have never and will never pay for football on TV on principle.

I asked the Match of the Day and 5live presenter Mark Chapman, one of the best broadcasters out there right now, why he thought the audiences of pay TV were so modest: "I think it has to be cost. It is ridiculously expensive. I also think as soon as you combine technology with something you have to pay for, there will always be people looking for a way round it, hence all the streaming sites and people accessing it illegally. I think we are also in a time where a lot of people are happy to see the goals and the red cards and nothing else. Look at how many people claim great knowledge of a player having seen a highlights reel on YouTube. 'Why would I sit through 90 minutes of Fulham vs Cardiff when I can just see Ryan Babel's goal?', will be the philosophy of a lot of people. I also think the Premier League has a massive problem with competitive balance, so if you know what's going to happen in Liverpool vs Huddersfield why would you pay for it? And also the league has a lot of clubs who frankly do not have massive fan bases."

I'm told by people in the industry that BT Sport are less likely to be in this for the long term and perhaps will not bid in the next round of rights sales. They only got involved in order to try and hook in customers for their broadband and, by all accounts, that simply has not worked well enough to justify them paying the current nine million quid per game. Whether that's true or not, I don't know for sure, but with such paltry numbers, Sky and BT Sport have absolutely no chance of covering the cost per game from advertising. That much seems sure and I have not found any proof to the contrary.

Of course, if you throw in income from subscriptions, divide that over the whole year and all the games broadcast, add in some advertising on other platforms etc. etc., it could crank the income per game up, but it still seems likely that the cost of buying the rights to show football has to be supported from profits elsewhere in the corporation's business. Sky and BT Sport are, of course, extremely squeamish about releasing any numbers at all in this regard, which only seems to further hint that it is dying on its arse.

But all of this is totally counterintuitive to us, isn't it? The popularity of the Premier League on TV is one of many pieces of propaganda that we have been fed and many of us believe to this day. I certainly used to. We have been brainwashed into thinking something that isn't very popular in absolute terms, is actually very popular. Clever.

OK, so we've established that despite Sky and currently BT Sport producing some superb programmes around the broadcasting of live football, almost no-one, as a percentage of the people who like football in this country, is interested in shelling out some hard-earned to watch them and that means we have to ask another important question: Is the Premier League actually popular globally? It tells us all the time it is. I think most of us think it is. 'Global Rights' is an expression often muttered as though it is the key to understanding everything. And the income from the sale of global rights put about £40 million into every Premier League club's bank account last season. I certainly assumed it isn't just popular globally, but phenomenally popular. So is it?

OK, well, err...Nope. It doesn't seem to be.

I hear you. Eh? What voodoo is this? Not that popular? Are you sure? Everywhere you go on earth, it's there. You've gone full hippie tonto on us,

Johnny. And now you're referring to yourself in the third person, which is the first sign of being psychotic, y'know. Of course it is globally popular.

Well, first we need to think about what the word popular means in this context. In 2013, it was said in The Times to be the most-watched football league in the world, broadcast in 212 territories to 643 million homes and a potential TV audience of 4.7 billion people. That word potential is doing all the heavy lifting in that sentence. It is also on the Premier League's Wikipedia page, which I think we must assume they have written for themselves or are happy to have written about them. However, I have seen it reproduced as though it is the actual audience for any game. These statistics are quoted all the time but where they originate from is less clear. As I say, regularly updated, verified numbers are elusive. But if true, that'd be a lot of people. Those numbers sound impressive, don't they?

Despite these muscular figures, in 2017 it was estimated in Forbes magazine that 12 million was the average TV viewership globally for a live game. The website www.e-soccer.com also states this number: "On average, every Premier League game has a global audience of over 12 million people." They go on in the same piece to say, "This season the Premier League will break all records for viewing numbers with an estimated 930 million fans watching the games during the 10 month period." They don't state the source of this, nor if they mean 930 million different people, or if this number is an add-up of the audiences for all broadcast games. I suspect it is the latter, possibly to make the number look huge. But if EastEnders attracts 10 million viewers twice a week, we wouldn't say that it had 20 million viewers in that week as most of them would be the same person, nor that over 52 weeks, one billion had watched it in a single year, would we? Not least because one billion could not have watched. I'm sure the 12 million number is the one to focus on. Obviously, it will be much higher for certain games and much lower for others. It is the one most often quoted as a typical or average global audience per broadcast game and I can find no-one who has said it is an average number in any way out of whack with reality.

So we're down to 12 million from a 'potential' 4.7 billion. I can't find out what that 4.7 billion represents. This is part of the problem with all these numbers and why there is so much cynicism about audience figures. They get quoted but without context. Is it 4.7 billion who have an existing subscription to watch football, or 4.7 billion who could literally have one if they wanted to but do not necessarily have one? It's recently been said Sky has 23 million subscribers for its services (many of whom will not have opted for the sports channels) in Europe, so I suspect it is very much the latter but I just can't drill any deeper than that. And as I said previously, I have the strong feeling that if

4.7 billion people were watching each game, the fact would be shouted from the rooftops and there could be no misunderstanding or obfuscation of the facts. The fact that everything is milky and opaque tells its own story.

Now, obviously sometimes as many as 10 games are shown live at the same time outside of the UK. More usually it'd be 5 or 6 on a Saturday afternoon with others spread out from Friday to Monday, which obviously means you have to choose one, as you can't watch them all simultaneously. But to be generous, even if we say that 12 million different people watch each match (which will not be the case but let's go with it to come up with a maximum number) that would be at the very, very, very most 120 million people worldwide as a total audience, for one round of games across a weekend. And it isn't unreasonable to assume that would largely be the same 120 million people most weeks. 120 million out of that proffered potential audience of 4.7 billion is just about 2.5 per cent. That 2.5 per cent is the largest possible estimate - and it will be much less than that in reality - of potential worldwide viewership. And that's only 2.5 per cent of the people who can potentially see it. The population of the world is around 7.7 billion. So to put it simply, any single game is likely to be watched by 12 million people out of 7.7 billion on the planet, which is approximately 0.02 per cent of the people on earth.

You can see that if these numbers are anywhere near true, almost no-one on earth watches the Premier League and we must presume that is because they either can't see it, do not want to pay for it, can't afford to pay for it, are streaming it illegally and thus not counted, or just don't give a shiny shite about it. Yes, you can see it all over the world. It has a big global presence. Search for it and you will find it. Maybe that's why it feels so big. But presence is not the same as popularity.

This all sounds familiar, doesn't it? Big numbers. Big money. Big everything. That's the Premier League's propaganda. But lift up the marketing blanket and peer underneath and things don't look so impressive.

But as you're reading this, like me, you'll be suffering from cognitive dissonance once again. Surely the Premier League is massive, right? Surely it's hugely popular, right? We're told this over and over again. We all believe it is true. All of us. It is a big thing in our lives. It is often said to be one of Britain's most successful exports. In 2010 the Premier League was awarded the 'Queen's Award for Enterprise in the International Trade category for its outstanding contribution to international trade and the value it brings to English football and the United Kingdom's broadcasting industry'.

We've all seen film from remote parts of the world with the locals in old Manchester United shirts crowded around a television showing Chelsea's latest game. That sort of imagery goes deep and it is great publicity for the league and further helps entrench the popularity myth. But let's not forget that 12 million per game global average viewing figure, more than 18 million fewer than watched England play Croatia in the World Cup Semi-final on ITV in the UK.

I think the league has been happy to have two very different things conflated: money and relative, not absolute, popularity.

The Premier League has been a brilliant generator of money. It is the richest league on earth. It pays everyone loads of cash. That is without doubt. It has done that largely through the sale of broadcast rights. Now, statistically there's no doubt they have sold those rights to more territories than any other league and in doing so have ensured that it is the most watched. It absolutely is the most watched league on earth. That 12 million figure is far higher than any global average audience for a game in any other league. This is their claim to fame and it is not insubstantial. Creating a product that more people watch than any other similar product is an incredible achievement. However, this is where a conflation has happened. Because it is the richest and most-watched league, we have all been shaped into thinking it is actually popular in and of itself.

It is more popular than any other league, yes, but still isn't very popular when viewed against its potential audience. By way of a popularity comparison, the global audience for an episode of Top Gear in 2015 was put by CNN at around 350 million per episode.

Surely those who are coughing out the big money to acquire broadcast rights have access to these detailed and accurate figures, and are happy to buy the rights for however much it is they've paid, but it looks to me like everyone has paid massively over the odds, at least if they wanted to make a profit from simply showing the games to the public, so we must assume this is not that important to them.

But then, profitability directly from showing football, for these broadcasters, does not seem to have been their primary concern. It can't have been. The Premier League, especially in the last decade, has been the beneficiary of a strange quirk in media economic history which has seen Sky and A.N. Others prepared to pay huge broadcast rights fees out of profits from elsewhere in their businesses for reasons other than to make money out of showing football, be it to expand subs to other services, harvest or keep broadband punters, or perhaps even to merely depict the company as important and virile. The rights fees therefore are not the proper reflection of the popularity of football that we all assume. When we see they go for billions, we naturally assume it is down to its popularity. Normally, no-one would pay big for something that only a tiny per cent of its potential audience actually watches. But this is what has happened.

As we continue our journey, do keep these numbers in mind in order to keep in perspective how successful the Premier League is, or indeed isn't. Not that anyone in the game especially cares about any of this.

"No-one in the football business understands, or indeed wants to understand how low those figures are. They don't actually care is the truth because of the money they receive. They have no interest in being the game's custodians," says Niall Sloane, Head of ITV Sport, and that is a damning but irresistible verdict. He offers further perspective on these numbers: "These [viewing] stats are all too often thrown out because there is very little chance of anyone asking for a verifiable breakdown. Sky never, ever talk in terms of how many people are watching their output as it is all too paltry. It's been suggested they actually tell Talent and Staff that the true figure is 4 x what BARB figures suggest."

Mark Chapman: "For what it's worth I have never trusted how TV or radio figures are worked out. Execs, producers and presenters love them when they tell them what they want to hear and hate them otherwise. I don't think it's an exact science. Give me someone who takes the time to come up to you and tell you they like what you do, over a spurious figure!"

As I've talked to a lot of such people for this book, the expression 'the Emperor's New Clothes' has been used more than once to describe this situation. It is odd. Possibly unique. But there you have it. Is it any wonder we feel queasy about the Premier League when it is founded on these shakey numbers. Still, even though it isn't as popular as perhaps we had all assumed, at least it's The Best League In The World. Hmm, well, let's have a chat about that next.

THE QUALITY AND COMPETITIVE MYTH

While the Premier League is not very popular on TV, Sky and the league itself have tried to bend our minds to think the exact opposite is true and it's totally worked. It really has. I suspect this is how and why the phrase 'in the Premier League era' came about. Within a few years this was how statistics were expressed and it remains even more the case now, as though it means something. It doesn't. It's an arbitrary parameter. Why define anything by the date of a brand name change? I'll tell you why: It's because it establishes the era as though it is different, separate and other. Special, even. It is nothing but a Maoist-style rewrite of history.

The Premier League isn't and never was some different, higher or special form of the game which required defining as its own era. It's the same game played with the same rules by men in unpleasant man-made fibres. And by the way, we loved football for 120 years before the Premier League and we will love football after we have overthrown it and replaced it with a People's Collective who play in hair shirts and whose wages are paid in turnips.

It's important to state this loudly and often because we have been hypnotised over the years by the propaganda. And I use the word hypnotised advisedly. I don't mean they've dangled a watch in front of our eyes and sent us into a trance, but rather in the more broad sense of making our minds pliant by constant marketing and propaganda up to and including altering the lexicon of football to define stats against the date of the brand change. It has created its own universe. Many of us are susceptible to this sort of unquestioning mind bending. It's not our fault per se, it's just the way we've been made.

I once went to a show by a nice chap called, improbably, Colin Cloud. From a long line of Clouds, presumably. He is an illusionist and a very good one at that. The only issue I have with illusionists is that all they're saying is, "I'm going to fool you, I'm going to fool you, oh look, I fooled you." It is very clever and I guess the enjoyment comes from trying to figure out how they've made the apparently impossible possible, but for me, there's limited pleasure in that. Of course in these days of pragmatism over magic, no-one can claim to be an actual Magic Man with special powers, though I'd rather like it more if they did. However, the brilliant thing about Colin's show was that despite the fact that he makes no claims to have a supernatural gift and is but a brilliant illusionist, some members of his audience continue to believe in his 'powers'.

He later told me part of his art was spotting people who were susceptible in various degrees to various types of suggestion and subconscious guiding. There are, apparently, people who are wide open for anything like this and people who just aren't. Part of the illusionist's art is to spot them. These were the people who found that their backsides were indeed stuck to their seats on his command and who yelped in amazement at every sleight of hand, as though he was performing miracles. He was brilliant at it and had clearly put in loads of work to get that good but I kept thinking, he's just an illusionist. I couldn't get wrapped up in it the way some clearly could, which is odd really as I'm away with the fairies so much of the time.

My point here is we have very malleable minds that will absorb and believe what the Premier League, or indeed anyone else, pushes at them if done with enough slickness, persistence and opacity. I know this because people Tweet me with regurgitations of the Premier League's 'Best League...' propaganda, presumably unaware they are doing it. Of course, all the best propaganda is repeated verbatim but believed to be individual thought. Indeed, until I started writing this, I believed a lot of it as well. I found it hard to conceive just how unpopular it is on TV worldwide but that is only because of their ceaseless mindwipe, forever pushing how big it is.

And another of their mindbenders - long promulgated - is that the league attracts 'the best players in the world' and now 'the best managers in the world' as well as being 'the best league in the world'; thus, speaking out against the league and the money in the league is speaking out against great football, is being a killjoy or a misery. Those who say this are exactly where the league wants them, doing all their work. Someone once told me, "I just want to see the world's finest athletes. If we don't pay them the big money, they won't play over here." This is what I mean about the profound effect of propaganda. The lad that said that to me had drunk deep of the Premier League Kool-Aid but didn't even know it.

I see the very idea of trying to establish this as a notion or truth is silly and merely league propaganda. You can dig out long lists of tedious statistics to prove and disprove whatever theory you're drumming up, but my long years watching the game has taught me one thing and one thing only about football; it is a subjective artform and objective truths are very few and far between. I'm not even sure the ball is round. So trying to prove one league is better than another on any basis you care to name is a total waste of valuable consciousness. Indeed, before the Premier League, no-one ever rated the First Division against any other league on earth. Why would you? There's simply no point at all. But now, it's an everyday thing. It's the league's invention, a seed it planted and it is impossible not to see it as part of the propaganda for Premier to mean, not just first, but best or premium and thus worth buying.

And anyway, just what is the difference between great football, entertaining football and good football? Are they all the same thing? Can you only play the best, great, entertaining or good football if players are likewise best, great, entertaining or good? Confusingly, all of these are true and also absolutely none are true.

As ever, football is a mercurial beast that resists definition. But marketers hate such vagaries. We've all seen football from the World Cup down to local amateur level that is largely tedious. We've also seen wonderfully entertaining games between local amateur sides as much as by title winners. Beyond some basics, any football can be wonderfully dramatic and thrilling and any can be simply awful. I've seen world-class goals scored by largely useless pub players, I've seen world-class players play like pub players. This is why football is so popular as entertainment.

We all think we know what a great player looks like, but whether we do or not, I'm not sure greatness is important to enjoying football. Clearly, some modicum of skill helps games to flow and I wouldn't recommend clubs play any fat old lummock, but football's entertaining qualities do not solely rest on whether you've got a Lionel Messi in your side to display outrageous skills and tricks. If it did, almost no-one would watch football. Yes, you need some ability. Some skill. Some way to more than occasionally kick the ball accurately. But other attractions also exist.

Take Mesut Ozil. Please. A World Cup winner with Germany and one of the finest footballers in Germany in the last decade. But at Arsenal he's been very patchy. Occasionally brilliant, mostly not. He can play very skilful football and has proven this in Germany. But as he's not doing it now very often, are we watching an elite player or not? I don't know and neither does anyone else. That's because there is no definite answer. He's a very good player who sometimes plays badly or ineffectively. That's it. In this way we see the pointlessness of endorsing the league's money model because it allows for the acquiring of talent like Ozil at £350,000 per week. What his lavish wages have delivered is some occasionally very good football, nothing more than that. Is that really what anyone who supports the existence of the Premier League and how it does its business really wants in return for this brutal money-first economic culture, which has hived off football to TV channels that few watch, hiked up ticket prices and put paying planet-breaking fees and wages at the centre of its philosophy? Is watching Ozil be good sometimes really what that is all about? That's just daft. It doesn't make any sense and I think we all know it doesn't.

Footballers are humans, not products, not robots or computer game avatars. And as such they are subject to the emotional stresses and strains of life. They can be ill, or be worried, happy or depressed. And all of these things will affect their ability to deploy their talents. Thus we can have a player who, when content and happy, can play 'elite' football but when not, won't. The game acknowledges this in these more enlightened days, with clubs employing sports psychologists to address mental health. Footballers are not a homogeneous product the way an upmarket car or sweater (most often) is.

Perhaps it is no wonder some fans get angry at players. Ozil and his ilk are just really good footballers who, like all footballers, will not play well sometimes. The fact they've been elevated to some god-like status by virtue of trousering £1.4 million per month is not criticism of them per se, but of the economic philosophy which made this happen. While it is true that broadly, the clubs that spend the most on fees and wages are most successful (depending on how you define successful), the idea that just coughing up £350,000 per week to a man like Ozil is a guarantee he'll be great, is madness. Indeed, I'd suggest the success of the richest clubs is as much down to how many times they can get it wrong without it impacting on them financially, as much as how much money they spend on a player per se. Ozil has been the recipient of this philosophy's immoral largesse and consequently he's being held to account against a standard that does not actually exist and which he can therefore never live up to. How crazy is that? Indeed, I think I should state clearly that while I consider the financial system that pays players so much money is downright wrong, I don't blame them for taking it. It isn't, or it hasn't been, their job to think about the economics or ecological impact of their income or of anything else. They're just geezers who turn up and kick a ball around. So all of these words are not an evisceration of them or their morals. They were just there when Pandora's Box was opened and let all these demons run amok.

So where does one start with these deep, DNA-level confusions? This idea that there is somehow a list of 'best players in the world' is all part of what I think of as the commodification of footballers brought about by the Premier League's money madness. It's repeated to try and justify the insane money. It is as though they are items for sale in a store. This orthodoxy believes that the ones who are worth the most, or are paid the most, must therefore be the best. It stands absolutely no scrutiny because, as I say, they're humans. Oh, and football is a team game, not a competition for individuals.

The Premier League (and quite possibly all the football management games over the years, too) has turned people into consumers or customers of football rather than fans. Football has become a form of shopping rather than sport. The league wants us to believe we're buying the best in the same way we want to buy the Taste the Difference range in Sainsbury's if we want a nice fillet of beef. I suppose when we're slaves to consumerism as a lifestyle, philosophy and mindset, that is quite understandable. Why wouldn't we think the one that costs the most is the best? Why wouldn't we think that lashing out money is the way to success, when we define our lives in the same way? If we default to the philosophy of 'the one with most stuff wins' then we're going to apply that to football as well.

I probably don't need to explain this to you, but I will do so anyway, just to make the point.

Football is not food shopping. All levels of football deliver great games, decent games and tedious, boring games. That's what the sport is all about. A side of 11 £100 million players will not inevitably deliver a 10 times more entertaining game than one with 11 £10 million players. That's just not how football works, even if we could accurately measure entertainment, which we can't.

Last season for example, under Jose Mourinho, we saw Manchester United field sides that cost upwards of £400 million in transfer fees getting beaten by sides that cost a quarter of that or less. We saw them playing terrible, boring football. How can this be when they'd spent so much money on great players? Because footballers are human, managers are human and money is not the measure of a human, that's how.

One player may cost £10 million, another £20 million, it doesn't mean they are twice as good. And even if they were, how could you even measure that to prove such a judgement? The truth is, you can't. There's no ruler to put alongside a player that measures their talent. There are no Top Trump cards. There is no way to prove that any player is worth whatever the fee that is paid for them. The only proof of his value there can ever be is merely that some club will pay that number. It has no greater profundity than that, and it never will. But the fierceness with which some fans assert they need a £50 million striker or goalkeeper, or more commonly still complain that a highly priced player has not played to a standard commensurate with the fee paid for him, illustrates just how deeply this notion has been swallowed.

I should also point out to everyone under the age of 35 that there was a time when we simply did not talk about players and money in this way. It only ever happened in extremis, such as when Trevor Francis became the first million-pound footballer. But the rest of the time it was barely mentioned and certainly not obsessed over as a measure of how ambitious your club was. This has all happened on the Premier League's watch. The league is the reason it happens. People might think it is natural or has always happened, but I'm here to tell you it hasn't.

If you remember football before this institutionalised money madness, you'll remember a thing called youth development, which involved coaching, training and teamwork. It was great. It was possible to regularly see 15-year-old players do well in the youth team, then the reserves and then the first team. Indeed, it was one of the best things about following a club. In fact, and this will shock you if you're under 30, there was a time some football fans thought buying players was a cheat, a shortcut to success, only necessary because you didn't have any local talent to bring on or because your coaching was rubbish, or both. Today, that sort of thinking has become all but outlawed. If you said that, people would look at you like you were insane. Not buy your way to success? What sort of fool thinks like that? Well, many of us used to. And we were not wrong. The money game the Premier League invented has taken that from us. This loss has made life worse, not better.

Money is now the be all and end all.

If you doubt me, as I write this, the story about Chelsea keeper Kepa Arrizabalaga refusing to come off the pitch in the League Cup Final against Manchester City is breaking. Almost every account of this states how much he cost and how much he's paid. And this is used by many as a reason Chelsea couldn't afford to get rid of the rebel player; they'd spent so much on him. This is merely one example, but nothing in the Premier League happens without being set into a financial context.

This isn't sport at all, it is high finance and banking. This is what the Premier League and its obsession with ever more huge amounts of income has bequeathed us. The language of finance is now the language of football. In the top flight, money culture isn't just part of the brand, it is pretty much the whole of it. That's why we need to smash the Premier League and replace it with something which has sport and fun at its core, not greed and money.

So ingrained in the football psyche has this commodification become that many do not even realise they're doing it. Time and again discussion on radio or TV turns to 'investment', to how much a manager has or hasn't spent, gross or net, to what a player cost or didn't cost. Were they too expensive, were they cheap? Partly this is because of the need to fill the expanded media with things to talk about, but it has become ceaseless. All of football is now seen through a financial lens.

Even despite the fact that clubs can only make transfers in the two windows, every newspaper and website is stuffed full of transfer speculation, along with fee and wage estimates, every day of the year. It's big business. It drives more traffic than literally anything else. You can have the most brilliantly written dissection of a player, a game, or of the culture of football, but it will not attract anywhere near the same interest as some made-up bullshit about Gareth

Bale going to Manchester United, even though these confected rumours are littered with caveat expressions like 'thought to be', 'could be interested in', 'monitoring the situation' and a hundred other ways to insert a get-out clause into some fiction made up by a newspaper in order to garner clicks from the gullible or careless. Or they just shamelessly make stuff up. This is another horrible consequence of the Premier League's celebration and pursuit of greed, another manifestation of commodification. Who is your club shopping for?

But hold on. The one who spends the most tends to win most things, right? Not always, but usually. So spending big is the way to success. So what are you on about, Nicholson you old fool? Of course clubs who have the big cash will spend it to get success. Of course money culture will become the dominant culture when this is the case.

This is certainly true. While money is wasted with appalling incontinence, it does still buy success most of the time. Which is why the Big Money culture, I find, is anti-sport. When the playing field is so uneven, it diminishes competition. The seemingly direct relationship between expenditure and success isn't a perfect equation. Plenty spend big and don't win anything, but the ones who do win usually have spent the most over time. Leicester City was a brilliant one-season outlier to this and has given hope to all clubs below the top six, but outside of that, we pretty much know which of the clubs will finish in the top places from now until the end of time (unless one of them absolutely implodes), if not the exact order. There is a chance other teams might break into the top six but the likelihood is receding. In other words, the league is ever more predictable even if the massive spending on any individual can be a terrible waste. Here I should mention the money pit that is Alexis Sanchez, more of whom later. So we're losing out on two fronts by Big Money culture becoming the totality of football culture in the top flight. Money becomes the focus through which is everything is seen. But even though it more or less guarantees a top six finish for the six biggest spending clubs, it sets players up to fail to meet the level of skill the money paid suggests they should have, thus engendering bitterness and unhappiness in fans, and hey, it also reduces competition. Great, huh?

Two very clever Americans, James P. Curley and Oliver Roeder, calculated in March 2016, that

"From 1995-96 to 2014-15, the same four teams account for an astonishing 80% of EPL, 76% of Eredivisie, 68% of La Liga, 65% of Bundesliga, 65% of Serie A and 58% of Ligue 1 top-four finishes. In terms of unique top-four finishers, 16 different teams have finished in the top four of Ligue 1 and 15 different teams in La Liga. Conversely, just 10 unique teams have finished in the top four of the EPL and Eredivisie. This analysis of the more successful sides in each league would actually suggest that the EPL is the least competitive league, while Ligue 1 is the most competitive.

"To get an even fuller picture of competitive balance, we can also look at the relative performance of all teams in a league in each season. To do this, we use a metric borrowed from the economics literature - the Gini coefficient. The Gini essentially describes the inequality in a group, and is often used to describe income inequality.

"If the relative difference between individuals of incremental ranks in some outcome measure (e.g., points gained in a season) is generally equal, then the Gini will be close to zero. But if this outcome measure is distributed highly unevenly then the Gini too will be higher. In this figure, striking trends emerge. Since the mid-1990s, the Gini of three leagues (England, Spain and Germany) have been steadily increasing. This means that more points are ending up in the hands of relatively fewer teams - the leagues are becoming more unbalanced. Among these, the EPL has consistently been the most unbalanced."

This was in 2016, before Leicester City's unexpected win. Since then the top six has been financially shored up to make sure such an interloper never has a chance again. So it will be even less competitive and even more unbalanced in 2019. This isn't to say that money will not be wasted and frittered away on overpriced, overpaid players. It will. But the richest clubs can always afford even expensive players to be flops and thus are insulated against their own bad decisions to a large degree.

Yes, that's the glorious Premier League, the least competitive and the most unbalanced. What an achievement! Anyone can't beat anyone, as is often said.

On top of that, we hear all the time that because the league has a top six who are notionally battling it out to win the title, this means the league overall is somehow more competitive, when all it's done is create 14 also-rans who have little or no chance, not just of winning the title but of getting into an elevated position. Fourteen who almost never beat the top six. The gap looks set to get ever wider as the biggest earners with the richest owners pouring seemingly limitless funds into their clubs to ensure it is a kind of closed league within itself. Leicester City acted as a powerful cattle prod in this regard. We now have discussions about which team has a chance of breaking into the top six. This is now A Thing. But in what other sporting world would we think a team finishing 6th was in any way important. As I write, which is before the 2019/20 season begins, some think for various reasons, mostly due to some of the top six being a bit rubbish, Wolves or Leicester or Everton might achieve this in terms which suggest this might be some sort of democratisation of the league. If they think this, they're fooling themselves. It might happen once or twice, every now and again, but such small cracks in the top six hegemony will never change anything for long.

Before the Premier League existed, things were different. The league was much more competitive and less predictable. Let me illustrate.

The first season I recall in detail is 1969-70. Everton won the title, Leeds United were runners-up, then came Chelsea, Derby, Liverpool, Coventry. The following season, Arsenal won the title after finishing 12th the previous campaign. Leeds were again second, then came Spurs, Wolves, Liverpool, Chelsea. In other words, half the top six were different from one season to the next. The following year, Manchester City and Derby County entered the top six, Derby being champions, Arsenal dropped to 5th. By 1972-73, it was all change again with Liverpool winning, and West Ham, Wolves and Ipswich entering the top six. Next year, Leeds won but we saw Stoke City finish 5th and Burnley 6th. A year later QPR rose from 11th, yes 11th, to almost beat Liverpool for the title.

You can see the point I'm making here. You had no idea who was going to win the title and in many ways, even better than that, you had no idea who would finish in the European places. Even when Liverpool began to win the league on a regular basis in the late 70s and into the 80s, the 'supporting' cast was always changing. From 1979 to 1992 Nottingham Forest, Ipswich, Watford, Southampton, Everton, Swansea, QPR, WBA, West Ham, Sheffield Wednesday, Norwich, Wimbledon, Crystal Palace, and Leeds United (the last winners of the First Division) all finished in the top six at some point. Aston Villa, Forest, Everton and Leeds United also won the title in those years.

What would we give for that level of unpredictability now? Change and variation was once the norm. We had no real idea who might do well and who might not before the season started. This is, by the way, a good thing and it is still very much the case in the Championship.

But of course when Big Money is involved, those spending the money do not want variation or unpredictability. They want to know they'll get a return on their investment. The last thing anyone wants is the placement shifts of yore. This is Big Business and Big Business likes predictability and, if possible, some sort of closed shop to ensure it is always thus because free money beats all the talk of free market capitalism and market forces that surrounds the game. Far better that your market is not free but rather is boxed off in your favour.

Yet, obviously, unpredictability is vital for sport. If you always know with a good amount of certainty what is going to be the outcome of most games, it defeats the point of even playing them. Without unpredictability, it becomes an exhibition rather than a competition. And this is the wonderful Premier

League: a greedy cartel of predictability. It's another reason why we must undermine it and bring it to an end.

However, this does not mean that there isn't good football to enjoy. I wouldn't want my critique to be framed as being curmudgeonly about the fun it offers. Football can be great fun at any level you watch it, and so it is in the top flight. As I write this, the Champions League semi-finals have just been played and a more thrilling couple of games you will likely never see. Inevitably it has been sold to us as 'a great advert for the Champions League' when it is nothing of the sort. It is a great advert for football. Not for any specific brand or tournament. What was thrilling was the sport. The fact I'm even having to state this shows how much brainwashing there is to constantly fight.

Clubs trying to get promoted to the Premier League are now sold the idea as a good thing because it's worth £200 million, or whatever the latest eye-widening number that has been confected to impress. Not for any other reason, though. No. Promotion = money. That's it. Thanks for the poetry. Thanks for the soul. Let's just have a hand shandy over the money. And that's why the fans at some clubs are realising what is going on and they don't care about the club getting a load of money because they know that it'll be horrible entertainment, that they'll try to hang onto 17th, win 7 games in a year, draw 10 and lose 21 and if they're lucky, survive to do it all over again.

They know it will be no fun and have no additional worth. Time and again I've been told by fans of clubs that have relatively recently been in the top flight, that they do not want to go back up, or rather, if they don't go up, they won't shed too many tears. Some would love to win the Championship but would opt to remain unpromoted, which doesn't seem unreasonable. This cynicism is even extending to clubs that don't struggle badly when promoted, who, after a couple of seasons of mid-table finishes, begin to wonder what on earth it is all for and that there is an impenetrable block on progress. We see this at the moment with the likes of Bournemouth and Burnley, both of whom have done really well to stay in the league. Burnley's 7th-place finish in 2018 was remarkable. But now what? The best they can hope for is to finish 7th again...and again...and again, with ever-diminishing degrees of satisfaction. But that won't happen. This thinking does not account for everyone of course but there has to be a waning of interest for many when all that lies ahead is trying to stay up.

Obviously, bad teams have never been able to compete in the top division at any time in the history of football. The bottom couple of sides are not bottom for no reason. Ever was it thus. But that's not what I'm talking about and it is all too typical to get misunderstood on an issue like this as the mindwipe kicks in and tells people to reject my criticism of the league. Those who think I'm looking back to the good old days instead of being all thrusting and modern as they perceive themselves to be, point to how half of the clubs in every league season have little to play for by the time spring rolls around. That's one of the natures of a league competition. And this is largely true - and I believe, is something that has always needed to be addressed by installing some sort of fight-out for those in the nothing-to-play-for central section of the league.

But what is new, compared to 30 or more years ago, is two-fold. First, 14 sides know in August that 7th is almost certainly the highest position to strive for. Yes, there is always a small possibility that one of the big six will have some sort of meltdown and one club can sneak into 6th for a season - an accidental improvement in position rather than a seized one born of performance. People are saying Leicester City might make 6th in the 2019/2020 season because Manchester United are so dysfunctional, but that in itself only illustrates where we are - that finishing 6th would be hailed as a big achievement for them. And even in this scenario it'll only be one big club that implodes and it'll only be for one season before the big club reasserts their primacy. Chelsea are the best example of this when they went from 1st to 10th to 1st a couple of seasons back.

So the vast majority start each season knowing the limits of their achievements. That can't be right. It is fundamentally dispiriting. Fans take to lying to themselves to pretend they could break into the top six and of course, Leicester City's 2016 win gives everyone hope that such a confluence of circumstances could happen again and gives them ammunition against people like me who argue against this status quo, even though I'm actually trying to create a situation where the lies they are telling themselves could actually come true. Which seems a bit harsh, all in all. But as I say, the Premier League hypnosis is strong.

And second, while it is true that the bottom two or three have always lost games in the same sort of volume as they do today, where the shift has happened is in the games the top six play against the 7th through 12th - the next six. Those games are much harder for the lower club to win or even draw, especially when playing away from home.

Bournemouth, as I write this, are 12th (they finished 13th, 50 points off the top, 30 off the bottom), that most catatonic of positions. Their season is over and done with 7 games to go. It was probably over with 12 games to go, in truth. The thrill is surely if not gone, then diminished. Who could blame their fans for wondering if this is how it will be forever now? As next season begins, what can they possibly hope for?

On the BBC, Jermaine Jenas inadvertently voiced this when he rhetorically asked, "What are Everton for?" As I write, Everton are 11th with 40 points (they finished 8th with 53 points, 13 off Manchester United in 6th) and have absolutely no chance of being relegated, but also absolutely no chance of finishing higher than 7th. They spent over £100 million on players in summer 2018. And for what? All of that money frittered away for what, exactly? Seventh is no different to 8th, 10th or 13th. Not really. OK you might get a Europa League place but so many fans, players and managers seem to think that's more a burden than a reward.

Some fans are disgruntled, but when you hear them call into 5live's 606 show they cannot articulate exactly why. It's sad, really. They've tried different managers, they've tried spending big, but still end up in that middle section. There's no obvious route to greater success for them, because there is no route at all. You can hear in their voices that they are a little perplexed, and that it all just feels wrong. Right there is the existential angst I've been talking about. A feeling of general unease and discontent with your club. Nothing to fight for. Nothing to gain. Only existing, nothing but existing with almost zero hope that it will ever be any other way. Everton's late run of decent results that gave them their 8th finish is now being offered up as hope for the next season along with some good summer signings. But that's just football's short-termism kicking in; a habit of judging not across the piece but by what has just happened. To finish 13 points off a poor United side was still a gulf and one that will not be impossible but will be very hard for them to cross unless United are even worse next season.

When JJ posed that question, it wasn't one anyone had an answer for, not even Everton. I feel melancholic about it because Everton were the side that won the First Division in 1969, the first season that I began to really take an interest in the game. Everton should have a chance of winning the league every season. But they don't have a hope in hell of doing that. They'd need hundreds of millions of pounds thrown at them for several years to even give themselves a fighting chance. I suppose it isn't impossible that someone will do that but it feels like an absolutely desperate thing to have to wish for in order to merely have a chance. It should not have to be that way. The league should be more fair and more even and then it would be less predictable and more enjoyable. This isn't deep thinking on my part, is it? It's just obvious.

I'll tell you someone who knows this all too well: Mike Ashley. Ashley owns Newcastle United, though he seems to wish he didn't. He won't put enough money into the club to make them a successful top-five side, but will put in just enough for them to survive in the top flight or enough to get them back in after relegation. Everyone loathes him, and rightly so, but he's not as stupid as his dress sense (those strange half mast, straight-up-and-down jeans worn with a white shirt and black shoes won't leave my mind). He knows that throwing a few hundred million at it and still ending up eight points short of 6th is a waste of money because 7th is the same in many ways as 17th, apart from the £20 million extra you get from your Merit Payment. Newcastle could be a huge club if someone put in a billion over the next five years, but short of that, there's no point in investing heavily to achieve nothing, especially when you want to sell the place. Ashley is just the most obvious example of the grotesque nature of modern football finances and ownership. But if you're him, and lord knows that would be a heinous curse, it makes sense.

However, when anyone critiques anything to do with football and football clubs, people get very defensive. Everton fans don't want to read someone who is saying that they've no chance of finishing above 7th in August and some would get angry at naysayers like me. They dig their heels in and insist it is possible for them to break the top six this year. And of course, it is possible, I don't deny that, but I strongly question the likelihood of it happening once, let alone consistently. And even if they do, it's not that much of an achievement. There's no cup for sixth or fifth. It seems bitterly ironic but entirely typical of how the Premier League's mind bending works that critics like me take all the flak for 'crushing' the dreams of those 14 clubs with our cynicism, when of course, it is the league that has ensured this is the case. It is their money-focused, money-hoovering, money-attracting economic philosophy which has brought this situation about, coupled with a cavalier attitude to who can own clubs. But the league is very good at deflecting the blame and casting those who see through its veil of propaganda as the villains and killjoys.

I once had someone raging at me on Twitter saying how great it was that there was a top six and that it used to be a top four, so that proved how much more competitive the league now was. When I pointed out that six clubs being so much better than the rest just made it harder for the rest than when it was four and has made 7th the peak finish possible, rather than 5th, he may have actually exploded. "But six is more than four, you moron!" he declaimed, not seeing that the league is 20 sides. I withdrew, feeling that if you're being rude to people on social media you deserve not to be interacted with. It's just wearing and depressing. But I thought at the time how the Premier League would have been delighted, even proud at his response to its mind medicine. Imagine getting cross at someone arguing for a more broadly spread, ambitious and fair competition? At someone who wants a more even playing field, someone who just wants it all to be more unpredictable. It's odd. When you've got the oppressed defending their right to be oppressed rather than celebrating those trying to free them, you've done a brilliant job of twisting people's minds. To understand this phenomenon, we have to establish where it fits in history. So let's just paddle in those historical waters for a little while.

THE HISTORY MYTH

While Premier League football may not be very popular behind the paywalls, it most certainly is popular in the grounds. Attendances are at high levels of capacity, season in and season out and Sky et al. will absolutely aggrandise themselves on the back of this if they can, as they've made the league part of their brand identity. Yet, sometimes it is forgotten that grounds could be full in part because half the stadiums are under 35,000 capacity; Bournemouth, for example, is 11,329. These are still big numbers by any other standards of public events, but selling out a 22,000-seat stadium is obviously easier than a 44,000-seat one. However, the fact remains, a heck of a lot of people attend the Premier League on match days.

Conditions and facilities have improved hugely since the dark days of football's crumbling and dangerous infrastructure in the 1980s when many grounds had barely been modernised since the second world war.

I talked to Pat Murphy, one of our veteran and very wise broadcasters: "You've got to remember the 80s was not a good time. Hooliganism was rampant, fans were staying away. I remember being at Aston Villa when there was 9,000 in the ground. I produced the outside broadcast at Hillsborough, so I don't see that period at all with a rosy glow. Thatcher's attitude to fans was inimical. Lord Justice Taylor was a hero."

Now, the Premier League propagandists would have you believe the improvement from these days is all because of The Greatest League In The World earning more money for clubs which could then be invested in the stadiums. And there is some truth in this. Of course there is. There's no doubt that as the financial power of the league grew, clubs began to update and modernise their stadia with the increased income.

What is less clear is what would have happened had the league never come into being. The Taylor Report post Hillsborough had made many recommendations to clubs in order to make grounds safer. It's also true that the police upgraded how they operate on match day. They learned to police crowds better, which made attending games safer. And some of these reforms were already in swing when the Premier League came into being in 1992. In other words, when it came to safety, the improvements may have happened anyway. After all, there has always been plenty of money going into popular successful football clubs. The sad fact is that too little of it was ever invested in facilities for fans. Typically we were treated by all and sundry like so much manky cattle and the lush profits were harvested by directors. Turnover was far smaller, of course, but then costs, especially wages, were as well.

It also needs saying that many feel the new grounds built in the last 25 years lack the atmosphere of yore. And while there may be lots of nice concrete concourses populated with outlets selling slices of pizza, somehow I find it hard to see that as an especially progressive advancement. However, one important thing about new grounds being built now is that they are far greener and more ecologically responsible. Spurs' new White Hart Lane stadium is a great example of this with recycling at the core of how it's run and low energy consumption a real consideration. Brilliant.

So in this regard, the finances drummed up in part by the Premier League - though also by super rich owners investing their own money - have been used to improve some aspects of match days. It would be churlish not to acknowledge that, though frankly, strictly in terms of facilities, going to see the Boro at the Riverside compared to going to Ayresome Park is, in and of itself, a far more soulless experience. I cannot prove this to you, of course. It is a metaphysical notion but it is one deeply felt by many. The Boro was never so packed that it was dangerous, or not in my experience. The improvements are in the lack of violence and the generally less malevolent air. That's a lot to do with many things, but not particularly the stadium that the football is being played in. So while we need to acknowledge the improvements investments in stadia delivered, we also need to acknowledge that something was lost in that process.

I do question whether creating the Premier League was the only way that this could've happened, but regardless, listen to how often the fact that grounds are largely full is used as an endorsement not just of the Premier League, but by extension its politics and economic model. Yes, we're back to the PR mindwipe. It is in play all the time and on every level and on every issue. It is worth pointing out again, in case anyone has forgotten, that football has a long history of being really popular well before the Premier League existed. It isn't called the People's Game for no reason.

It is also worth pointing out at this juncture that there is considerable cynicism about the attendance figures at Premier League grounds. This is largely because they're often declared to be a sell-out, or near sell-out, even when there are acres of empty seats clearly visible. This has especially been said at Arsenal, Manchester City and Manchester United. Greater Manchester Police records revealed the average crowd at Old Trafford during the 2012-13 season was almost 10,000 lower than Manchester United's figure. The feeling is that the clubs assess attendance by ticket sales, not by people actually being there. As an illustration of the Premier League mentality, that couldn't be better. Only paying counts, being there doesn't matter. It is an inversion of everything we understand by the word attendance. It's as plastic as the empty seats.

As I say, the truth is, football attracted huge crowds when we didn't even know the names of all of the players, let alone anyone from across the seas. In other words, we went because we loved football as a game, not as some sort of celebrity-spotting activity. Whether it does or doesn't feature the best players in the world, is largely irrelevant to most of us. If it were not, Sunderland would not have, as I write, just got 41,000 to watch them in the 3rd tier and Leyton Orient wouldn't be averaging over 5,000 in the National League. Think about it, if a band pulls a 5,000 audience, they have to be pretty popular. Orient are doing it in the unglamorous 5th tier.

If you still doubt that football love has nothing to do with the Premier League, a cursory look shows that the biggest attendances almost every club in the four leagues have registered happened between the 1920s and 1970s, the top 40 of which are all over 42,000 and the only ones set in the last 30 years are Arsenal and Spurs attendances whilst playing at Wembley when their new grounds were getting developed and West Ham United's at their new and widely disliked London Stadium. Manchester City would like you to think their expensive team and manager are incredibly popular, but in 1949 a 6th Round FA Cup game against Stoke City pulled in just under 90,000 to Maine Road.

When Huddersfield Town played Arsenal in a 1932 6th Round Cup game, the crowd was 67,037. When Bolton took on Manchester City in the FA Cup 5th Round in 1933 the crowd was 69,912. The Merseyside derby in 1948 pulled 78,299 into Goodison Park. This simply illustrates how popular football was. So I have to say it again: The Premier League did not make it popular with its magic stardust or - and this is important - with its money. But the league would have you believe there was nothing before 1992 and that its era is the only era. But then it is no respecter of any tradition it did not itself create and certainly not the League Cup and the FA Cup. So let's look at them and find out what's been going on.

THE CUP ISN'T DEVALUED MYTH

It is the fault of the Premier League that most clubs in the Premier League and many lower still, no longer play their strongest team in the FA or League Cup, or at least not until the later rounds, favouring resting players for the league fights. This would have shocked and appalled fans even just 20 years ago and it was never the case before the Premier League existed, even though clubs had far fewer resources. Indeed, a peculiarity of the riches that have flowed into football clubs via the broadcasting rights windfall is that it seems to have left them feeling less able to fight on two or more fronts. It is as though the money has made them poorer! Which is weird. How else to explain why some of the richest clubs in world football can't bring themselves to play as strong a team as possible in the cups and in the league? It is as if the money has bought them no advantage. And of course, that is absolutely true. It hasn't. Or at least not beyond a point. It isn't infinitely elastic in its effect. Indeed, anyone who watched Aberdeen take on Burnley in the Europa League qualifiers in 2018 at time when the Lancastrian club were rated as 30th richest on the planet, would not have known the difference between them. It was a 1-1 draw at Pittodrie and the Dons really should have won it. Although the return leg went in the Premier League club's favour 3-1, the financial gulf between the two suggested a walkover that never transpired. In other words, Burnley's Premier League income had bought them some superiority in that tie, but not much.

The really sickening thing is that even those mid-ranking clubs who are not threatened with relegation still put out the reserves in cup games. The money available to them by staying in the Premier League has blinded them to all and anything else. We even hear players saying that they'd rather stay in the league than win a trophy if they had to make a choice. This is how deep the indoctrination has gone. Get down on your knees and worship money, this is banking not sport. That is a wholly Premier League invention, or at best, a consequence of the economic philosophy on which its existence is based. Sometimes it feels like the football is just getting in the way of clubs making money and genuflecting at the feet of Mammon.

The 3rd Round of the FA Cup always was one of the greatest days in the season. Then it became the day when we said it used to be one of the greatest days in the season, but it was now devalued. And now, in a classic postmodern twist, it's the day we bemoan the fact that it's the day when everyone says the FA Cup is devalued. Indeed, possibly the worst thing about the FA Cup is the endless debate about it. But of course it is devalued to the point of being little but a stone in the shoe of the clubs. A manager can even win it and still get sacked for not doing well enough in the league. That's how little regard it is held in within football. Whether the fans do or don't love it - the truth is, opinions are mixed - the game itself at the Premier League level is almost wholly disinterested, with but a few exceptions. It's no use pointing to the latter stages when they play their best sides; that is just proof of its decline, not proof of its success.

The FA Cup is 147 years old, first being held in 1871-1872. It's still hanging on, and like all football, it can still deliver excitement and fun, but it's a fraud. It's the faux FA Cup. It's wearing FA Cup clothes, but it isn't the FA Cup any more and this is all the fault of the Premier League. Wherever you stand on the spectrum of affection for it, from total disinterest to romantic belief, it is not what it once was.

Hypocritically, the FA Cup trades off its history and traditions but can't or won't honour them. In 2019 only 10 of 32 3rd Round games kicked off at Saturday 3pm in order to accommodate various global rights holders and this was a classic example of its hypocrisy. All the heft and weight inculcated by a big schedule of games was lost. There was a palpable lack of 3rd Round vibe. As the 7 5.30pm games played out, it felt as though everyone just wanted it to be over.

Every club used to take it seriously, now they don't. Clubs always played their best side, now the top two divisions almost never do. Being in the Premier League makes you one of the top 30 richest clubs on earth, but win the FA Cup and you get £3.6 million, which will probably be eaten up in two months by your highest-paid player's wages.

The Premier League has ensured money matters to clubs more than anything else. So how can any competition have any credibility when many of those taking part are not trying their hardest to win it? Yes, fans of lower-league clubs enjoy beating a higher-placed club, of course they do; fans take their pleasure wherever they can find it, we all do. But once the excitement has died down, even they know that such wins are not what they once were and are conducted on a totally different basis.

Fans of all clubs universally loved the FA Cup, but now many just don't care at all. It has been demoted in the national football affection. TV and radio people can go on all they like about how great the cup is but many are just not buying it. It always pulled in big crowds, now it often doesn't.

Winning the cup was the most glamorous achievement of any season. Now, absolutely no-one thinks it is. Back in the day, people rarely minded replays, in fact they all added to the excitement. A second or third often became legendary, but today a replay is always 'the last thing they want' as though playing football is a burden that gets in the way of hoovering up loads of cash, as though winning in the cup is actually losing, as though they are impoverished of resources.

And even when the games are played, it is palpably a more predictable thing. The same clubs end up winning it by and large. Just 8 teams have won it in the last 27 years, whereas in the first 27 years of my life 16 different teams won it. The League Cup fares a little better, possibly because so many sides think even less of it and field reserves and youth team players. Thirteen have won it in the last 27 years, whereas 18 won it in my first 27 years.

Variables have been reduced. Pitches used to vary massively in quality, some all sand and mud, thus creating a skill-levelling factor. But that's rarely the case now and if a rough pitch does exist, it is even thought a bad thing and anti-football.

Income disparities between the various tiers were once much more narrow, giving lower-league sides more of a chance of victory by virtue of having good old veterans and talented young players. Now there is an absolute gulf. While lower-league sides do beat higher-placed teams, it is almost always because the bigger side hasn't played its first team and has 'rested' players, thus hugely reducing the achievement. We are invited to pretend this is still a giant-killing, but in our hearts, we know it isn't. Or at least it isn't 4th Division Colchester United beating 1st Division Leeds United in 1971. The expression "they've put out quite a strong side" is the very telling modern-day media apologia when it comes to cup football. The fact some keep shouting at us that the cup is not dead, is only proof that it is in its autumn years.

However, as I say, one thing cup football does provide for us is an illustration of how popular football can be when on terrestrial free-to-air TV.

BT Sport are sharing the broadcast rights with the BBC in 2019, but BT audiences are small. A Spurs cup game on a Friday night got an average of 357,000 viewers with a peak of 540,000. The BBC on the other hand got a peak of the best part of 8 million for the United vs Arsenal cup game.

Even though it was an early round in the competition, even though interest in the cup is much diminished, the BBC still got nearly 8 million watching. BT or Sky can only dream of such popularity.

Third Round day also used to be special because it was one single programme of unique games that all happened at the same time and were all governed on the same basis, but now with 9 of 32 games this year deploying VAR (video assistant referee), that can never ever be said again. As VAR will only ever be at Premier League grounds, any game played elsewhere will not be subjected to it. Hence the game will be officiated on two different bases. The competition is forever fractured. Broken into pieces, never to be put back together, the sense of community evaporated.

I'd like to take a sidebar here to discuss VAR. A product of the law of unintended consequences, the system, which is currently being trialled across Europe and will be brought in in 2019-20 season in the Premier League, is wholly a product of so much football being on TV. It is a consequence of the TV audience being the most important audience. I'm wholly against this on philosophical grounds. I do not care if it allows more decisions to be called correctly, I do not want everything fixed after the fact. Sport is a one-shot deal. You try and get it right in real time, but we all accept mistakes will happen. It is an expression of the randomness of humanity, not maths.

This does shock and annoy many people who just want things to be right. I don't. Not over and above anything else. It also means that the top flight, which is the only level it will be used at, will be governed on an entirely different basis to the rest of football, meaning we will now have an institutionalised inequality. It will be two different sports, in fact. I'm not going to go on about it too much here, but VAR is a direct result of the TV audience being regarded as more important than those at the grounds, and that attitude is a specific Premier League invention with its courting of TV money. If you listen to one of the main justifications for it, "because everyone at home can see what happened but the referee can't" is how it is typically expressed. See? That's the primacy of television, right there. So what if there's a wrong call made? "There's so much money in the game, so much riding on these decisions" is another imperative. See? That's your Premier League again. The league made it matter more because there's money on it.

Anyway, back to the FA Cup. They still drag it out as though all of these transformations have not even happened. But it doesn't matter how many clips of Ricky Villa or Ronnie Radford you show, now is not back then. The reason those clips are legendary and thrilling is because those games were rooted in a different time when the FA Cup genuinely mattered and didn't need selling to us. Trying to illuminate today's darkness with the glow from those distant suns only serves to illustrate how long the shadows are now that the FA Cup's sun is setting.

Also it's called The Emirates FA Cup now, the sponsor's name preceding the tournament's, and that symbolises much too. Sponsor first. Money first. Because of the Premier League's economic model, football lies prostrate and desperate at the feet of television's money, knowing the price of everything but the value of nothing, seemingly so hungry for cash that it is intent on killing the goose that lays the golden eggs just for one last big meal before its own execution.

We now have a media intent on the overselling of 'giant-killing' as the be-all and end-all cup USP. It is massively misplaced. You simply can't go from match to match forever asking, "Is this going to be the shock result? Is this one? Is this one?" and maintain it as an actual shock if it does go the way of the smaller side. But so obsessed are some with this that they want the top sides to be automatically drawn away so as to increase the chance of 'a cup shock'. How could it ever be a shock when you've done all you can to contrive it to be so?

All the talking up of the underdog games is getting embarrassing. "What a story that would be," said Jonathan Overend on 5live at the prospect of Rotherham beating Manchester City at the Etihad. He's not wrong, in the same way a five-legged pink horse doing origami would be a big story and equally as likely. It ended 7-0 to City.

I feel sorry that they're charged with pumping up the 'it could happen' quotient so much. Listen to how many times the word story is said. It is too knowing, too contrived, overcooked and over desired.

But even so, let's not pretend that it doesn't deliver some fun each year. It is, after all, football and that's what football does all the time, at any level, professional or amateur. But even as Newport County scored their winning penalty against Leicester City, 5live's excellent commentator Conor McNamara had to use the moment to defend the competition: "Anyone who thinks the FA Cup has lost its magic should be at Rodney Parade now." And of course no-one wants to churlishly deny them their moment of joy in beating Leicester City, but wins like this are fig leaves for the FA Cup to hide behind and for the Premier League to use in order to pretend it hasn't drowned the cup in its deep oceans of money. It may be an unintended consequence of Premier League riches but it is a consequence nonetheless.

The fact is, absolutely any cup competition will produce unlikely results at any level; the FA Cup is not special in this regard but seems deified for it, for no good reason. It is not visited with anything unique.

None of us want to be without those types of victories, we just want them to happen, as they once did, in a competition that everyone is trying their hardest to win by playing their best teams, not in one where sides have tied one arm and a leg behind their back in order to rather pathetically rest the other half.

There's no point in continually trying to blow on the ashes of a burnt-out concept to reignite them. The real FA Cup has gone to join the choir invisible and all we're doing now is trying to nail it to its perch to pretend it's still alive.

Today's FA Cup is pretending to be something it isn't. It is but a ghost of a long-dead, fondly recalled relative, now leeching off its own history, riding on the back of what it once was but isn't any more and can never be again.

To pretend it's still alive and well and we're all still in love with it is an act of sporting necrophilia and it is the Premier League who is abusing its corpse.

It is all down to money money money. It is all anyone ever talks about any more and it is sadly what I now have to talk about in more detail next.

THE MONEY MYTH

This section is the throbbing heart of the book. It is the most important because the money the league has injected into footballers' wage packets and transfer fees is the core of so much of our discontent and disgust, alienation and even anger. It is an extreme situation that has become normalised. But we're all human, and we all live in the same world, so I'd like to set the money paid to footballers into its proper context, which isn't by talking about it in a football context, but by comparing it with the society it relies on to exist.

However, I should also make it clear that this is not an attack on the players themselves. It really isn't. That would be wrong and would get us nowhere. I also do not want to think anyone considers me jealous of the wages paid. I know you might think I'm making this up to suit my argument. I know you might think that only a fool does not want to be rich. All I can tell you is I am telling you the truth of what is in my heart. It is really nothing at all to do with envy. These men have just ended up playing football in this era and have gone along with the prevailing trends and picked up as much money as possible, the way we're all told to do in life.

The received wisdom is that in Britain we don't like talking about money and that to do so is somehow bad form or vulgar. Of course, that is absolute nonsense. Every person I've ever known who is on normal money has never been especially shy or inhibited about talking about their spending largely because, as stats prove, almost all of us earn within about five or six grand of each other, probably somewhere between £22,000 and £27,000. Shamefully for the country, there are plenty on less, plenty who would see £27K as the sweet lush upland pastures of financial grazing, including employees of many football clubs.

If you doubt this, a poll commissioned by The Independent in 2018 revealed one in 14 Britons had to use a food bank! A major report by the Joseph Rowntree Foundation carried out by Heriot-Watt University revealed that more than 1.5 million people were destitute in the UK, including 365,000 children, and that 7 percent of the adult population - or 3.7 million people - have used a food bank to get a meal. In April 2018 the number of emergency meals handed out at food banks had risen at a higher rate than ever, soaring by 13 per cent in a year, with more than 1.3 million three-day emergency food supplies given to people in crisis in the 12 months to March. As shocking as these headline numbers are, they only hint at the hours, days, weeks, months and years of lived human misery, of wasted potential, of lives without hope or happiness. We live in a society with record employment and yet record post-war poverty and a new class called the working poor.

It is fucking disgusting.

This is how you create a population that is too distracted, too scared, too worried, too in physical and psychic pain to plan any sort of movement against the orthodoxies that have put us under the jackboot of this bitter, thoughtless, bigoted and dumb economic fascism. Put simply, they've got us where they want us and unless we fight back on both a micro and macro level, we will always be like this, forever hanging on in quiet desperation.

And it is in this very same world that top-flight football waltzes with £20 notes falling from its pockets, glorying in its obscene wealth and unfussed by the grotesque inequalities that exist in the very communities which surround the clubs in the league, seeking only to hoover up more and more and more money for itself in order to make the super rich even more rich and even less super.

Look, this is bloody well wrong. It is part of a whole economic culture, both political and financial, that is just immoral. We are allowing the wealthy to kneel on the throat of the poor while encouraging outrage if some poor sod is fiddling a few quid on the dole, even though we give a free pass to millionaires who find ways not to pay a few grand in tax, even though it would be impossible for them to notice the loss. It is obscene.

It gets worse. Did you know that in March 2018 only four of the 20 Premier League clubs were committed to paying the Living Wage, which at the time was £8.75 to all employees whether in-house or contracted? In other words they're making paltry savings off the backs of the labour of the poor at a time of financial incontinence when it comes to players' wages. Indeed, a typical weekly Premier League wage of £50,000 would be enough to pay one worker working a 40-hour week on the Living Wage for the best part of three years. And it is considered to be all fine and dandy. Can you conceive of anything more absolutely disgusting than opting to pay the poor less in order to pay the mega rich more? Of course, football is but one part of society where these sinful, these heinous, principles are being exercised. It is so common, we've numbed ourselves to it in order not to feel the pain of millions.

And even if we're lucky enough not to be destitute, one way or another, the majority of us are all relatively skint, all have broadly similar expenditure and all have similarly little left over at the end of the month. We all have few or no assets to our name outside of a house, and house ownership really shouldn't be the thing we have to rely on in life to have something to bail us out of the poor house. Ironically, the British obsession with home owning at all costs hasn't helped the situation as it's just endlessly driven prices up, with people ever more desperate to get on the property ladder. The mass selling-off of council houses by the Conservative government in the 1980s without replacing the housing stock just exacerbated the situation. So now, because people have little or nothing else to their name, they raise money against the capital in their house in order to buy a second house to rent out to people who can't afford to buy a house, because the prices are too high because people have raised money against their house to buy a second house to rent out to people who can't afford to buy a house etc.; repeat and fade.

This is often painted as greed and sometimes it is, but for many it is just a way to try and cover their ass because we all feel so alone and isolated. We all feel like the state is not there for us, afraid we will end our lives in poverty drooling in a care home, hoping for a quick death because it is being run by evil people who are exploiting our decrepitude for profit, encouraged to do so by a cruel political and economic system.

Indeed, many of us have little or no savings at all and pretty much live hand to mouth, or are one pay cheque from the streets. There is now a whole economic class of up to 10 million people termed 'the precariat', which is defined as 'a social class formed by people suffering from precarity, which is a condition of existence without predictability or security, affecting material or psychological welfare'. For many of us, this has been such a typical condition to be in for so long, that we think of it as everyday life, as normal. But it isn't. It is a deliberate willful oppression of the poor, or those with modest income, in order to benefit the asset and cash rich.

By and large, the majority of us are all in the same financial boat, so there's nothing to brag or to be ashamed about. That's why whenever any of us buys something that looks good, when a pal says, "That looks good," the first thing we will say in reply is "20 quid, Primark," or "Got it at a car boot for 50p." You never hear the rich do that.

So let's have none of this about the British not liking to talk about money. Perhaps the wealthy would like to pretend it is the case merely in order to hide their embarrassment, guilt or arrogant disregard of their self-indulgent profligacy, while many go hungry and live lives that are far worse than they need be through economic deprivation caused by political decisions.

And also let's not start creating false divisions amongst ourselves. Some of you will have £10,000 coming into the house, some maybe £30,000. Others still, £70,000. £70,000 puts you in the top five per cent of earners in the UK - a much lower number than people tend to assume. Indeed, many on £70,000 do not feel they are rich but nonetheless are richer than 95 per cent of the rest of the working population. Indeed every study into such issues finds that the more money you have, the more you overestimate how much other people have. The more you have, the more you think people get on benefits. The more you have, the less well-off you think you are. It's sick.

Let's not squabble about a few tens of thousands here or there. The levels of income I'm talking about in football make your £70K look like pitiful chicken feed. So let's not turn against each other. Do not let them divide and rule us. Let's not pit the £10K against the £70K earner. That's what the wealthy and the powerful want. They want us to distract ourselves with petty turf wars, distract ourselves from what they're doing. They rely on the £50K earner getting furious because the £10K earner is scamming £20 on a benefit somehow. They want us to fight amongst ourselves about who are the deserving poor and who are the undeserving poor. They want us to do that so we don't notice what they're pulling in, how they're doing it, or what they are doing with it. Don't forget, 50 per cent of the UK is owned by 1 per cent of the people. Do not forget that, as reported by Oxfam in 2017, the world's eight richest billionaires control the same wealth between them as the poorest half of the entire globe's population!

However, when it comes to football, all of these realities seem to get suspended. It is as though we put on a different head and suddenly see the world through a different financial lens. There is a widespread lack of perspective about the amounts of money being talked about. I was listening to an ex-player pundit talking about footballers' wages and saying that if you were "only" on £100K per week, why wouldn't you move to a club which paid £300K? Why wouldn't you move to China for £600K? More is always better. It did not seem to occur to him that perhaps, just perhaps, earning £5 million per year was simply more than enough for some of them and earning £15 or £30 million held no additional attraction, simply because enough is enough and too much is, well, y'know, much too bloody much actually.

"He's got to look after his family," the ex-player said, as though £5 million per year wouldn't do that. On a phone-in, a fan was complaining that his club's best players were "only" on about £30 grand a week and that showed the club's "lack of ambition" to attract good players; as though £30K every week was chump change. Again, it didn't seem to occur to him that this was £1.5 million per year and that by any standards is a phenomenally huge amount of money to earn, not just in one year but in every year, for years and years.

I'm not sure how it happened, but it seems that we've totally lost our understanding of the value of money when it comes to football. It is as though we wear a different pair of glasses. Astronomical wages have become totally normalised. Average pay in the Premier League is about £200,000 per month, £2.5 million per year. Obviously many are on £400,000 to £1.5 million per month. The total wage bill for the 20 top-flight clubs in 2016-2017 was over two billion pounds. Two billion in just one year. It will be even higher now, of course.

I am not reluctant to say that I think this is morally reprehensible. I think it is plain wrong. It is unnecessary and I believe it is the tap root of so much discontent, not just in football but in society more broadly. How much money does anyone need? And as you will read in the final section of this book, some footballers agree and simply have no idea what to do with all the money they earn.

Back in the real world it's a different story. In the UK our average wage is about £27K per year with, as I say, millions on far less. Forty per cent of people who live in Stoke, for example, exist on about £16,000 or less per year. The majority of Teessiders live off under £20K. Many of these are football fans and even though it may be a subconscious response, is it any wonder anger towards players bubbles away all the time, like a milk pan forever on the verge of boiling over? It just seems so unfair that they earn such huge numbers while life is so tough for many who watch them play, or who would like to, if they could but afford it.

Let's just get some perspective on all of this. It's important to do this because nothing exists in isolation. If you fall ill and have to go to hospital, when you are being looked after by a nurse, when they are caring for you when you are at your most vulnerable, when they may be helping you stay alive, how does it make you feel that they will likely be earning in a whole year what Manchester United's Alexis Sanchez earns in under eight hours? I believe we should be angry about this. We are entirely justified in being critical, less of Sanchez per se, but of a game, a club, a business and an economic system which allows this to be the case. People are dying because the rich are rich and the money paid to them could be better spent on a myriad of things to improve the life and health of thousands.

I don't know when we stopped being allowed to be outraged by wealth. We used to be, I'm sure we did. We should not shy away from this, we should not swallow it down or look away or say it's just the way of the world. It isn't. We make the world. So how does it really make us feel? Tell me it's right that it takes a nurse a year to earn what Alexis Sanchez earns in less than eight hours. You can't, can you? Of course you can't. That's because you're a decent person with standards. And that's because it isn't right. That's because it is very, very wrong. You know it, I know it, we all know it. Don't give me horseshit about there not being many great footballers but there are plenty of people to empty bed pans. Remuneration should not be about how many people can do any specific thing, but about the value of the thing you're doing. Wiping the shit-streaked arses of the dying in order to make their last moments on this mortal coil more comfortable is more valuable than kicking a ball into a net. And regardless of even that, £400,000 per week, which is Sanchez's weekly wage, is simply too much for anyone doing anything.

It is the very fact that we live under the yoke of an economic system fuelled by a philosophy of selfishness and meanness of spirit which dresses itself up as personal advancement, which reduces human life down to some supposed - though illusory - supply and demand relationship, that is at the very core of all unhappiness. The encouragement of the pursuit of personal wealth has turned us against each other. It has divided us. It has started wars and it is, and this is not an ounce of exaggeration, killing the very ecosystem we rely on to keep living on this planet.

This is how selfish we've become. So wrapped up in our own self-indulgence, fellating ourselves with our own materialistic lust, that we are killing the mother that birthed us. Well done everyone. We are, as Black Sabbath once put it, killing ourselves to live.

This is something which needs opposing on every level, in every walk of life and that most certainly includes football. Football has been allowed to indulge extreme greed without censure or discipline from the very people for whom the game is played. Us. There is nothing good about living in an amoral economic system which says grab all you can and the devil take the hindmost.

But we have to also accept that we have been complicit in this. We have not protested enough or at all. We have allowed it to happen without consequence. We may have moaned and groaned but we did nothing. We made no moral stand. So of course they just kept creaming it up more and more and more. We must object. We must take a stand to end this wholly unnecessary projectile money vomit.

Just a bit more perspective. God forbid you need the services of a neurosurgeon to operate on your brain, but if you do, they will likely earn about £100K per year. They will drill through your skull and with mastery of science and biology, they will operate on your grey matter and make you better. And for all that responsibility, learning and knowledge, they will earn in a year what Aaron Ramsey will earn at Juventus in less than two days. Even the highest-paid neurosurgeon will, in one year, get half of what another Welshman, Gareth Bale, gets from Real Madrid per week.

So tell me honestly, how does that make you feel about football? Tell me this disparity is right. Tell me this is the best of all worlds that we live in where a footballer earns more in a week than a neurosurgeon does in two years. Again, you can't, can you? Of course you can't. That's because it is wrong on every level. These are not separate universes, they exist in the same world. We are all here together. You can't amputate football from society and pretend that a footballer's wage is not part of it and that no ripples flow from that particular stone in the waters of life. Why? Because everything is related to everything else. Nothing is an island unto itself. You stuff one person's pocket with money, it comes from the pockets of many others.

Given this reality, it's no wonder that we see Premier League football entirely through the prism of money. How could we not, even though we don't want to? We can't get beyond it. The everyday discourse of the game gnaws at it like a dog with an overpriced bone. It is at the core of all our discontent, both conscious and subconscious.

We are constantly trying to assess player commitment versus income. Fees paid against performance. Is he putting in enough effort for his wages or transfer fee? Is he contributing enough? We make that calculation all the time, even before we know we've done it. As I write this someone is on the radio saying that Paul Pogba "doesn't play like a £90 million player." Possibly because he was an £89.3 million player.

But what does that even mean? How does he know what a £90 million player should play like? See? It's all about the money. This speaker is not making a judgement of the quality of his play, he's making a judgement on the worth or value of his play. That's very different. The judgement proffered is a financial one, not a football one. "It's all about money these days" is a cliché and in this instance we can see how true it is.

This is all the Premier League's doing. I feel this is how it's spoiled the game. It is all about knowing the price of everything, and the value of nothing. I find it depressing. This is sport. It's not high finance. Or it shouldn't be. Worse still, any discontent at this state of affairs is totally ignored by the industry itself, as though it is ungracious or mean of us to gainsay it, and not actually a well-reasoned moral objection, and not a genuine feeling that it has bloody well ruined the game in some deep, profound way.

Even the language used is designed to downplay the grotesque numbers. I must've heard pundits and observers make the statement, "Players are on good money these days" many times, as though they're just on 50 grand a year, a total most of us would consider 'good' and not 50 grand per bloody week and the rest of it. We simply don't use the correct language to describe such wages. Players are not on 'good' money, they'd be more rightly described as on 'astronomically high money'. That would be saying it right. Not to do so is, all moral pontificating aside, simply inaccurate.

Recently, when it was announced that West Ham's Marko Arnautović wanted to go to China for some outrageously massive amount of money, it shocked me that the first criticism many had was for his 'lack of ambition' in going to China, an inferior league, and not for his desire to suck down more cash. Here was a man earning £5 million per year in East London, wanting to leave to earn £10 million. It was left to Chris Sutton, to state it right, as the wrangle between player and club went on. "How much money does he need!?" he exploded on 5live's 606 show. That it had not been said so baldly until several weeks into the dispute tells us much about football's moral ease in the presence of stunning levels of remuneration.

I later spoke to Chris about this. He said, "Football is a working-class game and it is far too expensive. The money in the game can be viewed as vulgar, can't it? I understand that. I understand why people would feel like that. Ticket prices are a huge issue. If you can afford to pay someone £200,000 per week, you don't need to keep upping the prices, do you?"

Niall Sloane: "Clubs should be doing more to lower ticket prices. They don't give enough back to the fans."

Defenders of the steroidal wage levels will try and tell you it is just like the movie or music business, where stars earn big money, as though that might justify it. It wouldn't because the same arguments apply. But this is a totally spurious comparison anyway. No-one is paid £2.5 million in wages per year just for being, say, a singer and songwriter. You earn a royalty. Not a wage. Nothing is fixed. Your remuneration is directly related to sales. If you're injured, you don't get paid. If you're off form and write a song that no-one wants to buy, you don't get paid.

If you're a movie star, you get a fee for being in the film, not a guaranteed wage for five years. If you're injured and can't act, you don't keep being paid the same money year after year. If you're terrible in the film, you don't get the same money for the next five years' worth of films, regardless of how bad you are, or how poorly the movie performs.

But in football, you absolutely do.

Golfers, snooker players, boxers and tennis stars to name just four, earn big purses for winning tournaments or fights. I don't change my position on extreme wealth wherever it is found, but such sports people don't attract the same anger as footballers do because, and this is crucial, these are winnings and not wages. It is the fact that the gravy train pulls into Football Town every week loaded up with another delivery of lush cash regardless, that drives many football fans anger at underperforming players and has driven the existential angst about football that is now part of the fabric of our existence. The relationship, if you're looking for it, between performance and money earned, is not present in football, so absent that we're not even shocked by the high numbers any more. Alexis Sanchez earns a wage of at least £400,000 per week, some put it at £500,000. That's his basic. But he also earns £75,000 if he actually plays! Yes, I know. I feel like that, too. I mean...I mean...I mean...fucking hell, man.

Fucking hell. Y'know? If that doesn't make your blood run hot, then me and you can never be friends.

Isn't he being paid £400K to play? Apparently not. He's being paid £400K to merely exist at Manchester United and a pitiful £75K for every game when he does play.

It leaves you breathless, doesn't it?

A reminder: Football is a team game and how well you perform relies in large part on how well those around you also perform. If you're paid to score goals and no-one passes the ball to you anywhere near the goal, you can't score goals. It doesn't make you a bad player. There is no straight line you can draw between contribution and remuneration for every single player in every match over a whole season and most certainly not over the length of a four- or five-year contract.

Alexis Sanchez has played in 20-odd games and has scored three goals. When he's played he's been largely poor and contributed little. It happens in football. But it has not affected his income at all. Football isn't the music or movie business, so anyone who tells you it is, is deluded.

Oh, well, it's a short career, so they have to make hay while the sun shines, defenders of big money will also tell you. No it's not. Your career is likely to be 15 or 20 years long. If you're 20 today you almost certainly will not have the same job in any other industry for 20 years these days. Only in football is it even vaguely commonplace.

And anyway, even if it actually was a short career, this still is not an excuse for paying people such huge wages. They don't stop being able to earn a living once they've stopped playing football, do they? No. Why are footballers uniquely supposed to retire for life at 36 with enough money in their vaults to last the next 60 years without lifting a finger? Go and get a job you lazy shite.

I recently heard one of the big football agents, Jonathan Barnett, who has Gareth Bale on his books, saying his aim was to ensure players made so much money it would ensure they didn't have to work ever again if they didn't want to. I sat there and let that sink in. It sounded so old-fashioned. It sounded greedy. It sounded vulgar. But above and beyond all of these things it just sounded incredibly bizarre. Why on earth is he saying such a thing? At the root of it must be a belief that more money is always better. That, to put it crudely, being able to buy loads of things is the ultimate in lifestyle choices.

I mean, I hate to come on like some sort of trendy vicar here, but none of that is correct, is it? Life is not all about money beyond having your basics covered. Not for Bale or anyone else. Having millions in the bank will not make anyone happier. It has been proven time and again. Indeed, football agents and others are always keen to tell us their clients are just human beings like anyone else and are subject to the same fluctuations of mood and form as anyone might be, when it is suggested that in return for such huge money they should be performing better. What is that if not an admission that money is not relevant to peace of mind, contentment and mental stability? But when it comes to retiring with enough money to live off for perhaps 60 years it suddenly seems a different standard or understanding has to be applied. It's all utter bollocks.

Also, working is not a bad thing. Being useful in a societal context is important to humans as largely communal animals. Working to achieve something in return for an income is not some sort of reprehensible lifestyle choice that one needs freeing from, as Barnett implies is the case. Spending 60 years playing golf and shopping for curtains or playing X-Box is not really playing your part in the world. Ceaseless self-indulgence and gratification, as many have proven over the centuries, is for losers, not winners.

But hey! The rich footballer must pay a lot of tax, you might argue. The top 1 per cent of earners pay about 28 per cent of all tax taken in UK. Thus without rich people like footballers, where would all the money come from to pay for state spending? I'll tell you. Obviously, in a more fair, equitable society, the gap between rich and poor wouldn't be so wide, so that the poor who now pay little or no taxes because they're sodding skint and working on a zero hours contract for minimum wage, would actually have more money and be able to pay their share. And I've yet to meet anyone who is earning 20 or 30 grand who has a tax avoidance scheme or offshore investments to reduce their tax bill. But I have never met a rich person who doesn't.

Yeah, but we're all hypocrites because we'd all take the money, right? That's always the final get-out clause for those seeking to defend this outrageous financial situation, trying to paint us as hypocrites. But I'm here to tell you, if I was earning a typical football wage, I'd have to give away almost all of it. Give me, say, three grand a week, £150K per year. That is plenty for one person to live off, isn't it? What could you spend it all on? I'm serious. What?

This isn't some sort of attempt to paint myself as especially hair-shirted. I like having some financial velvet between my vertebrae as much as anyone. I just genuinely don't know what the hell I'd do with all the extra cash.

Even allowing for a few extravagances - I have no idea what, but let's assume I can find some - actually I don't see how it'd be possible to spend even the £150K per year, so what in God's name would you do with £1, 2, 5, 10 or 20 million per year for the next seven or eight years? How many houses, cars and suits can you buy before you're satiated? How much self-indulgence can you, well, indulge in, before you sicken yourself with your own shallow vapidity?

Once we articulate what this money means in normal life, once we put it into perspective, it helps us understand the numbers more. When they're isolated purely in a football context, they lose their real meaning. That's maybe why we all talk about them so lightly and use inappropriately modest language about them, why we think if a player is on £30,000 per week, the club is being stingy and unambitious.

As I say, I don't think we should be afraid of saying that we are opposed to such wealth and by extension to the business and economic system that facilitates such payments. After all, most of the world's great religions are opposed to it too. As the Bible says, "You cannot serve both God and Mammon."

Obviously, footballers have quite innocently fallen ass backwards into this giant pile of cash. Most would play for minimum wage, if the minimum wage was all that was on offer. And I'm fully aware that many do use their income for the greater good because they're obviously decent people. Juan Mata has been rightly praised for trying to get players to donate 1 per cent of their wages to Common Goal. Mind you, I hate to prick any virtuous bubbles, but if you're on five million per year, £100K per week, then you're donating 52 grand per annum, in other words half of one week's earnings.

If you're on £27,000, it's like you giving away £270, less than £6 per week. Though in truth, losing £6 per week would impact your life far more than losing £52,000 from your five million. Now, all the figures about donations to charity suggest the poor donate a higher percentage of their wages than the rich. And I wouldn't mind betting if you're on the average wage you've given away more than about 75p per day in this last year, one way or another. This isn't seeking to denigrate people like Mata for making the effort, but more to set it into its proper context.

More profoundly, is this really how we want society to be? Do we really want to rely on the mood and largesse of the wealthy to trickle down in order to make the lives of the poor and deprived better?

No, it isn't. Not least because it does not work. And that is another reason why we feel subconsciously queasy about the ugly financial dystopia that is Premier League football.

But, Johnny, surely being rich would great. Ok, but you're referring to yourself in the third person again. Sorry. "What's wrong with being rich?," you may ask.

Our whole society, our economy is certainly predicated on us believing this. The pursuit of wealth has been an important economic driver, since the Industrial Revolution. As I've said previously, I'd like to be financially comfortable as much as anyone, of course I would. But this isn't about such a modest ambition, it is simply about not being very, very rich.

Because here's another vitally important additional consideration: a lot of research has been done into wealth. Oh, yes it has. And you know what every bit of research tells us? Well I'm sorry to have to report this, but being rich doesn't make people happier. Sorry, money bags, I've almost nothing and I'm happier than you. Ha Ha. I win. Yeah, baby, how do you like them apples?

One report found that earning between £43,478 and £54,347 per year led to 'emotional well-being'. I like the sound of emotional well-being. We could all use some of that, couldn't we? Lord knows, so many of us don't have that. And we deserve to. It's time we redefined our society in terms of Gross National Happiness rather than Gross Domestic Product.

Because once you get over that £54K, the money stops working and you will never be any more happy or content. And surely happiness and contentment is all any of us want out of life. OK, I've previously asked for £150K, but, thinking about it now, I know it will not make me three times as happy, so maybe £50K will do, after all. As long as I've got my bills covered, I'm fine. That's how most of us feel, I suspect. I know I will not be happier if I buy more expensive trousers or whatever.

There is also some research that suggests the richer people become, for many there is a commensurate dropping off of contentment and an increase in negative feelings. People worry intensely that they might lose their wealth, they worry people only want to know them because of their wealth. They want respect for being wealthy but once you judge your own worth by your wealth, there is always somebody with more than you. Always someone with a bigger house, a bigger car, a bigger bank balance. And by your own standards, therefore, you are inferior to them. You are, in fact, the big fat loser. That's the self-induced psychological taunt. Indeed, as you will read in the final section of this book, there are footballers who are tortured by such concerns every day of their lives.

In an interview with The Guardian Watford striker, Troy Deeney, a man from the sort of background that is usually defined as 'troubled', made an important point.

"When I was younger I was just chasing money because I thought that would make me happy," he said. "And then, when I got my first house, when I started reaching those goals I'd set for myself, I was still miserable. Something was missing. Happiness comes from something deeper."

I know he's not the only footballer to have realised this profound truth.

OK, so talking money in a football context, how much should a top footballer be paid then?

This is not a precise science, but how about this?

In 1980 in the UK, it's been said that only eight players earned £50,000 per year. They entertained us every bit as much as anyone does today. In today's money that's about £220,000 per year, not per week.

How about that? £220,000 per year. That's loads and loads of money.

That doesn't seem unfair pay for a top player, does it? No human rights crime. The end of the world will not be nigh. That's at least £2.2 million over a 10-year career at the top. I'd call it generous, in fact. You and I have little hope of ever matching that, even if we wanted to.

By earning about 10 times the average wage, it recognises that you are the creme-de-la-creme of your profession, if that is important to you. Earning over £140,000 per year puts you in the top one per cent of earners in this country and you'll have plenty left over to grease the palms of friends and family. Tell me why that wouldn't be enough? You can't. That's because it is more than enough. OK, so £220K per year is the very most you can earn.

Of course, this is a kind of salary cap.

A salary cap isn't an original idea. It is how the NFL operates in the USA. All team spending on wages is capped at the same level. They can divvy it up any way they want, but every side has the same amount to spend. It's a simple and easy way to make sure the playing field is even and no-one can buy their way to success.

As long as the cap is set at a level affordable by the poorest side in the league, even if you're owned by someone as rich as Croesus, it will gain their team no advantage.

I'm all in favour of this and feel it absolutely should be adopted in football for exactly the same reasons. But I'd go a step further in capping not just the overall wage budget, but within that also deploy a maximum wage to avoid what happens in the NFL where a player can still be on an unnecessarily high, multi-million pound wage. And I'd like that to happen to address so many other destructive issues of wealth and inequality and opportunity that I'm outlining in this book.

When you're asking for a wage cap, it is important to be clear that this isn't a negative thing at all, nor is it that oldest of accusations, jealousy, nor is it that most dumb, mind-in-neutral, clichéd of accusations; the politics of envy. It is, rather, part of a positive movement towards a better, more fair, happier world. No footballers will be harmed in this revolution, unless not being able to buy a new Maserati every year is actually painful. All top footballers will still be rich by normal standards.

The principle that there is a set limit to both deprivation and luxury which none can fall below or exceed, is hardly revolutionary. Or rather, it should not be considered so. We should neither drive people into poverty nor allow them to luxuriate in extreme opulence, because no-one gains from either. The capitalist drive to maximise income at the expense of literally everything else is a huge problem because it ignores the basic truth that you cannot have infinite growth on a planet of finite resources. This doesn't mean we can't have nice things, or sit on a comfortable chair. Indeed, in a fairer world more people would have nice things and a comfortable chair, not fewer. It's just that you should not be able (or want) to have 222 comfortable chairs when you only use one.

However, I already know what some will say. Capping wages will sound to some like a denial of freedom or even of human rights. However, I'm sure if you asked the 99 per cent of people who do not earn £220,000 per year and have absolutely no chance of doing so, they'd rarely think it was anything of the sort. If you're on £16,000 you almost certainly will feel your lack of cash is exactly that; a denial of freedom and even of your human rights. After all, you are a child of the universe, no less than the trees and the stars; you have a right to be here, as the Desiderata says.

Others in football will say the capped wages would drive all the best players to other countries where they could earn bigger money. And of course it would, if this change happens unilaterally. But given the radical nature of this shift in thinking, that seems highly unlikely in the medium term. More likely is it becomes a wave of new thinking adopted throughout Europe, not just isolated in England. It is worth considering that in every other country, there are football fans who are just as sick of how things are. The money outside the Premier League in terms of wages and transfers may be less on average but is still, in many cases, interstellar.

The Premier League may be the most egregious example of ceaseless greed but it is not alone. In pretty much every country, many people want the same things I've been talking about here. And nothing exists in isolation. If one territory enacts such radical change, others will surely follow.

But just say they don't and the Premier League is populated only with footballers prepared to play for the new maximum wage or less. What then? Well, of course, numerically this is already the case in British football. The vast majority of professional players do so for less than £220k per year further down the leagues. But even if we could no longer watch the 'best' players - at least in person - so what? The joys of football would be undiminished. How do I know? Because until the Premier League came along no-one cared about such a vague notion anyway. We just turned up and watched a game and went home and were happy enough. Not being able to see the best Croatian on the planet meant nothing to us and we were none the worse for it. The league has inculcated this consumerist mindset into too many people in order to perpetuate itself and its values. But it is not worth sacrificing everything else we hold dear up to and including the viability of the earth as our home in order to be able to watch any footballer, is it? I mean, obviously.

The bottom line here is: Having enough is enough. Having a lot more than enough is too much.

If clubs cut wages to such a level, all other things being equal, they could spend the dividend this would release in the club's community, improving the lives of us all, spreading love and support instead of making rich people even more rich, whilst simultaneously condemning the rest of us to live lives that are far more impoverished than they need be. We are, after all, human too. Just like rich footballers. Who could say that would be a bad thing?

Ha ha, well, I may be an idealist but I'm not naïve. I know that's not going to happen, obviously. Even I am not that naïve. The clubs wouldn't spread the money around, they'd pocket it and build some more yachts for the directors to indulge even more expensive habits upon.

So, oh no, they are never, ever, ever, going to willingly do this. They are going to keep surfing the foaming wave of cash until it breaks on the shore. They have no idea where the shore is, of course, nor even if there is a shore. We will have to be that shore.

The only realistic way any such change will happen is if income into clubs drops markedly and they therefore quite simply have to pay players more responsibly in order to survive. I know that seems very unlikely, if not impossible. It might even seem as if the prevailing winds are blowing in the opposite direction. But cutting income to clubs massively is not as impossible as it might seem, it really isn't, but it will need a revolution of the economics, culture and even morality of football and more widely of society, to enact change for the greater good. We cannot go on as we have been doing. It is a cul de sac of existence. A dead end. Tinkering around at the edges will make little difference. Those of us who feel that there is something badly wrong with a sport which pays its performers so much, should take every opportunity to say so. If we don't, those who perpetuate this normalised extremism will think we approve, or that those of us who disapprove are merely jealous. We are not. In fact, it infuriates me when anyone who opposes gross wealth is accused of mere jealousy, as though it is not possible to have a moral stance on anything and that we all have a limitless desire to just keep buying more and more stuff, even though it is causing the ruination of the ecology of the planet. This isn't an argument for mean spiritedness but one for some degree of moderation.

I was talking to Pat Nevin about this. Pat is one of the most decent, thoughtful and erudite men in the media. He tells a funny story about how a bit of extra money into Scottish football clubs from UEFA - I mean about £750 - was, at one club, spent on a new drinks cabinet, rather than anything which would benefit the club itself! As we talked about the money in football, he pointed out wisely that we all have our own personal morality and that yes, he too thought the level of wages was morally objectionable. "But there are our own personal morals and then there is business. The two things are separate. Business sees these matters differently."

I see what Pat means. After all, I've never, ever had a waged job. I've been self-employed my whole life and quite deliberately so because I've always wanted to control my own time and to decide for myself what I was going to do on any given day. It has probably made life more financially difficult than it might have been if I'd just used my degree to get a job in education, which was the path set out for me, but I don't regret it for a minute.

So along with my partner, Dawn, we've always run our own businesses. That sounds more grand and entrepreneurially thrusting than it really has been over the last 35 years. It was more about making a living doing something we wanted to do at our own behest, not anyone else's.

Some years we've done relatively well, others not so much. We've pretty much lived hand to mouth for most of the time and any time we've had enough to live off for a few months, we just stopped working altogether until it ran out and then started again. But it means that I'm more than familiar with the profit motive. This sometimes means that when my critics learn of my desire to turn a pound, they seem to think it makes me a hypocrite as though selling t-shirts or books or art is no different to the behaviour of global asset-stripping companies, oligarchs of dubious means or oil-rich potentates. False equivalence is a poor way to try and justify the indefensible.

Whenever I've written about money and wealth, I notice it attracts some of the most aggressive, angry, rather bitter responses, given at core, all I'm really arguing for is a better, more fair world. And that's hardly a bad thing now, is it? For all of us to have a bit more, a few people must have a lot less. Is that such a bad thing? Why, especially if you're not one of the financial elite, would you defend those who are? Why get angry about some hairy freak like me arguing for a more fair and just world? I puzzled about this for a long time. Pat got me thinking.

"You're taking away their fantasy, aren't you? You're taking away their dream of being rich and famous. Of driving the big car, having the big house and all of that. That's why some people get defensive. They want their shot at it."

It's a very good point. It hadn't really occurred to me before, that the massive gap between rich and poor, the inequality and the unfairness ceases to outrage when it is so familiar; rather, it hardens the desire to get a slice of the money pie. That is how the powerful monied people control us and stop us storming the barricades, I guess.

Once you feel your back is against the wall, rather than band together communally for the greater good, the culture of the primacy of individualism we've all been indoctrinated in for at least 40 years, kicks in and tells us to grab what we can, when we can. Anyone who says anything which might stop you getting at least halfway up the greasy pole, even in theory, is to therefore be resisted.

Dawn and I were mulling this over during an open day at a stately home and estate. You know the sort of place - all very lovely, manicured and terraced gardens surrounding a 17th-century house. It opens the gardens up three days a year, a commitment so watery that I think we must presume it is done in order to gain some advantageous tax deal. I could research this but the very thought of investigating tax relief on property open to the public is already making my eyelids close in boredom. Anyway, it is not germane to my point here. We were having a flask of tea (like the old farts that we are) as we looked out from a terrace across a few acres of the enormous estate's land.

"How the fuck have they got all this?" asked Dawn. It's all owned by one man, whose family has owned it for hundreds of years. "And why haven't the people taken it off them and used it to benefit everyone's lives, not just one family's?"

It's a good question. There are a hell of a lot more of us than there are of them. We're people too. And while this isn't the place to indulge in detailed historical analysis about how so much of this country came to be owned by so few people and what the effect that has had on the lives we all have lived down the centuries, as I considered what she'd said I was struck powerfully by one thought.

What if we owned many thousands of acres of land and had a massive house but the two of us just live in a couple of rooms and shutter up the rest of it and are not even there much of the time. If we had all of that, I'd feel guilty. I'd feel guilty that just across the road people are living off £11,000 per year in a cramped one-bedroom flat. I'd feel guilty that loads of people would love a wee garden to call their own but can't afford a house that has one and here are tens of thousands of acres of land not doing much. How could you not feel bad? And I'll tell you what, opening my gardens up three days a year wouldn't assuage the guilt. How do you live in these sort of circumstances and ignore the poverty, hardship and unfairness all around you and plough on regardless?

Dawn, the yin to my yang, is not one for elaborate espousing of political or hippie psychological analysis, and had just two words to say on the matter: "They're twats."

I suppose we all have our hopes and dreams and why wouldn't those hopes and dreams find their expression in the big car, the big house, the big everything? It is, after all, what we've all been brought up to desire. We are relentlessly sold the notion of acquisition as the medicine for all of life's ills and as an ambition in and of itself. It is only in recent years that the impact of this ceaseless consumption, not just on our own psyche but also on the Earth, has begun to get more widespread consideration and that's something I'll discuss later.

THE GENEROSITY MYTH

Like most big corporates, the Premier League deploys a community strategy as an arm of its public relations, dressed up as social responsibility. Its primary purpose is to deflect criticism and to make the company look good. I don't think this is an overly cynical perspective. Yes, the league may well do some good with its investments, but mostly it's about looking responsible and trustworthy, noble even. McDonald's doesn't put money into grassroots and community football projects because it cares about football, why on earth would it? It does it to have something to point to when critics point to the McFlurry as one of the drivers of obesity. I mean, it's really obvious, isn't it? I don't think I'm being especially killjoyish in saying that. All big companies do this.

So when we read the league's puff piece on its website about how it is putting money into community facilities and the like, it is just more of an attempt to justify its existence and the economic philosophy that underpins it:

"The scale of Premier League support and investment in the wider game, and in communities and schools, is unprecedented in the world of professional sport.

"The League and its clubs fund community facilities across England and Wales, operate national and local sports participation projects, and last year launched Premier League Primary Stars, a primary-school education programme.

"Primary Stars uses the appeal of football to inspire children to learn, be active and develop important life skills through free teaching resources and support from 101 Premier League and other professional football clubs.

"The programme aimed to engage 10,000 primary schools by 2019 but has already exceeded that target by reaching 15,000 schools within its first year.

"This is part of the £100 million per season the Premier League invests to support the development of community facilities, sports participation programmes and schools."

All sounds very generous and wholesome, doesn't it? Who could gainsay such a gesture? Only a cruel beast. It cleverly invites us to believe this is all done in good faith. And when investment in schools, in community facilities has been cut and cut again by a succession of governments who all drink from the same economic and political bowl of beliefs, any money that comes from anywhere is always going to be utilized when and where possible by the people who really do have the public welfare in their hearts.

But we should not be relying on the largesse of huge corporations to fund such things. We don't want crumbs from their groaning table and we don't want to have to need the money so badly in the first place just because the public purse is so strapped for cash, as a result of deliberate and wilful spending choices by government. This £100 million per year is nothing for an administration which spends over £100 billion on the NHS alone that would likely pay for itself by improving health outcomes. Government fritters such money away on all manner of nonsense every day. This year alone it has already blown £4 billion on contracts that were never needed in order to cope with the consequences of a 'no deal' Brexit. Funny how they found the money for those, but not £100 million for supporting football in schools. And you can make this argument on so many issues so much of the time. It's been estimated by various organisations that the cost of replacing our Trident nuclear defence will be anything from £150 to £205 billion over 30 years, a cost governments seem happy to cover. It currently costs around £2 billion per year to maintain Trident. You can argue whether we need a nuclear deterrent, but one thing we can't argue about is that the state has enough money to do so. Thus it could be spent on something else. Thus there is absolutely no shortage of fucking money. Thus if there's no money for your community project, that is a deliberate and wilful choice of the government to deprive you of it. Never forget that.

Niall Sloane: "Governments do not care enough about sport and don't care enough about it getting a big audience."

The Tories gave £1 billion to the DUP in 2017 just to stay in power. Yeah, 'ave a bang on that. So there is plenty of money available and there should be no need to take the Premier League's corporate bribes.

Again, this is all part of our nausea around the Premier League. The forever feeling that something is wrong. There's the Premier League drumming up billions, dropping a few pennies in the public's begging bowl and keen to tell us how great it is for doing so. Go on, away with you.

On the one hand you don't want to not support projects to help kids play football or whatever it is, but on the other...well...where the hell is all that other money going? And the truth is it is mostly going to pay players. Yes, we're back to that again, but that is why we have that sinking feeling about all of this. Being kept afloat by gifts from rich people is not good for anyone's self-respect but that's where we are, that's what's going on.

And anyway, is there any independent scrutiny of these promo projects? Is there any setting of goals? Is there any way of measuring the success, efficiency or efficacy of Primary Stars?

A very pernicious thing about this is that the brand name of the Premier League is part of children's lives from an early age. This is exactly how you embed and inculcate a brand as the default or norm. It comes in like it's the not-for-profit third sector, as though it is part of the social services or welfare system. But obviously it isn't. It's doing this for its own self-promotion. Isn't that just, well, horrible?

I found myself wondering if it's just me who feels like this. When you're a writer, you do spend a lot of time in your own head breathing your own rarified air, or so you would like to believe. It is easy to get divorced from reality. So I walked down to the nearest pub, ordered a large single malt, perched on a stool and asked the barman what he thought about all of this Premier League largesse.

"It's all wrong," he said, dismissively, pulling a new arrival's pint.

"What, exactly?" I asked, pushing for more detail of his angst. He's in his late 40s and has the belly of a man who likes the good things in life and in large portions.

"Everything about it. Everything. The Premier League. Wages. Everything. All wrong. They can sod right off with all that bloody money."

It was about as comprehensive a judgement as you could wish for.

He pushed the lager across the bar at the new customer, who chipped in his own view.

"You talking about the Premier League?" he inquired, eyebrows raised.

"Yeah, did you know, they put £100 million a year into community projects?" I said.

The man, a youngish chap in his 20s who clearly did something in the building trade because he was wearing those work trousers that have the pockets flopping on the outside. The sort that a quick glance can deceive you into believing said chap's ball sack is on display. He took a drink and smacked his lips the way we all do when thirsty, often followed by the sentence, "Ah, I needed that."

"Oh, aye? Why do they do that then?"

"I think they fancy they're being a socially responsible business. Giving something back, like," I suggested.

"Bollocks," he hissed. "It's all PR if you ask me. How much money do they make a year?"

"Their turnover is over five billion." I said.

His eyebrows shot up. "Five billion? Aye, well, they can get tae fuck with their money. Bastards."

And there you have it. You can make any intellectual or economic arguments in favour of the Premier League that you want but those two men just had a gut reaction to it - to tell it to "sod right off" and "get tae fuck." When I talked a bit more to them, neither knew much, if anything, about the details of the functioning of the league but they both just had a profound feeling that it was wrong, that rich people were screwing over poor people, that the whole shooting match was one long venal stitch up. They saw through the bullshit and not even the league's biggest fan could have convinced them their view was one iota askew of the truth.

I feel powerfully that we should not have a football organisation that makes people feel like this. It is, after all, in theory, just an administrative organisation. The fact that people feel so hostile towards such a thing is a sign of just how much it curdles our guts. And when you get right down to it, the thing which offends most is, "all that bloody money".

But back to the Premier League's website. I note it also states, "Furthermore, Premier League football generates an estimated £3.3billion per year in taxes for the UK government."

Read that carefully. The writers are not saying the Premier League Ltd does, though that is how it could be understood if read quickly. The whiff of weasel words is ever present, as you would expect from a league which calls itself premier when it isn't. They state it is Premier League football which generates the tax, and that's very vague and woolly. To what does it extend? The players and managers? Does it include the tax paid by the workers at stadiums, the people who make football boots, strips and everything else that makes football tick, up to and including manufacturers of dubbing? OK, I doubt dubbing even exists any more, but you see my point.

This is all very icky. The fact the league even bothers to state how much tax is generated from its existence is the subtext: "You need the rich to pay taxes to pay for your life, so hands off the rich, OK?" Why put it there? It's not there for no reason.

The vibe is one which says look at all the money we pay to the state; but without any details of how and where these taxes are generated, from whom and from what percentage of income or profit, we can't really make a judgement. We don't even know if it is an accurate figure. What the league is obviously doing by even stating this is to aggrandise itself and plant the idea that it contributes a lot to the economy. It is further justification for its existence.

That's what is behind such a statement. Yes, everyone is stinking rich but without our taxes you'd have nothing. Thanks. Thank you very much. Is it any wonder so many feel that nameless angst and annoyance at the Premier League? All of this is knitted into an invisible subconscious matrix which shapes everything we feel and understand.

The very fact the league put this sweeping statement on its website shows how much it is always in the forefront of its corporate mind to keep pushing propaganda that justifies its model on multiple levels.

It's also worth reminding ourselves that whatever amounts of money the league donates to various good causes, its money does not come from nowhere. The league is, in a very real way, generating taxable profits from our money, however it has arrived in its coffers. Without us, this 'generosity' can't happen. The league wants the glory, but it's reliant on you and me. This is all too easily forgotten when as individuals we stand in front of such a financial behemoth. The numbers involved all seem to be so fantastical that it is hard to believe it even has anything to do with us at all. After all, we don't get a say in how it goes about its business, despite being axiomatic to it, and that is surely how its members like it. We're just busy trying to get through life as best we can and have some fun doing so. We're distracted. It's all above and beyond most of our lived experiences. So it seems like it's all happening independently of us and that we play no part.

But the league is just a corporation with 20 shareholders, comprised of the 20 teams who are in it at any time. We might also call that a union. It sells itself as though it isn't merely a collective bargainer for those 20. It's full name is actually Football Association Premier League Ltd (FAPL) but I suspect it is more typically seen as a company such as Marks and Spencer, who makes and sells football to the world, because it acts like it is something independent of the clubs: a business in and of itself. The Premier League is not needed for there to be top-flight football played, but it has been conflated with the actual playing of the game. All or any clubs could at least in theory quit the league the way the first 22 clubs did back in 1992 when they left the Football League. Quite what league they would be assigned to afterwards, I don't know and it isn't clear. Clubs could also refuse to join the league from the Championship. Wouldn't that be great? Sorry, no, we don't fancy becoming a zombie club in your money-obsessed league.

I know many people don't like to mix sport and politics, but politics is about life and sport is part of life, so to me, they are inextricably linked, the one informing the other. Our feelings about issues such as the environment and economics, even if we don't have a tag or title to apply to them such as socialist or capitalist or whatever, are political in the broadest sense. The trouble is, politics goes hand in hand with those labels and labels both attract and alienate us. They're too binary and often seem to require us to back one side on every issue. That's the problem I have with the user interface of politics.

The left/right/centre carve up seems ever more irrelevant as the years go by and isn't getting us anywhere. All that seems to happen is everyone looks for holes to pick in each others ideas, desperate to find that which divides us rather than that which unites. If football can teach politics anything it is not to allow tribalism to make you into a thoughtless, one-eyed dope.

It's a strange business. When you write about anything to do with life, some will interpret what you write as left wing, some right wing, as attacking them or supporting them. To a degree it is in the eye of the beholder. We throw the titles around as though we know what it means but beyond the extremes of fascism and communism (and even within those), I'm not sure anyone apart from political philosophy professors know what it all means. And anyway, tagging and branding ideas into this or that side just narrows down support.

For example, ask people if they're in favour of nationalising the railways and polls give it a huge majority, far bigger than those who think of themselves as socialist, even though nationalising the railways might be traditionally thought of as part of a socialist agenda. That just goes to show the problem with giving any ideas a political brand name.

Understanding what the Premier League is all about relies on some sort of political outlook and understanding. Indeed, when I read some of the reader input into F365 I often feel much of the frustration and discontent people have with any Premier League issue, be it financial or cultural, is because they lack a philosophical political framework into which they can place their experiences and understanding. So here's a little bit of my political thinking which has helped me draw back the veil on the football.

It is quite obvious to me that when you sell off publicly owned utilities - everything that benefits the majority of people such as public transport, water, power, prisons and everything else that we used to own but which is now contracted out - we lose that which binds us together. I can see what the idea was behind selling these assets and you can argue as much as you like about whether it has been better or worse value financially. However, more profound than that is the disharmony it has sewn. We no longer have a collective investment in the infrastructure of society.

Even the BBC have farmed out their complaints-handling service to a company called Capita. They are 'an international business process outsourcing and professional services company headquartered in London'. You can look them up. They've got their fingers in a lot of pies from education to NHS to being the people in the Department of Work and Pensions who decide on whether you will get a Personal Independence Payment, which replaced Disability Living Allowance - a task they were so terrible at doing that many people died while awaiting their collective getting-out-of finger. Civil servants had to be sent in to try and fix things. Not for nothing is Capita nicknamed Crapita. If you look into them it is a shocking tale. But they're still out there hoovering up public money. And there are other such sprawling private companies doing everything from emptying bins and mopping floors to answering the phones when people call up the BBC to complain about political bias on Question Time.

Because the political decision was made to run the country this way - because that's what it is, it is a political belief in what is sometimes called Free Market Capitalism which led them to choose this path - because of that belief, everything that should bind us together now feels distant and fragmented. We don't know who is responsible for doing what. We do not know who to hold to account. And above all, in these public services, which are exactly that, services for the public, the public are secondary to shareholders. This cannot be right. Things like PIP are about we the people, not their shareholders. And this is all a political choice. It does not have to be this way but it has been this way for up to the best part of 40 years and has never been as extreme as it is today.

Here's a simple illustration of how remote everything now feels. What do you call the railway service? What name do you give to the company that runs the trains? You call it British Rail, don't you? We all do. That's the name it had when it was run by the state for the people. They kept the brilliant logo but British Rail hasn't actually existed for over 20 years. It is now National Rail. I don't think I've ever heard anyone refer to National Rail. And of course, just to confuse matters further, they only run the trains, not the track. That is the responsibility of Network Rail, which are a publicly owned and funded body.

Sometimes it seems to me that all this fragmentation is merely to prevent us knowing who is to blame for anything. If a train was late we blamed British Rail. They ran the railways so it had to be them. As frustrating as it might be to have a train be late, it is only compounded when you don't know who to blame. Is it National Rail or Network Rail or is it the company that runs your specific route? We don't know. This, as much as anything else, gives us that sense of unease and of society being dissolved and, if not lawless, then unaccountable. It feels like everyone is being pitted against everyone else. It is every person for themselves. That is the underlying political driver. I firmly believe this is deeply upsetting to our psyche. We don't want to live our lives as competitive consumers, forever searching for the best deal, the cheapest ticket, the lowest tariff as though life is one big game show that we're trying to win. Life is about much more than that.

And it is this feeling of cold abandonment, of everything being for the profit of distant faceless people and not for the benefit of you and me and our friends and family, that I get from the Premier League, too. It's the same model. Like those companies that sell us water, gas and electricity, it feels beyond us, not part of us. It feels like it exists without our control or influence even though without us, they have no business. We are constantly subjected to a feeling of powerlessness and this does not come for free.

This isn't to say we left behind a land of milk and honey. Far from it. Just as in football, change was needed, reforms had to be made. But we're a long way down this road now and it isn't leading to anywhere we want to go or anywhere we want to be. We desperately need to find a new map and take a new direction. The pursuit of profit in every walk of society destroys that society, slowly but surely. The evidence is all around us, not least in football. All the money in the game has not made us, the fans, any happier. We still love football for the reasons we always did. And yet we're sold the notion of this big money football as though it had given us access to some lush upland pasture of enjoyment that was previously denied to us. It hasn't. And it isn't needed to deliver it.

I have used the terms capitalism and capitalists throughout this book to describe the philosophy behind the Premier League because of how the league does business and makes profits. But on further consideration I'm not sure it actually fits the dictionary definition: An economic system characterized by private or corporate ownership of capital goods, by investments that are determined by private decision, and by prices, production, and the distribution of goods that are determined mainly by competition in a free market.

The league itself doesn't own any goods, it doesn't really own anything other than intellectual property and some offices. And there is nothing about the league or the clubs which is decided by the free market as we might normally understand it because clubs get paid money for just participating. That seems more akin to a weird sort of privatised sponsoring and nothing at all to do with market forces. And when clubs don't need to make a profit to survive because they're funded in this way and also funded by people so wealthy that money has little meaning to them, that also sounds nothing like traditional capitalism at all. It all sounds much more like a private club or cartel.

Similarly, it is often said player wages and transfer fees are dictated by market forces. But that isn't true, or rather it isn't true if you understand what market forces usually refers to. Yes, they are if you think that market forces are purely what someone will pay, when there are two clubs competing for a player, for example; but when that amount is not dictated by any of the usual market considerations such as having to fund the purchase from profits, then it needs another descriptive term. When there is so much of what is in effect a subsidy in the cash flow of the business, comparing it to genuine free market trading seems inappropriate.

One of the unforeseen consequences of the Premier League's invention was that the promise of big money inevitably drew big-money people to buy clubs. And the ownership of many of our clubs makes many of us feel very uncomfortable. Rightly or wrongly it affects how we feel about the clubs and the money they use to leverage power and success.

Now, there are plenty of people researching the sources of owners' money. David Conn of The Guardian has written extensively about such matters. I don't intend to do so here. My point about the owners and their money is a moral one, a philosophical one and a sporting one.

Let's take the last of those first. The wealth of owners combined with ability to earn money from myriad other sources, means there is a huge disparity in wealth even within the league. Burnley's owner is worth about $80 million, which is less than Liverpool paid for Virgil Van Dyke. And whereas Liverpool can sell merchandise all over the world, Burnley can't. So there is a built-in financial unfairness internally within the league. It isn't an even playing field. There is an institutionalised bias towards the richest clubs and owners. And while a rich club like Chelsea FC can have a meltdown occasionally and have a terrible season as they did in 2015-2016 and finish 10th, their resources mean they can buy their way back to the top immediately, not just through an ability to buy good players, but to be able to afford to buy players who perform poorly and not financially cripple themselves. But that's a luxury Burnley or Huddersfield don't have in the same way, despite their presence in the league making both among the top 40 richest clubs on earth. The Financial Fair Play 'rules' only entrench this with its break-even requirement, where clubs are ordered to not spend more than the income that they generate, and that they must balance their books over the course of three years. It does nothing to even things up, rather it hardens inequality, even if we presume it is being enforced and not got around in one way or another, which is by no means unlikely.

The Premier League's success in hoovering up money is, ironically enough, reducing competition and making the league less interesting. It is eating itself. It's why the 6th place ceiling exists. It's why now almost no club ever wins away to a top six club. As I write this in early April 2019 someone kindly did some stat mining for me. Taking the top 6 sides playing the next 6 at home, they have played 33, won 24, drawn 6, lost 3. They racked up 78 points at a 2.36 points per game average, scored 75 and conceded 26. That is pretty one-sided. OK, it does not account for how enjoyable any of those games are, which is the most important factor, really. But in terms of trying to sell the league on an 'everyone-can-beat-everyone-else' basis, it has never been less true. While coaching plays a part and intelligent recruitment also, the knowledge that even so, by and large, the money keeps the money is basically very, very dispiriting. You can argue all you want that Manchester City, or Chelsea or whoever you want to name, haven't 'bought' the league but almost everyone feels that, yes they bloody well have. And they have. Not uniquely, obviously. Yes, there are other factors at play that can prevent a club winning the league, but the fact is, to be in with a chance at all is down to the money spent. The club that can afford to spend and also lose the most money has the advantage. It isn't unreasonable to acknowledge that. And that knowledge alone, however unreasonably or unrealistically, does ruin it for some people, at least to some degree. It is a core problem.

What sort of competition is it when there are several layers of financial apartheid which will 99 times out of a hundred stop 14 out of 20 sides even having a chance of winning it?

As I write this, City are playing Brighton in the FA Cup Semi-final and it feels weird. It feels like Brighton are a lower-league club, despite being in the top flight and that they have little or no chance at all, and it feels like everyone watching knows that. It doesn't feel like a fair fight. It feels like a big bully taking on a small kid. For Brighton to have a chance, they are relying on City having an off day. They cannot compete with them otherwise. Now, that's not right. That's why we shrug and feel a diminished passion for such games whether in the cup or the league. As it happens, City won 1-0 and it was a more even game than the mismatch might have suggested when the City squad cost seven times more than Brighton's. But that changes nothing because they still won and Brighton had just two shots on target. City never looked like losing. The tattoo of unfairness has been inked and won't be removed by such a result. The most it proves is that football, being a mercurial sport, can even out a lot of inequalities in one-off cup games and there is a law of diminishing returns on money spent.

In his piece about this match, The Guardian's Barney Ronay puts it perfectly:

"And yet for all the closeness of the final score, Brighton were never really that close. The Cup was once a great leveller. It isn't any more. Nothing is a great leveller. There isn't enough levelling available to breach the gap between a team that has been built with what the budget allows, and one that has been built with no limit to the possibilities, no break on the imagination."

Some fans will just accuse others of being jealous of their wealth, but it's not that at all. Aside from all the other issues, there is one that is rarely addressed and even less frequently talked about in relation to football: the environment. So let's have a blether about that.

THE ECOLOGICAL TRUTH

This next bit might seem a bit odd because I'm going to bring environmentalism into this discussion of the Premier League. Yes I am. And you can't stop me. Look, it isn't odd at all, but it just might seem like it is because we're not really used to thinking about a widescreen holistic vision of life and certainly not football's place in it. We focus on the rights and wrongs of this and that detail, but rarely are able to lift our eyes to the horizon and see the bigger, more long-term picture. Because I'm a pretentious git, I call this the atomisation of idealism.

This seems to be largely the way our headbanger monkey brains are wired. We live in the moment and as long as now is OK, that'll do for us. Football itself shows us this. Fans get fed up of their manager and want them removed after four or five losses, but as soon as there's a couple of wins all that is forgotten. When people say football is a results business, that in itself is an expression of our inability to see beyond today. Today's score matters more than anything else.

We'll happily do something for the greater good if it affects us right here and now but anything longer than that is a bit of a stretch. I'm sure this is why so many, even now, find it hard to take climate change seriously enough. Big issues are hard to grasp. We can organise a protest about the cutting down of an old oak tree in the park, but stopping millions of trees being cut down 6,000 miles away just seems somehow too out there, too elusive and hard to feel as strongly about as the old tree you kissed your first girlfriend or boyfriend under when you were 15.

By cultural and perhaps even by biological instinct we don't want to be told we can't do anything we want to do, wherever and whenever we want to do it, and that is essentially what we're being told by climate change experts. We've got to stop living how we have been living, or even how we might have hoped to live, and instead, adopt a radically different way of life, if we're going to even have a chance of avoiding terrible environmental consequences. Not a wee change of how we live but a radical fundamental core change. We have to do a 180-degree volte face and go against everything we have understood to have been a marker of progress.

We have to take this very, very seriously. The world's leading climate scientists, in a report by the UN Intergovernmental Panel on Climate Change, warned in October 2018 that there are only a dozen years for global warming to be kept to a maximum of 1.5°C, beyond which even half a degree will significantly worsen the risks of drought, floods, extreme heat and poverty for hundreds of millions of people.

"It's a line in the sand and what it says to our species is that this is the moment and we must act now," said Debra Roberts, a co-chair of the working group on impacts. "This is the largest clarion bell from the science community and I hope it mobilises people and dents the mood of complacency."

On 3rd May 2019 Robert Watson, the chair of the Intergovernmental Science-Policy Platform on Biodiversity and Ecosystem Services (IPBES) said,

"There is no question we are losing biodiversity at a truly unsustainable rate that will affect human wellbeing both for current and future generations. We are in trouble if we don't act, but there are a range of actions that can be taken to protect nature and meet human goals for health and development.

"The health of the ecosystems on which we and other species depend is deteriorating more rapidly than ever. We are eroding the very foundations of economies, livelihoods, food security, health and quality of life worldwide. We have lost time. We must act now."

"We tried to document how far in trouble we are to focus people's minds, but also to say it is not too late if we put a huge amount into transformational behavioural change," said David Obura, one of the main authors on the report and a global authority on corals. "This is fundamental to humanity. We are not just talking about nice species out there; this is our life support system."

I don't quite know how much more telling we need about this. It feels like we've been told about it in ever-more apocalyptic terms for 20 years, but because the bad stuff only happens incrementally and not to everyone equally, if you don't feel it affects you personally, it is just a little bit tricky to take seriously. I get that. I live beside a harbour where the North Sea meets the Firth of Forth. Rising water would seriously affect us here, so maybe it is more in the forefront of my mind now compared to when I lived 100 feet up at the top of a building in Edinburgh. But we really need to shake ourselves out of this self-centred selfishness. It is happening. We know why. We know how to slow it down and how to reverse it. We just have to pull out our fingers and do it. But will we? As I write this, Extinction: Rebellion, a pressure group dedicated to raising awareness of the crisis that is upon us, have been disrupting the main thoroughfares of central London for the last week to try and make everyone wake up to the issue.

It's a largely selfless, non-violent protest and it's not something those taking part stand to gain much from apart from a sense that they are doing something and having a laugh with like minds. They're just concerned about the planet. OK, some might find the hippie elements a bit hard to swallow. There are only so many jugglers anyone wants to encounter in one day. And while there are always people who attach themselves to any movement as a kind of fashionable pose, mostly these are simply people who care. Being good to the earth isn't a bad thing, whether you're wearing a jester's hat and tie-dyed hemp trousers or a three-piece suit. So what's the general public's response? Some were supportive, some just complained it was taking them longer to get to work and it was a bloody inconvenience and very selfish of the protestors to do this. As if not having enough water in a few years' time wouldn't be. As if food shortages wouldn't be. As if tens of thousands of people drowning in floods wouldn't be. See? There's your short-termist, headbanger monkey brain, right there. Can't see the bigger picture, can only see the now. But with climate change, when the issue gets so serious it cannot be ignored, it will already be way too late. On this one, we have to have a greater vision. We have to go against our most basic instinct to live in the moment.

This isn't a book about the environment, there are plenty of those already written by people who know far more than I do. But in essence, as far as I understand it, things boil down to a few easily understood basics; the long and the short of it is that the principle that we must consume less, pollute less, recycle and renew more is now well established as the way forward. We have to live different lives. Current models of economic growth are unsustainable. Infinite growth based on finite resources is impossible.

So how does this come back to football? Well, first and most obviously, football is part of the problem as much as anything is on a day-to-day basis in terms of its contribution to climate change and biodiversity destruction. It is all part of human activity and human activity as we have been pursuing it in the last 150 years is the problem.

Football is part of how we live. We have to make changes to our lives and how we live, so we must make changes to football. When we're told to consume less and pollute less, football and footballers are not excused. So it needs addressing. So how do we address it? Well, top-flight football both literally and emblematically represents the glorification of materialism, of consumption and of wealth. The only point in earning a lot of money is to give you the ability to buy stuff. That is literally the only use money has. So given rampant consumerism is killing the planet, it follows that rampant wealth is killing the planet. By paying people so much money all we're doing is giving them a licence to damage the climate with impunity. Why should we do that?

I'm not naïve to think paying the hundreds of footballers who are so massively remunerated a lot less will arrest climate change, of course not; however, it would be a symbolic statement that such income and such consumption is no longer acceptable. And if it is not going to apply to them, who is it going to apply to? Since the rest of us have almost nothing, the rich have to give up the most. There's nothing unfair about that. And frankly, even if there is, sorry pal, something's got to be done. None of us can live how we've been living and just being a multi-millionaire footballer should not insulate you from that fact.

Let's put it as simply as possible: At a time when we need to consume less, football is fostering a culture of consuming more more more more.

The Premier League has fostered an extreme money culture. Indeed, that was the whole point of its creation. It glories in huge fees and wages and it loves to be known for this. It is its big claim to fame. It is the first thing anyone thinks about the league, its clubs and its players. Money. Big money. Big big big money.

Footballers' shopping habits are reported on in minute detail every day of the week by cheap, mind-numbing tabloids. Footballer excess is part of football's entertainment. If you doubt this, Peter Crouch's podcast - which is wonderfully funny and entertaining - in documenting the life of modern top-flight footballers, details just how excessive and ridiculous this life is. From massive expensive cars, to massive expensive houses, flying first class everywhere, staying in huge expensive hotels with every whim on beck and call. The clubs even provide them with matchday underpants. Yes. Yes, they do.

The Premier League, by elevating these people as the winners in life's game because they earn so much money, has therefore endorsed and inculcated a culture of massive, earth-snapping consumerism. And the climate crisis means we simply cannot go on consuming the planet's resources like this. We can no longer build an economy on consumerism. I will say it once again, it is simply impossible to consume infinitely on a planet of finite resources. It just has to stop. We can't get away with it any longer. As I write this Europe is burning up under extreme summer heat. Because no-one can point to any one weather event being 'caused' by climate change, it has allowed some of us to be anything from sceptical to disbelieving. It is so easy to ignore or fail to grasp the magnitude of the situation and that is exactly what we've been doing for so long. But no more. No longer. Children are taking to the streets to urge us into action to behave responsibly towards the planet they are about to inherit. We must not let them down and football and footballers have their part to play.

Just look at the typically huge footballer car, to take but one example. Those cars are killing the planet with pollution from exhaust fumes and, just as bad, from the micro rubber dust from tyres which embeds into children's lungs and causes respiratory problems. It's not funny or clever or fashionable to kill the ecosystem, is it? Here we can see that, contrary to what may normally be claimed, big money is not buying more freedom, it is buying the very opposite. When we see children's lungs racked with pollution-driven asthma how the hell do we live with ourselves for putting them through that, merely to drive around in luxury? Worse still, now we know it is happening, how do we happily keep on causing it? It is fucking obscene. Clearly, they are not the only ones who buy those cars, and I don't want to pick on such purchases uniquely, but they are high-profile people who inspire and define what success looks like and those cars are very much symbols of that. They set standards and perceptions. They are success emblems. But they are killing machines.

The relationship between money and environmental destruction is well established. I am simplifying things here, I know, and you can point to those who spend money on green choices, and that's all fine and dandy, but we've been brought to the precipice by a couple of hundred years of massive consumption of resources.

These notions might be painted by some as green extremism, as if damaging the ecosystem which gives us life is entirely sane and normal and not in any way wacko. And yet earning huge money is still set out to us as a kind of Holy Grail in football and in life in general. It is understandable of course, because this is how it has always been since the Industrial Revolution. Get more, get more, get more. And we've all had a go at it, more or less successfully. But now my question is, Why? We know happiness and contentment are above and beyond mere materialism, once you are comfortable and warm and have enough to eat. This isn't an argument for frugality or for living in a windy tunnel huddled under a towel. No. But it is an argument against the ceaseless acquisition and massive consumption that top-flight football promulgates and which we have had uploaded to our synapses as the way to live.

We must change our default settings. We must uncouple ourselves from materialism in a profound way. Having loads of money and acquiring loads of stuff is undermining the viability of earth. Who ever thought anyone could write that and it not be science fiction? And if knowing our lifestyles are destroying the Mother that birthed our species is not inspiring enough to change how we think and how we live, then we are destined as a species to be but a cul de sac of evolution; a freaky fungus that killed itself trying to live.

We can't go against the planet. Well, we can, but there is only going to be one winner and it won't be us. Perhaps the Earth is already taking action to kill us off as a species in order to protect itself. It is a living organism that is finding ways to stop the pathogen that is doing so much damage. There is no sympathy from the life force, it is kill or be killed and if we're in danger of killing the earth, the earth will surely kill us first. And indeed, is busy doing so in a myriad of ways, even as I write. It is rising up against us. Right now, we are the enemy. But we don't have to be.

Wiser, greener choices to try and respect and embrace nature, to live modestly and to understand that money can't buy you love have been painted as a loser's outlook by those who promulgate wealth seeking. "Get more, get bigger, get more powerful. More. More. More." It's been an orthodoxy for a long time, but it is time that changed.

The way I see this is that anything which perpetuates this situation is part of the problem and must be brought to an end. It's that simple. The Premier League, its values and economics, its financial largesse, must be shown as destructive and replaced with something more holistic, green, fair and healthy. I must state again, this isn't the product of envy, or jealousy, nor is it some sort of puritanical philosophy. I don't seek to be superior or sneering. How could I? I'm as much a part of the problem as anyone is. Mine is just an argument to return to some sort of consumer sanity. It is a call for this sector of society to set an example for the good of all life on earth. After all, while we can all do our bit in terms of polluting less, recycling and making less demands on the planet, we're mostly quite skint. We're the ones who average £27,000 per year, remember. Compared to rich people, we consume relatively little, even if, compared to developing world nations, we really do consume a lot.

The concept of choice has come to dominate our lives and this is a core consumption driver. I grew up in the 1960s, born to working-class parents who grew up in back-to-back terraces sleeping five to a bed. This was not unusual. It was typical 1920s and 1930s poverty, so by the time the 1960s happened and there was a little bit more choice and a little bit more money, it must've seemed a lot to them. The fact that they no longer had to have dripping on bread but could buy Blue Band margarine instead, as humble as that sounds, was a big lifestyle upgrade from their perspective. Bought rather than homemade, made them feel like they were getting on. For them, having a tiny bit of choice was an amazing thing after having almost nothing as kids, having fought in the war, and then having gone through post-war rationing when you lived off powdered egg and wore trousers made out of turnips.

Fast forward to 2019 and my local supermarket has a 25-foot long shelf dedicated only to crisps. To. Crisps!! It has 62 different cooking oils from olive to avocado to macadamia nut to soya and I can buy green beans from Egypt in the middle of winter and avocados from Peru in March. There's not much I can't get. Apply this to every sector of society and it is totally and utterly overwhelming. I enjoy cooking and while I make no claims to a huge gastronomic education, I fancy that I'm quite good at making edible scran. But even so, all this choice is just too much.

When I was a kid, we used to eat seasonally. You only got strawberries in summer, likewise tomatoes. In winter we lived off root crops. We couldn't get everything, all the time. And while I'm as guilty as anyone of buying food out of season, I'm not convinced that life is so much better as a result. And yet we have an economy set up to deliver anything we want, no matter the cost to the planet.

Basically, I've realised quite profoundly that although I want some choice, I don't want that much, and I do not want ever more. Choice has been elevated to the status of a moral imperative and tied into some kind of notion about living in a free society. And it is this very concept which has driven us to the brink of environmental destruction. And were my parents alive today, they, despite being brought up in poverty, would agree. It's all gone too far. It is all illusion and lies. Freedom is in the mind, not in the supermarket. Choice in everything has ballooned massively, to the point where I'm genuinely sick of having to make choices. Tell me I'm not alone in this. Please!

The basic things we all need for life should be owned by the nation for the nation, not owned by shareholders for dividend payments. That's mad. To think otherwise is just very extreme political dogmatism, though ironically those same people would paint my simple by-the-people-for-the-people approach as some weird radical form of communism. It's not. It's just sensible and addresses the fact that we don't want to have to keep making choices. When the government tells me I need to choose between a dozen electricity suppliers and a dozen gas suppliers, that is absolutely not a choice I want to have to make. It does not deliver a better quality of life or better gas or electricity. All you get is the same power, no matter who is sending you the bill. And if you doubt this, I should tell you that here in Scotland, water is still owned by the state. It has not been sold off. We get the water we get, we know who is responsible for delivering it, and we don't have to choose from any number of companies to send us a bill for it. Is life worse for this? Of course not. It is one less thing to think about. We all use water, so we should all pay for it and all have a stake in it. Private ownership of the water supply in order to make profit for shareholders absolutely bloody well disgusts me and I believe all decent people should feel likewise. Making money out of supplying water seems a godless act of greed.

So if I'm presented with a huge choice of football providers on TV or on various other platforms, I really don't want to have to make that choice. I'm tired of choosing. If how I feel is commonplace, then the very notion of choosing from up to five different subscriptions in order to be able to watch football is ridiculously out of touch with us, and quite possibly goes some way to explain the low rates of take-up in itself.

Before I return to the football, I need to tell you that all of this thinking about the environment is not a new 21st century thing. It is not a fashionable or trendy thing. Is not part of being, in that horrible new term, 'woke'. People have been telling us about all the current ecological issues for a long time. From a personal ecological perspective, I feel like I've gone a full 360 degrees on these matters since I was 21.

In late 1982 as full-blown hippies, Dawn and I moved to the Black Isle, north of Inverness to, in essence, get back to the land. Under the influence of John Seymour's Self-Sufficiency books we grew our own food organically, kept hens, hand-dyed and spun wool and knitted the yarn into jumpers which we sold. And all the while being on the dole. Ah yes, these were the glory days of mass unemployment for those of us who wanted to walk a different path in life. It allowed you time to find yourself and work out your own future. There was little or no pressure to get work.

During that period we absorbed a lot of what was considered at the time to be very extreme green, ecological, environmental thinking. Organic was a by-word for the hippie weirdo. But we just wanted to work with nature, not against her. That's all. It doesn't sound mad, does it? Not now it doesn't, but back then it did. I take a football lesson from this. All of the proposals in this book may sound extreme, radical or odd, but so did organic farming in 1984 and it moved very much into the mainstream within a generation, showing radical change is possible.

We were vegans for much of the time from 1984 to 2011, excusing eating our own hen's eggs by virtue of some sort of philosophic caveat we had to concoct for ourselves. We quit the diet just when it was getting fashionable! We grew a lot of food and it all made sense. It was a virtuous circle. But being anti-petrochemicals and pro-renewable energy was laughed at back then. We were losers. Freaks. We cycled everywhere. We bought paint without lead in it. We only used plastic carrier bags that would decompose - the Spar had them back in 1983. We used biodegradable detergents. We even ground our own wheat, though I can't exactly remember why now! It is easy to laugh at all of this and right that we should do so because you can't take anything seriously unless you can laugh at it. Dawn even made her own sanitary protection so as not to have to use tampons and the like. This was all part of being natural, not plundering the earth's resources and polluting the planet. So she would cut strips of towelling and use them instead like we were living in 1803. And it was then down to me to wash them. As we didn't have a washing machine at the time, all of this had to be done by hand. The bloody water was, of course, poured onto the compost heap to enrich the soil. I wasn't in the least squeamish about this, (possibly because I was always a fan of liver as a boy) seeing it all part of nature, seeing us as humans as no more or less a part of nature than the birds and bees. Now that's some green credentials, huh!

Of course, we were hopelessly idealistic, somewhat naïve and totally against every prevailing economic and cultural trends of the time. We didn't even have a TV for the best part of four years, though again, I can't remember what our opposition to that was, other than it would melt your brain with its mind-numbing output. So maybe it was that.

Back then, anti-materialism was thought to be the stuff of hippie madness, and that was one of the reasons we liked it as an idea as we were firmly of the view that The Man had caused war and devastation, so whatever The Man did, we didn't want to do. The whole get a job, go to work, get a house, family and pension gig held no truth for us. It felt like it'd be a very heavy overcoat to wear through life.

So we had got off the conveyor belt of normality (albeit still relying on those who were on it to pay tax to provide our dole money). We wanted to reject what we thought of as the old ways of organising a society and economy and wanted to live simply but differently. We wanted to live in harmony with the planet, not in opposition to it. We saw nature in a pantheistic way, as not just beautiful but as divine, infinite and mystical. We felt that everything was comprised of everything else. That we were stardust, golden, billion year-old carbon and we had to get ourselves back to the garden. And while this may partly have all been down to exposure to magic mushrooms and Steve Hillage albums, it was a genuine, honest, soulful thing. Not a pose or a fashion. But the idea that the earth was a finite resource that we had to take care of wasn't on any mainstream radar at all. It still wasn't trendy to be a friend of the earth.

But all these years later, all of these things are now very much in play. If you've ever wondered why there is soya milk, almond milk and oat milk in supermarkets as well as organically grown brown rice, well, I'm here to tell you that's all down to us. We demanded it for years, we made it happen. See also: veggie burgers, carob powder, mung beans and alfalfa sprouts.

As David Crosby once rhetorically asked, "What did the hippies get wrong? Almost nothing." While Croz is famous for a degree of self-righteousness, it's hard to disagree with his central contention and I wish we'd stayed closer to our hippie ideals for longer. We were young and idealistic but we were onto something.

James Lovelock's Gaia hypothesis made total sense, or at least more sense than the prevailing free market monetarist economics that drove the Tory government of the time and which allowed the current extreme economic model to become so normalised that you'd think there was no other option at all.

One windy cold winter's day we were cycling into our nearest village, Munlochy. Many of the fields on the Black Isle were huge, all the hedgerows having been dug out to allow for more efficient crop production and harvesting. As we rode down a steep hill into the village, the wind was whipping across open fields that had been ploughed in the autumn and were now bare to the winter weather. The topsoil was visibly being removed by the elements. Clouds of it swept down the hill and were deposited on the road. Whereas once it was all held in place by the interlocking root systems of the hedges and trees, now it had nothing to protect it and was simply being eroded by the rain and wind. We pulled into a passing place and watched this very visible erosion of the land's fertility, the full horror of both what this was and what it also symbolised dawning on us. You didn't need to be some sort of eco-loon to see this was wrong and that long term, it was not sustainable and more than that, the custodians of the land were either knowingly irresponsible or knew not what they were doing. That was 36 long years ago now.

But we were young, barely in our 20s and of course as time moved on, we got drawn away from this vision of life. We didn't know how to progress it while earning a living and we knew we couldn't live on the dole forever. So after three and a half years we rejoined society, took some of the values with us, left some of them behind. We were taken away by the pursuit of more upmarket living, more material wealth and a general desire to live higher on the hog. In our defence, it is hard to swim against the tide all the time. Also, we'd both grown up with very little and at some point wanted a lick of the cream. But now, much older and wider as well as wiser, with those wilder days behind us, I feel much more equipped to make the fight.

But despite, or indeed because of, my early green lifestyle choices, it really annoys me when some nascent environmentalist wags a finger at one of my current choices and says, now now, this is no good for the planet, you know. It is rather galling. I mean, I didn't fly on a plane until I was 32 years old, so don't come to me and tell me I've been the one wrecking the world. Also I've got 26 vegan years in the bank, so if you want to blame me for all the cows farting us into an environmental Armageddon, then I've got serious credit built up, so if I want to take a flight and eat a steak whilst doing so, I bloody well will!! I do see this is unreasonable, though.

This might sound like I have lost my mind or have resumed eating magic mushrooms after a 35-year break and yes OK, I am still listening to Steve Hillage's 'Glorious Om Riff', but I haven't made this stuff up and I'm not some sort of fool on the hill.

But let's leave planet hippie and get back to the football. I know this seems a long way from talking about the Premier League and footballers wages, but it really isn't. Never forget my mantra, forged in those days: Everything is related to everything else. Whilst the rich and privileged may have frittered away our environmental inheritance (and we should never forget that and never fail to hold them to account for that), frittered it away on their entropic lifestyles, we won't be excluded by the earth's response to their profligacy. If we continue to actively endorse incomes and lifestyles that facilitate ceaseless consumption, we are just taking a few more steps to an environmental apocalypse and let's face it, an environmental apocalypse will put a severe cramp in the fixture lists.

Obviously, this isn't a vendetta against footballers over and above anyone else. This isn't to persecute them alone for some perceived sins. But imagine the example it would set for profoundly rich high-profile sports people to give up their wealth for the sake of the planet and for the leagues they play in to operate on modest income. Imagine the societal and cultural reverberations of an en masse surrendering of wealth - possibly the most revolutionary act anyone can do in a society so obsessed with acquiring it. There are plenty of green organisations that are advocating nothing less than a revolution in how we think about economics and lifestyle. That we must replace economic growth with sustainability. Football is not excluded from this.

Thinking again of many footballers' luxury automobiles, I can easily imagine a not too distant future when routinely owning a car is looked upon as being ridiculous and reckless. That we would waste so many resources, pollute the air we breathe, and kill both ourselves and our planet, merely to convey ourselves around in a small piece of metal-enshrined personal space - a metal space that kills 1.3 million of us on earth every year and injures 20-50 million more purely in accidents. That's before you build in all the early deaths caused by car pollution.

Any objective look at this situation would judge us insane, especially when we have perfectly good, far less polluting options available to convey us communally. But we live in the now. And cars are brilliant. God knows, it isn't hard to see the attraction. Dawn and I have had our share of motors over the last 39 years. We sold the last one three years ago and haven't bought a replacement. We didn't really need a car. All shopping gets delivered to our door, one way or another. So today we get around on push bikes, buses and trains. We've also signed up for e-car, which is basically an electric car club which you pay for by the hour, just in case I find a massive record haul that needs taking home. Having a car available in this way seems so much more efficient than having a big lump of metal sitting out the front of the house doing nothing for days or weeks on end. It's a halfway house until we get a properly efficient and comprehensive public transport system.

And I can genuinely say that this sacrifice of not having a car has not made life worse in any way. Quite the opposite. It's one less thing to think about. One less expense. One less choice. Time and again I find the more stuff you shed yourself of, the lighter and more simple life seems to become.

I can't say this more clearly, the old ways of thinking about wealth, money, materialism and resources are already outmoded - they do not address our real needs. People are being born today who will live in a world that has in part or in total rejected these redundant values. Change might be forced upon most of us, but it will come. We either surf into the future of a breaking wave of green understanding, or we drown in the polluted waters of yesterday. And this applies to football as much as anything else.

Our children (not mine, obviously, as we don't have any) and their children, will not forgive us for surrendering to our worst, if totally understandable, party-now-fuck-tomorrow instincts that have been the economic driver for my whole adult life.

But the bottom line here is, having enough is enough. Having a lot more than enough is too much for you, for me, for all of us, for the planet. So when someone protests that the huge reduction in wages in football that I'm proposing is somehow a denial of human rights, of ambition and of achievement, tell them the planet sent you.

THE GAMBLING TRUTH

It wouldn't be fair to lay the problems created by the flourishing online betting industry wholly at the door of the Premier League, but it has become the main platform for driving the growth of some of the most venal, amoral capitalist businesses which will seek to make profit out of anything, no matter how destructive. Betting found its spiritual and economic home in the Premier League and has spread its tentacles far and wide. Saying that it might ruin lives of gamblers and their friends and families will not get you a sympathetic ear. It's all about money and if you're vulnerable to addiction, it is even better for them because they'll just exploit you until you have less than nothing. Hand in hand with ending the Premier League, we must uncouple gambling from the game itself.

The Premier League's profit-first culture has set a standard and opened all the doors to them and it appears to care not one jot for the consequences. And it's surely another reason for our existential crisis in top-flight football. Another reason we feel so queasy at the thought of another game broadcast live in between a cavalcade of enticements to place a bet. A game played by people whose shirts and grounds are covered pretty much from head to vote in betting company logos. This has just reached a new nadir with Wayne Rooney taking a role as player-coach for Derby County, wearing the number 32 on his back because his wages are in part being paid for by a betting company called 32Red. He is now a weird hybrid footballer, being employed by both a football club and a gambling organisation. What the Hell is going on? His net worth is currently estimated at $160 million. I could not have invented a better illustration of the amoral, perverted financial culture of modern football. Is it any wonder that we regular people look on at this with astonishment and increased alienation?

It doesn't have to be like this.

Football and gambling have become so inextricably interwoven in the last 10 years that the language of gambling is now part of the language of football. Outside of the actual ads for gambling, odds-on scores and results are now routinely referred to in this context. "The bookies had them as 4/1 favourites," someone on TV or radio will say in response to an unexpected result. TalkSport actually dispenses in-game betting odds as the match unfolds.

I've called it the ' 'ave a bang on that' culture after the Ray Winstone-fronted adverts which used this as a tagline and it is absolutely everywhere, all the time. Sky Bet used to have "It matters more when there's money on it" for their advertising tagline, as though football couldn't satisfy you in itself, and you needed the additional fix to briefly thaw out your frozen soul. It always seemed a pernicious statement, speaking of dull, pointless lives, needing the adrenalin of the threat of money lost or, less likely, the glory of money won.

Who wants to buy into that? As it turns out, a lot of people. Why? Well, gambling has always been with us, but I suspect it is flourishing so radically right here and now as one more symptom of our dysfunctional society, riven with economic and cultural desperation and inequality. The Premier League has never been in the slightest bit bothered by the full, complete and comprehensive exploitation of football fans for money, so why would any industry which orbits it? Anything and anyone which brings in more money, no matter what, is welcomed as a Very Good Thing indeed..

A more socially responsible organisation would have some regulations in place as to what and who its members can and can't have as a sponsor, what TV companies can and can't advertise around its games. But no. God forbid anyone should have any standards. No, it's an advertising free-for-all and the league is more than happy with it like that. Anything goes as long as there's a bit more money to be made off the back of football.

As ever, it is all about the primacy of the individual over the community, the customer is always right even when they are wrong and have lost all their money betting on football. We are but units of wealth production, not people. This is now a huge, huge problem and the Premier League must accept much of the blame for it, not least because it is so wedded to the free-market philosophy which sees all human activity, all human desires, all human lusts, all human weakness as a chance to make a profit. It is moist and fertile soil for such industries to plant their seeds in.

Although I don't now gamble, I do know how addictive gambling is. Ten years ago, Dawn and I rented a house in Las Vegas for five weeks. We were doing quite well at the time, or at least, we had access to a giant fuck-tonne of credit, which I know isn't quite the same thing, but which we treated as though it was. Back then, as now, we were dedicated boozers, and we soon worked out that you got free drinks in most casinos if you sat at a poker machine and pushed enough money into it. Like so many before us, we thought we could balance gambling losses out against free drink. But of course, no matter how much we drank, and we drank a hell of a lot, we couldn't quite manage it.

Like Jonny Wong in the song, we knew we could never win, we were just trying to lose a little more slowly. We could no more hold on to our money than grab mercury. And it went on like this for 36 days. We just couldn't stop. As we drank more and more free liquor, we lost more and more money, but kept pumping more and more in to try and stem the losses. A few big wins deluded us into feeling we were getting close to even. We weren't.

This is how we dug ourselves a £35,000 hole and jumped into it, drunk and screaming wildly into the infinite black velvet desert night sky. Climbing out would take years.

Now when I look back, it feels like it was one long period of psychosis. We should've realised that being fully paid-up members of the If a Thing Is Worth Doing It's Worth Overdoing Club, gambling would get its hooks into us and would only let us go once it had cleaned us out, stripped us naked and left us on our knees in the desert with only a loaded pistol as a way to solve our problems.

Losing money whilst pissed on free tequila and gin feels perversely like a win, when in reality, you're just a big fat loser. Yet it was so compulsive.

And because I felt its lure so strongly, I worry about gambling being so pervasive in our football lives. Games are preceded and followed by TV ads for betting companies. Ten Premier League clubs are sponsored by international gambling firms. They are crucial enablers in the gambling industry. The second, third and fourth tiers of English league football are all sponsored by Sky Bet. As I say, if you listen to TalkSport they're giving you in-game and half-time odds, telling you how much you could win if x, y, and z happens. The same goes for TV: up pops Ray Winstone with pre-match and half-time suggestions for bets to place and encouragement to feel that you are master of your domain; a betting overlord, traversing the globe in search of profit, when really you are Kevin from Wakefield sitting on your sofa in stained trackie bottoms, unable to pay your rent and badly needing your acca to come through so you can buy some dope in order to forget you're about to be evicted.

At every single football ad break, the first ad is usually for gambling: Betfred, BetVictor, Bet365, William Hill, Paddy Power, Unibet, which is now pitching for the educated middle-class male market (it's always aimed at me; it seems women do not gamble, possibly because they're not advertised to), or Coral, with the fat bloke and the blonde woman - and that is just a small selection. There are all those heinous, Ladbrokes Life ads where they try to establish different characters, such as Generous John and The Professor, who just look like people that have a horrible existence, their pain only numbed by lager and gambling.

Lad Broke, indeed.

I note that as I write this in late April 2019, Ladbrokes are suggesting they will no longer put ads encouraging betting at football matches or on TV during games. This is a clear indication of two things. First, they know it is destructive, second, they know the public are sick of seeing so many ads.

What we should gain from this more broadly is the proof that public pressure can produce change.

Update: As of 2nd July 2019 The Mirror reports, "Five of the UK's biggest gambling companies have committed to a series of measures to address problem gambling, including a major increase in funding for addiction, following government criticism. The companies - Bet365, Paddy Power-owner Flutter, Ladbrokes-owner GVC, Sky Betting and Gaming and William Hill - have agreed to the proposals after discussions with the Department for Digital, Culture, Media and Sport (DCMS). The gambling firms will significantly boost their financial support for safer gambling, increasing their commitment from 0.1% of their gross gambling yield to 1% by 2023. This will result in roughly £60 million in funding support from the firms in 2023, and it will remain at that level for the future." All of which sounds like an industry which knows it's pushed its luck too far and is now trying to appear caring and responsible. It is, in effect, tantamount to admitting how ruinous it has been. But let's be clear, this is just a PR exercise. It's trying to buy off criticism in order to preserve its very existence.

Gambling is a terrible addiction which can destroy lives every bit as comprehensively as any drug you can mainline. And like a confection designed to melt at just the right temperature in your mouth, so deliciously compulsive that you inevitably overindulge, the betting industry knows just how to press our psychological buttons, even offering up ready-made excuses for our losses. The Ladbrokes Life caption, for example: "When you win, it's skill, when you lose it's bad luck."

"Where's the fun in form?" says one of the 'characters' from the Ladbrokes Life adverts. "When you know, you know you know...you know?"

This is what we really know: You will lose. Now or tomorrow or later. You will lose. You are, or you will be a loser.

Anywhere from 0.5 to 3 per cent of the population of Europe has a gambling problem. This isn't a harmless bit of fun. In fact, it's so not a harmless bit of fun that the industry has had to pretend to care about its punters' welfare with vacuous advice such as, "When the fun stops, stop." Well, frankly, if the fun has stopped, that advice is already too late. You've already got a problem.

"Please bet responsibly," says Ray, in a knowing tone, which is just as pointless as 'please drink responsibly' on a bottle of vodka. People without a problem don't need telling; people with a problem can't take the advice.

It's just PR. It's faux caring from a vampiric industry.

Betting used to be something you had to enter a bookie's to do. You had to brave the smoke-filled, gadgee crowds to put your money down. Now, it's intentionally been made so easy to lose your money that you hardly notice it's even happened. At least in Vegas you know you're on a Fear and Loathing, Electric Kool Aid Acid Test in a Kandy-Kolored Tangerine-Flake Streamline Baby. You know it's not normal life and that this is one big freak out which will end. Yet football betting has deliberately become unremarkable through its persistent omnipresence, the encouragement to gratuitously lose your money made standard, as though it's just a natural part of life.

What is this doing to the quality of all our lives, whether we do or don't gamble? Do the grubby, downmarket values not cheapen all of us? Surely there are plenty more fulfilling intellectual and emotional stimuli available, without pretending that pointlessly throwing money away is fun. But time and again men tell me they can no longer face watching a game without having a bet on it. The addiction is that DNA deep now.

At least in Vegas we were being social. We laughed, we had the time of our lives, we rocked. By contrast, football betting on a phone seems like a desperate, solitary, sad little habit carried out in a Wetherspoons with the piercing screams of a hen party from Middlesbrough as a soundtrack.

Compulsive gambling, like compulsive drinking, is clever. It sneaks up on you, tells you you're having a good time, tells you anyone who says you aren't is part of the bleeding heart, PC, bedwetter, hand-wringing, do-gooder nanny state. You haven't got a problem, or at least not a problem that one more big bet or one more bottle won't fix.

That's why football's addiction to betting is so dangerous. We should be grateful that the Premier League actually isn't seen by many people on TV because if it were, the problems would only be far larger than they already are. It has put gambling front and centre, has encouraged and completely normalised extreme behaviour, as all the while it drums up huge profits by preying on the vulnerable and the poor. This will have actively provoked and fed many thousands of people's addictions, making their lives worse and worse. And that isn't just a pain the gambler alone endures, it spreads out to friends and families.

When the fun stops, stop? Well, the fun has stopped, but there seems to be no stopping the takeover of football by the gambling industry, and that's to the benefit of no-one except those who feast on the profits it carves out of its low-rent, shallow, debased culture, and still, more importantly, carves mercilessly out of human misery.

But it's not only down to the Premier League. A couple of years back, Ladbrokes, incredibly, became the FA's 'official betting partner'. In this context the word partner is one of those horrible and inaccurate marketing terms, designed to dress up common or garden advertising as something more than it really is.

Ladbrokes' CEO: "Football is the holy grail of sporting sponsorship opportunities. We are absolutely delighted to have secured exclusive rights that will see Ladbrokes at the beating heart of the beautiful game."

They always call it 'the beautiful game'. It's gone beyond cliché. What do you call something that is beyond being a cliché? Cliché plus, perhaps. Anway, there you have it. Gambling is very much embedded into the body politic of football. By binding itself to the governors of the game, it has brilliantly continued to normalise something which, when you stand back and look at it dispassionately, is quite an extreme and rather odd lifestyle choice. Extreme made normal: that is very Premier League.

In 2017, Britons lost £12.6 billion through gambling, almost £300 per person, with 48 per cent of people questioned by the Gambling Commission having admitted to gambling "at least once in the previous month".

That's £12.6 billion just thrown away, £12.6 billion spent with absolutely nothing to show for it. And if that 48 per cent figure is anywhere near accurate, we can see just how widespread it's become in society. What's more, the industry is expanding all the time, so much so that it has become a kind of financial matrix holding the whole of the game in its grip, handsomely funding it in order to profit from it, to ever greater degrees.

Before we think about how this has happened, let's consider the consequences of this financial colonisation. Clubs are boosted by gambling company money via multiple streams of sponsorship - aka 'partnership opportunities' - allowing them to spend more on players and improve the club. The gambling ads surrounding football on commercial TV put money into those broadcasters' coffers, who in turn use it to bid for rights in order to provide us with football on our televisions, where the betting firms advertise even more to further expand the market. A circle of sickness.

Betting firms also provide revenue to myriad websites which rely wholly on advertising income for their existence, such as ourselves at Football365. com. You may think it's hypocritical to worry about gambling whilst taking money from the industry, but what are we to do? We have to take advertising money because, at least traditionally, readers resist paying for content on the internet, despite the concept of paying for consumption being well established elsewhere in life.

And it's important to realise that while it might feel this is all being imposed onto us, it really isn't. Our choices are feeding it. If no-one did ' 'ave a bang on that', then it all goes away. If you paid a website such as F365 a subscription fee, then all the betting ads could go away. If you don't object to your club having less money to spend through not taking gambling sponsorship etc., then their presence evaporates.

But how easy is it really to make a choice not to gamble? This isn't a matter of having enough moral fibre and just taking responsibility for your actions, as if addiction is that easily addressed. Such failures of understanding only exacerbate the situation.

When something becomes ubiquitous, it's easy to get sucked in. Most people are doing the school run, doing the 9 to 5, working too hard to make life easy, and even if they have the energy and understanding, just accepting the status quo is the path of least resistance. So people sit back, soak it up and before you know it, gambling seems normal and unthreatening and we let it into our lives. Well-funded, clever and ceaseless marketing can make anything irresistible to most people. When the lexicon of gambling and discussing 'the odds' becomes a common currency, which it has, when the language of betting is softened to make 'a cheeky flutter' seem unthreatening, when the FA has an official betting partner, when William Hill sponsor the Football Writers' Association and the Sports Book of the Year (for which I was once long-listed), when Sky Bet is a commercial partner of the League Managers' Association, when Sky Bet sponsor the Football League, when Gamble Aware, the organisation tasked with helping people with gambling problems, is actually funded by the gambling industry, what hope has the punter to not get involved and start losing money?

Each of us is vulnerable to quiet, internal psychological pressure and peer pressure, too. Indeed, marketing's job is to encourage both. Some might say this is a form of soft bullying, so seductive that we've let it happen without protest and maybe without even realising. Gambling is now at the heart of apparently respectable institutions and thus acquires respectability by cultural osmosis.

Paul MacInnes wrote a piece for The Guardian about the issue with some revealing statistics:

"Dr Sean Cowlishaw of Bristol University interviewed 1,000 men aged 18-24 [and] found at least a quarter were showing signs of having a gambling problem. Cowlishaw says, 'Most of what we know (about gambling harm) is through research and evidence heavily influenced by industry. Industry funds all the research in the country through Gamble Aware. The amount of money put up is incredibly small and the industry has been able to maintain control over the topics addressed.'

"Five of Gamble Aware's 13 trustees have direct links to the gambling industry. In the financial year 2015-16, it raised £7.6 million in contributions from the gambling industry. Of that, it spent £919,654 on research. Meanwhile, £3,788,698 was given to the gambling harm treatment charity Gamcare. Of Gamcare's 11 trustees, six have direct connections to the gambling industry."

Now that sounds like one big mess of conflicts of interest. Many might think the industry sees Gamcare as little more than a PR defence measure (again very much a Premier League corporate strategy), born from the full knowledge that problems are being stored up for the future by the online betting boom when 25 per cent of 18-24 year-old men are already exhibiting issues around betting.

So what do we do? One way or another, we're all hooked on the gambling pound. If football was filleted of gambling money, many would be poorer and out of work. Its roots are now very deep and wide. And yet there are signs that problems are growing, that it is making lives worse, making people worried, unhappy, and ironically spoiling the enjoyment of the sport itself.

Is this an addiction we're prepared or able to break? I wouldn't like to bet on it.

When the FA announced that new long-term sponsorship deal with Ladbrokes, FA Chief Executive Martin Glenn, said, "Ladbrokes join an outstanding portfolio of official FA partners, providing support across the England team, and the most famous cup competition in the world, The Emirates FA Cup. We are delighted to welcome them on board."

It was to be a five-year deal. Nine months later, after a three-month review (what were they doing for three whole months?) the FA ended the deal. Shamefully, to the point of moral cowardice, there has been no detailed reasoning given for this change of policy. Their press release was an exercise in nothing-to-see-here obfuscation.

Something major must have happened for the FA to conduct such a massive volte face. What was it? They don't have the courage to say, but I think we can make some educated guesses.

Opposition mounted against the deal from the start. Could they have changed their minds because they then banned Joey Barton for 18 months for gambling on games and then realised their hypocrisy because it was the very thing the FA endorsed as a leisure activity by taking Ladbrokes' money?

Y'see, to go back to my point that I started this book out making, all of these issues are the underpinnings to our feelings about the Premier League and indeed modern commercialised football more broadly. Advertising is everywhere and has been for many decades around the pitch - though it was controversial in the late 70s when first introduced onto shirts, as many felt it defiled the colours - but when you get the FA having 'partners' it takes it to a whole new level and demands a lot of questions.

Questions such as, Why you are taking money from confectionery companies who sell sugar and refined carbohydrates at a time when child obesity is at an all-time high? Why are you taking money from fizzy pop manufacturers when the rising consumption of its empty calories is so controversial in encouraging that obesity? Why are you taking money from snack food and confectionery purveyors when more than two-thirds of men and almost 6 in 10 women are overweight or obese, and when the country is in the grip of a Type 2 diabetes epidemic which threatens to quite literally bankrupt the NHS, a condition that we now know is fundamentally caused by over-consumption of sugar and refined carbohydrates?

We know sugar and carbs can become addictive for some, just as gambling can. Surely the FA knows this. And if they don't, they should. In an era where selling all manner of crud and awful lifestyle choices on the back of football is so commonplace, it doesn't even seem weird that an administrative organisation is taking such sponsorship. But it should.

It doesn't end there. Why are the FA taking money from alcohol producers, a product again entirely inseparable from so many public health issues, from obesity, diabetes, public disorder, through to some horrific domestic abuse statistics? And again, there are addiction issues.

The FA seems financially addicted to the addiction industry, doesn't it?

Quietly, but relentlessly, the FA has sucked in millions in corporate cash from highly inappropriate sources. Did they realise the error of their ways, or was dropping Ladbrokes just a detoxifying PR stunt? I suspect that is exactly what it was.

If you don't think we are in an extreme situation where terrible lifestyle choices are being pushed as perfectly fine and normal, that is a testament to the indoctrination we have all been subjected to for so long. What is actually extreme, through ceaseless, generation-long marketing, has been made to seem normal.

It is a free for all and it was the Premier League which brought all of this about. It is a 27-year-long culture which has been dedicated philosophically, economically and morally to the pursuit of profit over and above everything else. It inculcated the notion, or at the very least promulgated the belief that everything was for sale to the highest bidder. After all, top-flight football most certainly is. They'll sell it to you if you've got enough money, regardless of if you only want to broadcast it to your friends and family. Lay your billions down and you can broadcast it exclusively to your own shed if you so wish. They don't care. Only the money matters. This is where we are now, so it is no surprise that the gambling industry has invaded and occupied the territory.

Surely it isn't crazy to feel this is all wrong? For the game to be so commercially exploited at every single turn by so many negative forces makes it feel as if football is played for the sponsors and not for the fans. Football is now a guest at the sponsors' table and not vice versa.

To illustrate just how ludicrous sponsorship has become in the Premier League, clubs are now allowed to have 'sleeve sponsors', that is, companies whose logo is placed only on the sleeve. Yes, it's true. Well, you probably knew that anyway. Sleeve sponsorship is cheaper than having it on the front of the shirt or even on a pre-game training top. Where will this stop? Shorts sponsors? Socks sponsors? Official underwear gusset partner?

Top clubs are now choked with 'partners'. Here are just five. Have a guess which one I've invented:

"Official noodle partner"

"Official coconut water partner"

"Official casual footwear partner of South Korea"

"Global handbag and accessories partner"

"Financial services affinity partner"

The answer?

None of them.

They are all real.

It is the Premier League which marches at the front of this cavalcade of commerciality, and very loud and very proud it is to do so. So we know where the blame lies. However, it tries to offset this with ongoing PR to paint itself as a responsible and positive force in society and thus should not be challenged. However, this ceaseless exploitation does not come without consequences. Indeed, so much of the toxicity around the league is birthed from its economic culture and the exponential growth in an abuse culture at and around football hasn't happened for no reason. So let's just have a think about that for a moment.

THE ABUSIVE TRUTH

We live in very odd times. I don't recall any period in my life where Britain was so divided against itself. This is evidenced especially in the Brexit referendum. Don't worry, I'm not going to mention the B-word again. Whether or not we have always been split down the middle so profoundly and we're just seeing it more nakedly now, nonetheless it is hardly adding to our good mood. This manifests itself profoundly on social media, where we seem intent on either hunting down and abusing those we disagree with or finding those we agree with and over-praising their wisdom. I would postulate, with my hippie philosopher's hat on, that in both cases this is to aggrandise our own view and establish how great we are. In other words, it is an over-compensation for feeling insecure, for being a tiny voice in a cavernous world. Perhaps also because our communities are very fractured and many of us feel quite lonely, it is a natural way to reach out and feel some warmth. We don't like to feel alone and isolated but all too often to one degree or another, that is what the culture of the primacy of the individual has brought about. This may also explain the huge growth in football podcasts. It isn't just an expanding desire for football content, but rather for sympathetic voices that entertain and in doing so assuage loneliness.

It seems to me that many have not learned how to use this technology and are simply wasting valuable living time telling people who don't care, what they think of them in insulting and horrible terms. This seems to be serving the needs of the abuser to abuse. When one suffers from these sorts of attacks it always strikes me powerfully how much the people doing it must really need to do it. It is easy to think they are just nasty people using the anonymity of Twitter to call people names and worse, and that is correct in one way. But underneath the ugliness of their attitude, something is going on. Something is driving the behaviour. The need to have agency and power must be something to do with not having either element in everyday life. It is not too fanciful to think it is people shouting, "I'm here!! I'm here! Don't ignore me!"

As someone with a modest 13,000 followers on Twitter I only occasionally suffer this, though I have been subjected to the occasional bit of timeline mining in order to try and find something off-colour. Memorably someone accused me of being a homophobe because in 2011 I had Tweeted how Luka Modric has the look of a lesbian hockey player. Why hockey, I don't know. It was the sort of attempt at comic observation that I simply wouldn't do on

Twitter eight years later, even though I have an exemplary record of being pro-lesbian, pro-hockey and pro-Modric, because it is all too easily taken either out of context or just wilfully presented as though this is proof of your secret gay bigotry, when it's just a daft comment and not intended to be anything else than that. If you're properly famous, you can now expect this to be done not just by the public but by the newspapers, desperate to unearth something you said when young, when drunk or when mentally unwell and hold you to account for it. It is very weird and kind of sad, too. That people would waste time doing this suggests lives not being well lived.

Chris Sutton: "We're in an age where everyone is offended by everything. So I've learned to temper myself a little bit. You do have to be careful. One single word out of place and you could be sacked."

However, it is not all bad, many people are actually really interesting and will chip in with good observations and anecdotes on any issue I'm writing about. That just proves it can be a positive thing. The black cloud is always lurking, but so is the silver lining.

I've used Twitter on and off for 10 years. And at first I got caught up, endlessly trying to fight battles and being sarcastic to people who said things I found idiotic. Then I realised it just was not worth it, that I wasn't making the world a nicer place, that I was just feeding the negative beast and souring my own peace of mind. Perpetuating unpleasantness is no way to live your life. So for the last few years I've just adopted a policy of never being nasty, trying to be as polite and appreciative as possible and just ignoring those who are horrible. As soon as someone calls me a name, I tune them out. Why wouldn't I? That's my Red Card offence. As soon as abuse comes, I mute them or ignore them. It does still sometimes ruffle my feathers, of course. It is part of the 'if you're not perfect, you're shit' culture. It would seem no longer is anyone allowed to learn and grow and change. Some would have you forever defined by your worst moments, your worst judgements, your worst language. What a world to be born into. Can you imagine if there was a record of all your most silly, rude or stupid comments? I mean, you're reading the words of a man who once got thrown out of someone's flat aged 20 for vehemently arguing that Bob Seger was both musically and indeed morally superior to Depeche Mode. I believed it, too. So I feel sorry for young people today who are not allowed room to grow, and to grow you've got to make mistakes and get things wrong. No-one should be harsh on people for doing that.

So given this trend, it isn't surprising that football's abuse culture has reached some sort of heinous fever pitch where people seem to feel empowered to be racist and sexist towards footballers and any amount of horrible abuse is hurled at referees. Why is this happening? Why now?

Chris Sutton, again. As a high-profile man in the media, he suffers more abuse than most, especially on Twitter, and has even had a death threat.

"I do think it's getting worse because of social media. In all honesty I understand why people don't like it and steer clear of it. People feel entitled to abuse you in any shape or form. If I took it all seriously, I'd never get out of bed in the morning. Twitter is extreme. There's no grey, everything is black or white. People don't want balance. There are people who are witty and funny with it but many more who are not.

"Players and officials definitely get more abuse than they once did. More than when I was a player, even. Mind you, when I was at Chelsea my own fans used to abuse me! I think today, people pay so much money for a ticket and feel it entitles them to be as abusive as they want. Football culture is so vicious now.

"I think things are going to get worse, I do. It's all down to personal responsibility and knowing boundaries, isn't it? I took my boy to a Norwich game and the bile and abuse that the adults around us were shouting was incredible. You can see that will rub off on the younger generation and they copy what they've grown up hearing. Kids are so easily influenced."

One of the consequences of the massive wealth in the league is our emotional and intellectual alienation from the players. It is hard to relate to someone who you only see from behind the tinted windows of privilege. It is even harder to imagine what it is like to get so rich by just kicking a ball around. As I've been saying, we see the Premier League almost wholly through a financial lens. In turn this has caused a ramping up of anger directed at officials and players, recently leading to fans getting on the pitch and even punching players in an act of what I am sure they would describe as banter.

Now, I know this seems as old as time but it really isn't. Yes, the terraces have always been up in arms at a penalty given against them, or something similar, but as Chris confirms, the levels of sheer personal abuse directed at players and officials has never been as it is now and it happens right through all of the game. Here's just a small smorgasbord of the abuse hurled at the referee during my local amateur club games. Played out most weeks to a few dozen people on a windswept field with the rain lashing in off the North Sea, the abuse directed at the referee - there aren't any other officials at this level - is almost ceaseless for 90 minutes from players, coaches and many of the observers.

"Face it, ref, you're shite! I could do better than you with my eyes closed!"

"Hey! Prick! You've got another one wrong, haven't you?!"

"You're an absolute fucking tube, referee!!!"

Calling someone a tube is a very Scottish thing. Almost poetic, really.

And this is all entirely normal and all as predictable as that guy on a YouTube video who always says, "How come 14 people gave this a thumbs down?" or some variant thereof. It happens every week, at pretty much every single game, at every single level, from the top flight down to amateur-league kickabouts. At all age groups, at all levels, it's all abuse. But extreme behaviour has been so normalised in football that if you pointed out just how unreasonable it is, you would receive blank looks from many.

We all get inculcated into this culture, few of us are innocent; it's not something that's even questioned much of the time. Every radio phone-in will feature people saying the ref was a disgrace at their game, as though they - the fans - are always objectively right. It's childish, not least because it's really, really hard being an official. I can't believe they get so much right, frankly.

The fella reffing my game was middle aged. He had to administer the game without help from anyone else. This makes offside calls especially tricky. Does he get sympathy for not being able to be close to the play, as well as level with the play, at one and the same time? Oh no. Rather, he gets ceaseless abuse from people who are no more able to accurately judge an offside from where they're standing, feet turning to slabs of cold dead meat in the freezing rain, than the referee.

As if to add insult to injury, if this fella wasn't prepared to referee the game for a few quid, the game couldn't actually happen. It's like getting insulted by a thirsty drinker for letting them into a pub. I don't think he made a bad call all game. He was a good ref. Not a hapless amateur. Not a "useless cunt".

I felt really sorry for him. It was like being 14 again and witnessing a gang of lads bullying a boy who couldn't fight back, watching him gulping down his fears and tears as his tormentors grinned amongst themselves at the upset they were inflicting.

As he walked off the pitch on the final whistle, I intercepted him, patted him on the back, said, "Well played, ref," and smiled. Sadly, after an hour and a half of abuse, he obviously thought this was an ironic comment and as such, just more crap, so he blanked me, emotionally numbed to my niceness and positivity. And that is awful.

I have a feeling that those who perform the relentless abuse would tell me "it's just banter". But I don't believe that. I think the abuse culture has escalated into a whole psychosis where the referee is always shite, always against your team, always no good. The banter defence only applies when the blood isn't high, but during the game, it is a deliberate attempt to intimidate. It is intentional.

It's not phoney or fake. It's not a joke. And those doing it derive some kind of pleasure from it. Indeed, they seem to need to do it.

There are many stories of officials being assaulted at amateur levels. What on earth is happening to our society that people are being driven to behave like this? The dogs of war have been let slip, it sometimes seems.

But what do we do? As individuals we can't walk up to the abusers and suggest they don't do it. That's not going to work, it's too widespread and it would put people in danger. Abuse needs to be eradicated from the culture of football at all levels. Top-level players need to stop protesting every decision, stop throwing a strop, stop swearing at refs, stop trying to cheat, stop lying; basically change their behaviour entirely because it is perpetuating and normalising bad behaviour everywhere else, via their example.

But this isn't an argument for a lavender-scented, sanitised game devoid of expletives or passion. It is possible to be noisy without being abusive. You can express frustration impersonally. You can bitch about a player or official to your pals or to yourself. You don't have to do it publicly. You can bellow out the rage that life's injustices build within you during the week without it being a verbal baseball bat to the head of one person.

It can be fun to take a different approach. For example in one amateur game I saw, after a decision to award a penalty, a fan shouted, "Which pub have you been drinking in, ref?" Now that's funny. It's not nasty or aggressive.

It's time both we and the authorities became radically proactive in breaking this culture. Whether that means equipping officials with body cameras to record the abuse and abusers, or instant red cards for abusing or intimidating a ref, or obliging clubs to enforce and police a non-abuse policy, it has to be done. With referees at amateur levels reporting it's getting worse and having no faith in the system to protect them, it's not hard to say we stand in the middle of some sort of crisis.

Without people to referee a game, we will have no football at all, so we should grow up and appreciate the officials' efforts, not use them as some sort of piñata upon which to unleash our own inner demons.

However, this is just one strand of the flourishing football abuse culture. I wouldn't pretend things were a land of peace and love in the past. There was certainly racist abuse, and chanting at black players. There were bananas thrown on the pitch. Violence was rife in everyday life and fighting between fans and indeed players was far more common. However, anger towards officials and players simply did not have the same sort of expression or presence as today. We were not so quick to be so furious at a misfiring player or to eviscerate someone as a useless or biased official. It seems counterintuitive, really.

Violence was commonplace but anger towards the participants, at least those who were not black, wasn't.

I don't think you need a degree in psychology to see what is going on here. It is another poison that the Premier League's money culture has pumped into the body of football, one which stems from the consumer mentality the league has inculcated and glorified. The money paid for a ticket and the money paid to players makes some feel entitled to hurl abuse around as much as they like on the 'I've paid my money, I'll do what I like' principle. Again, this is part of the washout from a culture that puts a price ticket on anything and everything. You've paid, so they owe you something and if you're not getting what you want, then you reach for the abuse gun to try and make things right. It is football's equivalent of complaining about faulty goods. Football is shopping, shopping for players, for tickets, for pizza at half-time. So we shouldn't be surprised when this finds a manifestation in how the customers feel about what they're being sold and how they respond.

When players are phenomenally rich, in the minds of many, it legitimises indulging in the abuse culture, as though the money is armour against it. The money dehumanises them. Obviously, this is wrong and unfair but I would also suggest that it is an angry response at the unequal nature of a society where you can sit and watch a player being paid more in a week than you might earn in up to 10 years; perhaps not consciously, every time, but the fact is, nothing happens in isolation with no consequence and one extreme tends to beget another. So if a player fails to trap a ball or misplaces a pass, fans feel they have been shortchanged. They're getting all that money and are making the same mistakes we might make. That cognitive dissonance kicks in once again and upsets our mentality. You can hear this all the time in the tone of phone-in callers. The gap between reward for the player's talent and the actual talent is huge. They are paid as though they're gods but are performing like humans and that's why the abuse culture has flourished. It spills onto social media and from there goes nuclear because of the perceived anonymity and available platform to vent anger.

It all goes to make for a horrible culture; a horrible atmosphere that surely none of us want to experience. This is another reason to object to the Premier League money culture and, I feel, illustrates the negativity extreme wealth poisons us all with. We want to feel at ease, we want to feel happy, but when we're faced with radical inequality and invited to celebrate it, it simply doesn't feel right.

THE JUST BEING HERE TRUTH

So why do we go to football? It is to be entertained, it is to have fun and also, often most importantly, just to be there. None of these things are reliant on watching the best or elite players. If it was, why do people watch lower-league football, which is anything but elite, in such huge nationwide numbers? Why can I watch 5th-tier Scottish football with about 500 others? Why do games below the Premier League comprise the majority of football's overall attendances? It's because people enjoy it, and enjoying it is what it is all about. Indeed, many times, the 'worse' the football is, the more enjoyable it is.

The words enjoy and enjoyment need a little discussion at this point, as they are somewhat evasive. We use them liberally but when you think about it, they do become hard to pin down. Let's go back to that classic line from the start of the book about why the pitch at Ayresome Park was so green: "Because there's been so much shite on it over the years." That and comments like it are all certainly part of the enjoyment of football. Even when the game is dull and not much happens, we find a way to enjoy it in a way we rarely would in any other walk of life. You don't sit through a band who can't even tune up properly, but you do sit and watch the football equivalent.

Gallows humour in the face of a terrible thrashing is another flavour of enjoyment. Bemoaning a terrible player, laughing at one of those shots which is sliced so badly it goes out for a throw in and a referee who falls over, are but three other things we enjoy at football. This could be a big list, but my point is made.

I was recently watching my local amateur team, Pittenweem Rovers, who have been in existence for 100 years. They were 2-nil down and playing poorly. But they pulled one back. Suddenly the vibe changed from weary if good-humoured resignation of defeat to the excitement of the chance of a draw. And when they did score the equalizer with little more than a toe-poke, the release of emotion and joy for me was as big as it would have for any goal at any level. Seeing your team score, no matter what level it happens at, is an equally enjoyable thing. All of this can happen at any level and has nothing at all to do with paying big money to big players. Nothing to do with so-called elite players or 'premier' football. The enjoyment of it is far wider, broader and more universal than such frothy frivolous notions as 'skill'. The Premier League has ceaselessly promoted the idea that their football is some sort of exhibition sport where we watch the most skilful strut their stuff, but it simply isn't that and even if you want it to be, it won't be.

Of course there are really great, exciting games played in the Premier League, really arresting, exciting football despite everything. Football remains a great sport. However, whenever one such game is broadcast on Sky or anywhere else, it will with 100 per cent certainty be described by someone as "a great advert for the Premier League." This is accidentally and subconsciously very revealing, showing as it does that marketing the league is a kind of mental default for broadcasters. All is part of the invisible matrix that is forever shaping how we see and feel about the league. Somewhere deep in the mind, the propaganda kicks in and says, "Don't forget to say how great this shows the league is." Do you ever hear that said about any other sport? I've never heard it said in any other circumstances other than the Premier League or as a part of the desperation to re-inflate the FA Cup.

I don't think I ever heard anyone say, "That was a great advert for Division One." Indeed, it would have sounded very odd and been treated as so. So why did it change? It changed because football became a product that the Premier League and broadcasters needed to persuade people was worth paying for. Ever since, this has been the core of everything Sky and now BT Sport have done. The principle of paying must have primacy and not be questioned. It is the same reason that for many years absolutely terrible games between terrible teams were still given the big build up. It's why we have Super Sunday. It was why over the years there have been any number of oddly branded days, like Red Monday. They have commoditised every aspect of the game and are never not trying to sell it to us, even when it involves nakedly pretending something that probably won't be very good is actually going to be really great. It's such a shame really that we can't just be trusted to watch football without all this cajoling. I really think it diminishes the experience, not increases it. After all, on the radio, the games are rarely given this treatment, everyone is honest about it, great, good or indifferent. We're all grown ups, we understand what football is and can be. We don't need gloss paint lashed onto everything.

As in all levels of football, games can be thrilling and dull and everything in between. This is why it is such folly to try and pretend any league is 'Premier'. To what is that even referring? And it cannot be given such a value judgement, simply because football isn't quantifiable in that way. You can watch a boring draw between the top two sides and an exciting game two divisions below. Who's Premier there?

When the league was called the First Division, it was factually that. There was no subjective value judgement placed on it. That just seems more honest and simple.

But we have all been hypnotised and marketed into a state of mind where we stop questioning and accept even the most egregious weirdness as though it is normal. Once you strip out the marketing hype you're left with a product - and that's how they themselves refer to it - which is not vastly different to any other time in the past. Football is remarkably constant in how it attracts people to it. The main changes that have happened are consequences of rule changes, such as where once you could tackle, take the ball first and then the man, launching him over the stand in the process and not be penalised, nowadays you can't.

Similarly, stamping on the calf of the opposition's most tricky skilful winger, the way Chopper Harris did to Eddie Gray in the 1970 FA Cup Final, is also outlawed. The pass-back rule has sped the game up, but players are no more skilful now than they've ever been and if you think they are then you never saw the likes of Tony Currie, Stan Bowles, Rodney Marsh, Duncan McKenzie or any number of incredibly entertaining skilful players ply their trade in the 1960s and 70s. They had to have brilliant ball control because they were playing on uneven surfaces and risked having an ankle kicked off by a defender. They were, if it were possible to measure such a thing, more skilful if anything, just because they had to be. And in McKenzie's case, he could also jump over a Mini. Show me a player who can do that now. In fact, I would happily pay money to watch footballers attempt to jump over a car and I'm sure we all would.

Pat Murphy has reported on football for over 40 years: "We see far more skilful goals these days, with the better pitches, but back in the day, we had so many entertainers and unlike today, they all connected with the fans. Men like Marsh, Bowles and Best. I can see a time when clubs take total control of their media outlets and so not let the press into conferences at all, unless they're a proven lickspittle. Press officers are fans with dictaphones. They're the gatekeepers and that's how the clubs like it. They want to push their narrative and don't want anyone going against it. I feel sorry for the press these days. If you're critical of the club, players or manager in any way at all, suddenly you're an apostate. It's pathetic. The annoying thing is, fans believe the club rather than the press, even though the club is spinning everything all the time and all we're trying to do is get to the truth. But nobody wants to talk honestly. The public should be more intelligent about what they are being force-fed. There's a journalist at Leicester City who hasn't had one interview since 2014 because he had a dispute with Nigel Pearson back then. It's shoddy and childish."

In this and so many other ways we are being kept at arm's length from the players and the game. They are on the TV, or behind the PR wall, aloof and distant and it's much easier to abuse someone who is aloof and distant, isn't it? Nobody should be doing that, of course. Let's just be nice to each other. We should not be angry at any footballer just for being a footballer and I can't believe I've felt it necessary to actually say that, and yet it is not unsurprising that we stop seeing them as people like us when they are not treated, are not paid and do not live like us. They feel more like emblems and less like humans.

Put simply, the argument that that if we destroy the model the Premier League has been built on, it will somehow less to less enjoyment of football, will lead to football being less popular or will in any way damage the game, it is simply a lie. It will not.

As the old terrace chant has it. "We're here because we're here, because we're here, because we're here." And it really is as profound and existential as that.

At the beginning of this book I talked about the uneasy, uncomfortable feeling that we have about top flight football. I hope I have drawn back the veil on why this might be. Is it any surprise? We are watching a league that sells itself as hugely popular on TV when it isn't. It sells itself as great football, when it often isn't. It sells itself as a great competition, when it is ever more predictable. It has reshaped history in its own name so 'the Premier League era' is now all but the only era. It is awash with vast unearned wealth at a time of austerity and yet its clubs often won't pay staff the Living Wage. This unnecessary and grotesque wealth has made fans more impatient and abusive to players, managers and officials. It has also undermined once great cup competitions and via the transfer culture turned football into shopping not sport.

And despite all of these things, the league sells itself as a generous benefactor even though fans concerns are disregarded in favour of catering to the paltry TV audience who are counted by the league as viewers if they watch three consecutive minutes across a nine month season.

On top of that, its shameless promotion of a greedy culture of consumerism is terrible for the planet and for our mental health. And if all of this were still not enough, it has fearlessly got into bed with the gambling industry to wreck perfectly decent people's lives even further.

This is the wonderland we watch football in and it's why we have that gnawing nauseous feeling I talked about at the start of all this. I'm right aren't I? And it's why we need a revolution. So it's time to talk about how we create a new future, what it might look like and why we should work to make it a reality. Get yourself a big drink, you're really going to need it.

PART TWO:
A NEW COUNTRY

TALKING ABOUT A REVOLUTION

Change is a weird thing. It's everywhere, all the time, from season to season. From the sun to the rain. From the dusk to the dawn. From the seedling to the fruit. But we fear it. The thing that we know right now, that's the thing we want cling to. Change threatens the known with the unknown. So we hang onto the known and it becomes everything, like it is fixed. Like it is real. But it isn't real. As Bill Hicks said, it's just a ride. It's just a blink of the cosmic eye. Here today, gone today, because there is only today. We pass the impermanence of now off as forever; that is the nature of the human condition. So when the curtain is pulled back and a new now is revealed, we tend to look not for the freedoms it offers but to attack the unfamiliar as dangerous or just plain stupid. That's why change is so fought against, even though logically we know that what we perceive to be the status quo in this moment was arrived at as a new thing at some point.

So when I talk about a revolution of football and of the society it exists in, be in no doubt that everything we take for granted as being 'the way things are' was very much not the way things were at some point in the past. In other words, no matter how extreme you may think this section of the book might be, in the past where we are now would have seemed equally preposterous. So change, radical and profound, can, does and will happen. And for this reason, I hope you will not quickly dismiss these ideas.

Because it's time to begin to knit ourselves a new reality out of all these homespun yarns I've been plying together. I have begun to suggest what can be done to begin a revolution in terms of wage caps and maximum wages, but it's time to get down to what my mother would've called brass tacks. Time to start inventing a complete vision about the world we're striving for when it comes to Premier League football. How do we go about smashing it up and tearing it down and what do we put in its place? We want this to be the most velvet of revolutions. Who doesn't like velvet? Like George Costanza, I would drape myself in velvet if it was socially acceptable.

OK, here we go.

As we've seen, there are many different issues at play, many levers to pull to change this ride to a better ride, but the biggest brick in the wall is the paywall concept. It is what the whole edifice is built on and is still the driver for all the money that has caused so many problems and led to so much disaffection and discontent. We need to shatter that first and foremost. It must be our first target. So to do that we cancel our direct debits to whichever paywall football provider or broadcaster we pay them to. This will be a radical act, and seldom will cancelling a direct debit be so revolutionary in our lives. No barricades to storm. No blood shed. We come in peace but we change everything. Just by unticking that box on your bank account, if we do it en masse over a relatively short period, we halt that which has become the norm. We begin to unpick the matrix and we restore the values of humble community and oneness to all our lives and to the sport itself. Nothing bad will happen, that's important to remember.

It's easy. It takes seconds to do, but in doing that one small act we will be starting a major change, not just to football, but to the society we live in, and the world we live on. And we will be financially richer for doing so. Not bad, huh?

So that being done, what does our future broadcast football dream world look like? What are we aiming at by cancelling the subscription? Let's pretend we can flush the broadcasting toilet and apply a toilet duck to cleanse the whole environment and start again. How would we really like things to be?

I am convinced the dream world should have the live games available on BBC and ITV terrestrial channels with the broadcasters sharing the coverage. They and they alone would have sole broadcasting rights for all live football, every league, every tournament, domestic and Europe. No longer should access to football be sold for huge profits. That's our basic principle.

To maximise audiences it has to be on both BBC One and ITV1 at least some of the time. I know this is insane but the fact is that many people simply won't press the other buttons in as big numbers as they will press 1 and 3 or whatever digital number the channels lie under. Put a programme on 2 or 4 and it will get a smaller audience. This is a well-established fact borne out by the viewing figures over many years. It may be because some people just have a TV on in the background. They're not viewers in the conventional sense, it's just on as wallpaper. I can understand that as a principle, but why use 1 and 3 as your wallpaper? Obviously, it makes absolutely no sense at all. There is little rationalising it. It's obviously as easy to press one button as another, but there it is. It is nonetheless true and, if nothing else, proves just how illogical humans are.

I talked to Mark Chapman about this: "There would be plenty of scheduling issues. There are big programmes like Strictly, Britain's Got Talent and others who also want to broadcast at the same time in order to get their big audiences. Football couldn't just take over every top slot. You also have to bear in mind that if they are going to do it properly, they've got to give it some time and space and you have that on a dedicated channel in a way you rarely will on BBC or ITV main channels. The problem with putting the Champions League on the BBC is all the advertising around it. Gazprom et cetera. However, against that, the games on the main channels would be real watercooler moments that everyone would be talking about the next day. That's got to be worth something. There are so few of those these days."

I'm not so sure the advertising would be such a big issue for the BBC. After all, any football they now show is littered with advertising and sponsorship all around the pitch and all over the players, and that hasn't stopped them. Being frit of any further exposure would be little more than posing and given their coverage would be very much be marketed as for the greater good, I don't think this is a deal-breaking compromise.

The re-engagement of the general public in football, while being harder to calculate financially in advance, would boost engagement on all levels. While some people do watch games on catch-up, the vast majority want to do so live, as some want to use social media whilst doing so, something you just can't do if you're watching it in any delayed way. Beyond that, feeling part of an unfolding event is important. Seeing games in real time is part of the essence of the game. And in the fractured world of modern digital TV, as Mark says, those collectively experienced watercooler moments are very rare, and as such would have a premium to them when it comes to pricing advertising for ITV and that advertising income across a season would provide a substantial contribution to paying for the rights, in a way that no digital broadcaster could hope to get near.

For the clubs themselves, there would be knock-on value in the massively increased exposure they would receive by a move to terrestrial. Remember, no-one has ever seen any Premier League side playing a Premier League game live on terrestrial television. Such hugely increased exposure must in itself have a monetised value to clubs whether that's through increased sales of shirts or tickets, or increased revenue from sponsors keen to ride on the back of the additional millions of pairs of eyes now seeing their team. We might argue this isn't a good thing, of course, however, such funding might be important in the transition phase as we sober football up from its toxic addiction to mainlining big hits of cash. But my point here is that terrestrial broadcasting of live football wouldn't be a financial backwater or cul de sac.

League football would make itself more popular and by the way, the same thing would apply to the Champions League and Europa League coverage. That should please everyone. Because what are the alternatives? More platforms, more subscriptions, more channels? That's not working and it isn't suddenly going to start working.

Right, so that's settled then! The broadcasters share the rights and costs. All the biggest games would play on buttons 1 and 3 and in addition there would be one or two dedicated free-to-air channels for the more niche games which would be co-owned between the BBC and ITV. Just let it sink in for a moment. No longer would anyone have to work out who was broadcasting any particular game, you would always know where to find it. There would be no more subscriptions to keep up to date with. No money to pay anyone. Football would now be inclusive and accessible by the whole country. And when it is on, we know there are millions watching it with us. We move away from all being in our own little financial cliques and once again football becomes a community activity by and of the people. The distance between us all begins to narrow and we stop thinking about everything through some sort of financial equation. There is no us and them any more, only we.

If you doubt how positive this would be, this summer the broadcasting of the Women's World Cup on the BBC has been a huge success, attracting record audiences for what is still a development sport. It has brought millions of people together to watch the England games; it is, in the BBC's old maxim, entertaining, educating and inspiring. Now imagine what this World Cup would've been like if on paywall TV. Audiences would've been small, the excitement about England's progress very limited. There would have been little or no spread of interest in the women's game. Kids would not be seeing role models that they can aspire to be like and adults would not feel similarly excited by their sporting success. At a time when the public needs to be more active more often, a World Cup can get kids out onto the playing fields and make we adults feel inspired to get off our backsides. But none of this can happen when the audience is small. In this way we can see that the BBC showing the Women's World Cup will improve the health of the nation and that will have reduced cost implications for the health service. In other words, even if it was paid for by the government, which it isn't, it would pay for itself many times over. It has also allowed us to have something in common and that is a priceless commodity in this fractured modern world.

Mark Chapman: "It always surprises me when I'm walking through working-class areas to go to a game just how many people recognise me, and you'll hear them say, 'It's the guy off Match of the Day.' I also get lots of recognition for the NFL coverage I present. It is all simply because it is free-to-air."

His experience well illustrates just how free-to-air turns television into a communal experience. How it brings us together rather than pushing us away into little purchaser bubbles.

It seems like the stuff of fantasy, doesn't it? I know it does. It does to me and I'm the one who is supposed to believe it is possible! But let us remember that this is how it once was and this summer's World Cup, just as last summer's did too, has proven again how it can be.

So how could this happen? We can't just light some joss sticks, chant Om and hope that everyone will see that we are all one in the universal mind and that paying to watch football on television is having a corrosive effect on our society. Surely it will never happen because, if for no other reason, the rights cost too much for ITV or BBC to afford. That is certainly the traditional thinking on this matter. But, let me remind us all once again, all such reflexes are just the Premier League virus checker kicking in, telling us to repel the idea of change. Telling us to decry any deviation from the established norms. But I'm not here to do traditional thinking. So let's swim in these waters for a while and see how on earth we can make this happen.

I've been talking to the great and the good of football broadcasting - you will read some of those discussions in the final section of this book - and the first thing that almost everyone agrees about is that the old subscription model is falling apart at the seams. As I've documented here in detail, the audience simply isn't expanding in any meaningful way - though the Premier League does claim a 10% increase in people watching in the 2018-19 season. However, I suspect that 10% isn't a serious expansion of interest. When you count someone as a viewer because they have watched three continuous minutes of a game, it is not proper engagement the way we would normally expect a 'viewer' to have. So there's nothing Sky or BT Sport or anyone else seems to be able to do about their lack of an audience. The vast majority of people just won't pay to watch football on any device. They can try and roll it into other packages, sell 90-second clips to us of goals and red cards or knock out other sliced and diced versions of the game direct to our smartphones in order to try and tempt us, but that simple fact remains. And I think that is the maximum point of weakness in their defences which we exploit first by cancelling the direct debits.

Let's just say that those of us who do still pay, take this opportunity to quit paying for football TV altogether, so that within a few months, almost no income is being derived from it. Symbolically, that would be a very forceful rejection, albeit one that Sky et al. would try to suppress from public knowledge with their milky, opaque subscription figures. But the headline audience numbers would reveal it, one way or another.

Now, there is much talk of other platforms such as Netflix, Facebook, Google and Amazon entering the market and becoming major players. And indeed, Amazon has already done so, buying a whole round of games to be shown on Prime simultaneously in 2019-2020 in something that smacks of novelty and gimmick more than commitment. It already feels like The Old Way. But the problem with any of these is that they will still essentially be the same subscription model. However it is dressed up, we're still going to need to cough up somewhere along the line. So the same problems will remain.

The football industry is slow to change now. The club's executives, grown fat on the sweet rich cream lo these last 27 years, are very conservative and just want the money to keep flowing. Simon Jordan, the ex-Crystal Palace chairman and now a very good broadcaster on talkSPORT told me a funny, but revealing, story about giving a speech about the future of broadcasting football to Premier League executives. At one point he asked them what plans they had to future proof their broadcast income. They had none. None, sir. None other than to hold out their hands to receive more free money.

Simon told me, "The lack of creative thinking was shocking to me. They were so complacent, it's untrue."

But the big wheel keeps on turning. Simon's idea, and it's one that has an obvious appeal, is for the Premier League to make itself the Netflix of football: set up its own broadcast platform and take the games direct to the public. Whether it is a runner or not, Simon is certain the existing Sky model set up in 1992 is in its end game. "The domestic broadcast rights are tapped out. There is more supply than demand."

His calculations are that 100 million people would buy this and deliver substantially more money to clubs.

Pat Nevin agrees. "I can see that being extremely attractive to clubs. In some ways it is the obvious way to go. I can't see the current model lasting too much longer. Things are changing. Other companies may enter the market."

However, doing the whole thing in house in this way would mean giving up a guaranteed broadcaster's income and gambling on Simon's calculations of how many would buy it and for how much being correct. Given that Sky and all concerned are very cagey about viewing figures it means no-one is in any way certain how big the audience might or could be. So to move from the predictable model where they know exactly how much they're going to get from a three-year deal to what is basically just a regular roll of the dice, which would rise and fall with sales, which in turn would rise and fall with the quality of the team's play, dropping off when they're awful to watch, or just losing a lot, is scary for the clubs, not least because audiences can fall substantially if a big club like Chelsea or Manchester United are not very good one season. The clubs want their broadcast income insulated from such unpredictability. So getting 20 clubs' conservative execs to agree to this looks tricky, as many will think it too risky and insecure and would rather take less but secure money rather than gamble on more but insecure money.

Even if they could agree to set up 'Premier League TV', how would they distribute the income? At the moment all 20 clubs get the same cut of the

'Equal Share', which is their wanky term for UK broadcasting rights - £34.8 million in 2017-2018 and the same share of overseas rights (£40.7 million) and Commercial Rights (£4.7 million). The only income that fluctuates is the 'Facility Fee' which is payments for games shown live - the big clubs are shown more and get more cash as a result - and the end-of-season 'Merit Payment' which goes up roughly £2 million per finishing place.

While this division means the top six earn £40 to £50 million more than the bottom sides, I suspect that would not survive a new regime. The biggest clubs feel they drive the whole league and want the largest portion of the money by far. That was their goal from the start, even going back to the late 1980s. They believe people are tuning in to see their team play A.N. Other and that without them, the smaller teams will have a tiny audience for TV games - which is certainly true in the UK. So the new PLTV would be under huge pressure to give a majority of the slices of the revenue pie to those big six sides. In other words, a lot of the smaller clubs would risk getting a lot less money than they do now. (It's all about money now, it's all they think about, dontcha just hate it?) So are they really going to vote for that?

Another problem would crop up too. Would the Premier League even need to exist? Its main job is that of collective bargaining in the sale of rights. Those big clubs know that collective bargaining has benefitted them least of all and thus would love to see an end to it. In other words, if the current model is to be broken up, they would rather broadcast their own games direct to the public, pocket all the money and not be part of some PLTV conglomerate which may try and distribute income more evenly.

So is Simon Jordan's Netflix of Football concept a runner? I doubt it. I don't think anywhere near a majority of the Premier League clubs would vote for it.

Niall Sloane: "The Premier League is only going to set up a Netflix of Football if shareholders can make more money. Shareholders are the ones that matter. For example, BT shareholders have questioned the company's policy [of buying Premier League rights]."

The fact remains, as soon as you put any paywall in place, the amount who will watch drops off massively. Why would that change? It is well established over many years. Interestingly, this isn't always to do with price, it is rather to do with just having to put your details into a system. It is the admin of keeping on top of who you have to pay what to. OK, the hardcore football fans will do what needs doing, but that isn't most people. So while it sounds like a good idea for the Premier League to broadcast its own games there are absolutely no guarantees that it would provide anywhere near the sort of incomes the clubs have got used to. And like anyone who keeps receiving a lot of cash for doing nothing, they won't be keen to give the current model up until there is literally no money coming in any other way. It might not be in their best long-term interests but I suspect they will be afraid to let go of nurse for fear of something worse.

As I say, the other innovation could be for each club to broadcast their own games, to take control of their own output and content on their own TV channels and derive their money that way. This is obviously of most interest to the likes of Manchester United and Liverpool with a huge global fan base keen to see them. But where does it leave Burnley or Norwich? To get the £100 million they get now, as a fag packet calculation, for each of their 38 Premier League games they'd need an income of about £2.6 million per game. Even if you could persuade people to pay £10 per game, they'd need to get a minimum of 260,000 people to pay for each and every game they play. Unless you have a global fan base, and many clubs like Burnley, Watford, Huddersfield and any number of others just don't, that is a lot of people and again, a very unpredictable financial outcome. I'm pretty sure if you're a small club just promoted from the Championship, the very idea of acting as your own broadcaster would just be totally outside of your skillset and a complete distraction. This is a job for professionals and they'd need paying. So even if you could get that £2.6 million from viewers, how much would it cost them in terms of buying in broadcast expertise? Suddenly they will need to generate a lot more money and need a lot more viewers to do that. Would they really vote for that knowing how few people watch paywall games at the moment?

There is currently no legal provision for clubs to do their own deals and they would be breaking up the Premier League if they did, as it is specifically outlawed. This is why some of the big clubs have discussed, and probably still want to, break away to form a European Super League, do their own broadcast deals and keep it all in-house. They've got the numbers to possibly make it work but they would need to cede from the Premier League and they know many fans would not like the prospect of their club not being in a domestic league, not least because having to get to Germany or Italy or Spain for an away game is not achievable for most. It's also true that fans like their club to play English clubs and would not feel the same if they were not doing so. So clubs selling their own games looks unlikely outside of the creation of a European Super League and it is very much the nuclear option and only for the top six. And even then, we still know that paywalls scare people away, so would they really be any better off? You might be selling your games direct but have hugely narrowed your audience, not expanded it, especially once the novelty has worn off. How many times do you see Chelsea playing Real Madrid before it gets routine and not special and not worth buying?

So that's two oft-touted ideas for a new model dismissed. What else is there?

They've all got a major problem because the league has been able to sell broadcast rights at massively inflated prices, and they've been too high to make broadcasting the game profitable, so they have set themselves an unsustainable bar.

Here's the truth. If the subscription model in any current or future configuration no longer works well and can't be made to generate anywhere near the amount of money that broadcasters have paid up until now, and here the financial implications of us all ending our paywall contracts also kicks in, there are only two options remaining:

1. Sell the rights for much less money to make it profitable for a digital platform to run a subscription option with the small remaining audience.

2. Sell the rights for much less money to terrestrial TV and get a relatively huge audience and perhaps some cut of the advertising revenue.

That is the future choice. There isn't anything else. We either pay for it or we don't (except via the licence fee). And if we increasingly don't, there is absolutely nothing any of the clubs or broadcasters can do about it. They can invent new and varied ways to bring the games to our TV or other devices but if we have to pay for them and refuse, then it all has to change. That is the bottom line. No pay. No money. No Premier League. Good, huh? Yes. We're in charge. We are the bosses.

Many will tell you that the future is all about putting games on people's phones in China and India and placing content clips on social media. And although that sounds like a hellish world, maybe it is. Maybe no-one wants to watch 90 minutes of football on TV anymore. They'll be happy with goals and red cards only in a 90-second download. Maybe. And the short attention span generation may well drive that. But if 90 minutes of football isn't popular, why are the grounds still full? Why are Orient getting 5,000 in the 5th tier? Why do cup games on BBC get 8 million? Why did England's 2018 semi-final against Croatia get over 30 million? No, the demand is still there. We have not all become butterfly minds just yet.

This is where things get really interesting.

"I think the future is all about the battle between reach and income," says Mark Chapman: "They have not thought about the reach, they've just been happy to take the money but in American sports they've realised that they don't want to trade reach for a few bucks more. In football in this country, the model has runs its course. Look at the cricket and how small those audiences have been on Sky and BT and what the implications for the sport has been. There's a lot of discontent about it. The rugby was the same and then it went back on free-to-air and got eight million per game."

This wrestling match between reach and income is a fascinating one. How valuable to all parties is the audience of 8.1 million which the BBC got for Chelsea vs Manchester United in the FA Cup, against BT Sport's 357,000 for the Spurs game? And how do we measure that value?

Clearly, the terrestrial broadcasters would love to have league football on their channels because it would give them big numbers and make them more culturally and sportingly important. ITV would like the numbers in order to be able to sell more advertising and grow income markedly. The BBC would see it as being in the bosom of the country's favourite sport - at the beating heart of the nation and, in a way, that is where the BBC should be and is mandated to be.

And by withdrawing our support for paywall TV, this is where live football would end up. Some money and a big audience is far better than some money are no audience. Rights fees would have to drop massively but that is exactly what we want.

What about the income to clubs? What about their ability to mainline a big hit of cash every year from the broadcasting rights money? There's no dressing this up, those days will be over. And thank god for that. This will be our first step away from the current extremism.

It is not as if there would be no money, just less, a lot less. And you know what? That will just mean the clubs have to pay less for players and in wages. When the rest of the world knows you are stuffed to the gills with cash, the cost of everything and everyone goes up. When they know you aren't, it goes down. This is the irony of clubs craving for wealth; it gains little advantage. Clearly, there would need to be some tapering as football stops toking on the big money crack pipe, but sooner or later, things would settle down at a new, much lower, financial level. This reduction in income fits perfectly with the introduction of the salary cap and maximum wage too. No longer would clubs need interstellar turnover to pay interstellar wages. The playing field would become far more level. The competition far greater. With this double lock on wages, meaning all clubs are spending the same total amount of money on wages and are paying the same maximum wage, we will finally free the game from the curse of financial hegemony reducing competition and entrenching an elite. In other words, it will once again be about the sport and not the money.

I'm sitting here trying to think what the argument against this might be. In this new regime we've created a game that is conducted on a more level playing field, which means coaching and managing is fundamental, and means the games will be less predictable, the winners will not be drawn from the same pool every year. I suppose it goes against every economic cultural imperative that we've been sold for 40 years and there would be a negative reflex against that, but that really holds no water. No human rights will have been abused in this revolution. Footballers will still be rich, but rich in a way that we normally understand that word to mean.

Putting the league on terrestrial TV makes total sense for we the people and though it might not initially seem so, because all concerned still have pound signs in their eyes, it makes sense for the clubs as well. No longer will anyone have to break the bank to compete, nor would they risk bankrupting the club to get into the monied house on the hill.

Yes, this would absolutely destroy the elite clubs' ability to outspend everyone. Yes, it would mean you couldn't leverage wealth to gain superiority. Yes, it'd mean top players earning no more than £220K per year, so no, we'd not be getting so angry about players' unearned wealth. We'd stop judging performance against fees and wages. We'd stop being angry. Stop feeling the injustice of paying more and more to make the rich, richer while the poor remain poor. Doesn't it all sound brilliant? All so much better than today. Football would be back in the bosom of the people, which it should never have been ripped from.

Once we stop paying for paywall TV, how long it will take to effect change is hard to say but if it's part of a public campaign where we are all clear why we are doing this and what we're trying to bring about, then Sky or whoever holds broadcast rights at the time, will be forced to address it quickly; likely within weeks. It isn't just the financial loss they'd suffer, they can probably amortise that across the corporation, it is the evaporation of belief in the concept of paywall football and everything that has gone hand in hand with it. That is the significant thing.

I suspect they would move quickly to broadcast the games for free as a holding position while they work out what to do next. They'd remove the paywall rather than surrender the rights and at least get some customers to their channels in the hope it will break the will of the people. Once they understand this isn't a fad or a pose, but a cool, relaxed but determined revolution, they will be faced with a choice to give up the rights early (which may not be legally possible), broadcast them for free, or keep charging a shrivelling few thousand to watch. They could also just try to live off the overseas income while it lasts. But you can be sure this will be a movement that once it takes hold will spread like wildfire to many territories, so long term, likely it wouldn't be sustainable.

They will almost certainly try to fight back with an advertising and propaganda campaign by detailing what their money has created for our football entertainment and what good their riches do in society. We've seen that on the Premier League website. But that will be easily ignored and will only inform us that we are winning.

135

Our actions should also have the effect of scaring off those other potential rights holders such as Netflix, Facebook and Amazon. After all, they're already doing great trade. They don't need the hassle of trying to beat life into something that has passed away. Once they see the way the public have mobilised to reject paywall football, their interest in it should fade away too. Who is going to risk buying rights to something that people have already rejected on principle?

All of which will open the football broadcast landscape up to terrestrial TV to acquire the rights at a now vastly-reduced cost. Good this revolution business, isn't it? We're already better off and we've only just started.

But what if Sky just keeps on paying huge fees for broadcasting rights, paying for it from across the Sky empire? If BT Sport do pull out and the other platforms are peripheral, leaving all or the bulk of Premier League broadcasting to Sky - which I'm sure they'd love - they'd presumably be happy enough to keep pumping billions into the Premier League's coffers, allowing the days of wine and roses to continue. What if that happens? That would be a bulwark against any democratising of the game on terrestrial TV, it would prevent the collapse of the financial structure of the league and we the people would be no better off. Our nameless existential nausea would still exist.

It might seem like a sort of business madness for Sky to think of doing that in an era of radically declining viewers but they might just do it in order not to lose face; in order to be important. Just when we thought we were free, we'd be pulled back into the mire. Even though broadcasting to dwindling numbers in the face of a moral objection might seem like madness, they still might do it.

However, things are changing. Many do not realise that in the autumn of 2018, Comcast won an auction to acquire Sky, bidding $38.8 billion to beat Rupert Murdoch's 21st Century Fox after a lengthy bidding war. Industry observers say Comcast have spent this huge amount of money in order to give them major television and programming assets, which will help it compete against the likes of Netflix and Amazon, which have invested heavily in original entertainment programmes. Jim Waterson, media editor of The Guardian: "Sky is a very profitable business, with 23 million customers across Europe and produces its own content. Opportunities to buy such a business are increasingly rare, helping to drive up the price to an extraordinary £30 billion."

As a sidebar, 23 million Sky subscribers across a total European population of 741.4 million, reinforces just how low audiences for football must be. Those 23 million will not all be signed up for the football, but even if we say they are, we're looking at just 2-3 per cent of the population of Europe as a maximum audience.

Given the UK-only rights for five of seven packages last time cost around £4.4 billion for a three-year period and likely can't deliver a profit per se, how much value will Comcast even place in football? When one sporting rights contract costs 15 per cent of the valuation of the asset itself, it begins to look less and less sustainable. It isn't impossible that Comcast will think their billions will be better spent in other areas which can deliver far bigger audiences and will not pay the league the huge fees it has before.

Anyway, that is for the future, and to a degree, irrelevant to us because we the people can break the will of any company. However, in order to make sure that our football revolution actually happens, we do need a Plan B. And I have one. Indeed, perhaps this should be Plan A.

OK, let's do a bit more radical thinking. Strap yourself in. I warn you, what I'm about to suggest will sound absolutely bonkers. Yes, again. It does to me, too. But that's only because we've all swallowed free-market capitalism as the only route to a happy life. But given Britain currently eats up 71.5 million prescriptions for antidepressants per year, at a cost of half a billion pounds to the NHS, that clearly is not working, now is it?

Who knew endlessly buying stuff or feeling the pressure to buy stuff wouldn't make us content, huh? Who knew choice would be depressing? Who knew that fracturing the collective in favour of the primacy of the individual would lead to such a fragmented, isolated society? Who knew farming every social service out to companies who have been charged to make a profit out of any indignity of human life would turn out to create such an appallingly slavish addiction to profit? Who knew making a small elite very rich off the labours of the many, and in so doing consigning a sixth of the population - over 10 million people - into the precariat, forever teetering, one financial crisis, one pay packet from homelessness and the dissolution of their lives, would make us all so damn unhappy?

We've been sold a lie. It's as simple as that. The lie of money and materialism. So it's time to look for new routes to new realities. Time to turn off your mind and relax, float downstream if you wish, because we're going into tomorrow and if there's one thing we know about tomorrow it is that tomorrow never knows, as me old granny used to say while rolling joints on Beatles albums.

OK, so here's an idea which sounds crazy but isn't.

If Sky or any other non-terrestrial broadcaster wants to buy football rights, even at a lower cost, they can't.

It will be outlawed.

Sorry, not for sale to you.

Why should it be? There's absolutely no reason it should.

Instead, a sympathetic government would assign 'listed' status to all live football and would justify it in part because it will be absolutely great for the health of the nation in many different ways.

The Broadcasting Act of 1996 gives the Secretary of State for Digital, Culture, Media and Sport the power to designate key sporting events as "listed events". This ensures that the broadcast rights to these events must be offered to the main free-to-air terrestrial broadcasters on "fair and reasonable terms".

Currently holding listed status guaranteeing each is free-to-air and available to 95 per cent of the population are these sporting events: the Olympic Games, the FIFA World Cup Finals Tournament, the European Football Championship Finals Tournament, the FA Cup Final, the Scottish FA Cup Final (in Scotland), the Grand National, the Derby, the Wimbledon Tennis Finals, the Rugby League Challenge Cup Final, and the Rugby World Cup Final. So why not all live football?

This would mean that never again could football rights be bought by a private company and broadcasting it be charged for via a subscription. Now, just as you probably do, I already know what the problem with this is: How on earth does any government justify the cost of buying the rights to broadcast live football, whatever that may be? Obviously, given the circumstances (in my new world) with the public having pulled the lever to stop buying paywall football, the amount it would cost would be hugely lower than the last splurge. We've devalued the rights markedly with our collective action. But whatever the total would be, how can any administration defend such spending against the inevitable accusations that they are wasting the public's money on buying sporting rights?

I already know the defence to deploy to fend off those who would oppose such a life-changing move. There are a lot of really good reasons to do this, especially when you look at it from our new wider, more holistic perspective.

Think about this.

Just think about it.

The cost every year, to the NHS in treating Type 2 diabetes, a condition that is very much rooted in inactive lifestyles, as well as dietary choices is - deep breath - £14 billion. Fourteen billion pounds! And that is set to rise as more are diagnosed with the condition. It is a crisis that needs tackling on many different fronts.

You know where I'm going with this, don't you?

By bringing football back to the masses as an everyday part of everyday life, if it can inspire children and adults to take up the game, or just inspire them to kick a ball around more, inspire them to become more active and fitter, to play sports, even to walk more, as a result there would be a consequent knock on in reduction of health expenditure.

The launch of the new First Division, the first season after The People's Football Revolution happens and the Premier League is abolished, could be tied into a huge public health campaign called Football Free For All. Instead of football being an exercise in greed, it will become a positive force for good. The sense of freedom as the nation is unburdened of the paywall culture would be tremendous. We'd all feel as though we'd been gifted something. We would all feel like we had an investment in the most popular sport in the country. No longer would it be the private property of billionaire's communications companies. Once again, football is ours, the People's. In the embrace of the common good for the greater good. That is a beautiful feeling.

There are more benefits yet. More exercise also helps with low mood and depression, so we may be able to reduce the half-billion pound expenditure on the 71.5 million antidepressant prescriptions dispensed every year and that is without calculating arresting the cost of lost income through lost production caused by these conditions. There are only savings to make. The opportunity is there to save billions in future healthcare expenditure, not just for one year but for decades. All that is required to get on board with this sort of idea is stop looking at everything as an isolated individual problem costed out separately from other expenditure and tackle them more comprehensively and from different angles.

And we must also factor in that millions of people who are excluded from enjoying football now, especially economically, will be brought back into the mainstream. This is really important. Social isolation is a destructive thing and not without health cost implications as well. People get pushed to the margins because they don't have the money to take part in that which others have a choice about. You might choose not to buy Sky, but it's a different thing altogether if you do not have that choice due to poverty and you are excluded from that degree of autonomy. Such issues are at the root of the fragmentation of society. It is how we have cut adrift a whole economic class of people. By restoring football to free-to-air TV, we extinguish just one of those fires of deprivation and replace it with the cool waters of inclusivity.

Just think about this for a moment.

Think about it.

When the state is spending £42 billion over three years on Type 2 diabetes alone, it throws the 2018 sale of five out of seven UK broadcast rights packages of Premier League football for three years at £4.464 billion into sharper focus. And of course, as we have already discussed, that most certainly will not be the price paid in the future.

Frankly, were nothing else to change, it still makes total sense for the government to buy the rights for all live football. With an annual £14 billion bill to pay for diabetes, are we to seriously believe that a more active, happier population wouldn't shave just £1.5 billion off that bill per year? For buying live football rights, even at the current cost, to be revenue neutral, a 10 per cent saving is all that needs to be made on that one bill alone. C'mon, it is taking the piss to think this is not possible when married up to a public health campaign. We already know that broadcasting women's football highlights on the BBC last season has led to a big uptake in participation in the game amongst girls. In acquiring live football rights, the state isn't merely frittering away our money (though it does that quite routinely), it is investing it in the future health of the nation.

Who would speak against this?

I do not believe it is possible to make an argument that holds any water as to why this should not be done. It is an open and shut case. Writ large and really bloody obvious.

Yes, a government needs to have a holistic approach to understand and support this, but it is hardly difficult to grasp. You don't need to be big giant brain to see the basic numbers involved here.

And to indulge in a bit of base politics, the political party which offers this would be on to the biggest vote winner ever, not just because it makes sense but also because, put simply, it's giving the public a lot for no extra cost to them. Even the most venal, opportunist politician would be insane not to get on board with this. It makes sense from any angle you want to look at it. Indeed, it is staggering that it has never been suggested and yet another example of how much all concerned are in thrall to an extreme form of economic and political thinking.

In 1992, when the Premier League hijacked top-flight football, no-one was talking about an obesity crisis, a Type 2 diabetes epidemic. That isn't to say we were a skinny nation the way we were in the 1970s, thanks in part to 'healthy' eating advice from the NHS being changed in the early 80s from suggesting diets based on protein and fat, to being based on low fat and plenty of carbohydrates, and also because of cheaper food and especially cheaper sugar, we were all bloating up nicely by 1992 but were still less bulky than today.

When top-flight football disappeared from our TV screens and went behind a paywall, what did that do to the nation's health, and especially to children? It can't have inspired kids to play more football, can it? It must only have had a negative effect. If you can't see what you're being sold as the premium-quality game, you're more likely to drift away from it. It doesn't seem like a huge leap of faith to think that if all kids could see Harry Kane banging in goals every week and not just for England or on Match of the Day highlights, more would want to try and copy him. And do we not care about our children? Do we not care about the health of the nation? Do we really want football to be behind a paywall more than we want a healthy, active, engaged country? No, we don't.

This isn't radical or extreme thinking at all, really. It's just practical, that's all. It's just human. It's just being nice, being good, being caring about our children, about our people, about ourselves. It is a soft revolution. It just considers the greater good to be of primary importance and not the dividend paid to shareholders, or the astronomic wages paid to agents, players and managers.

This is what I mean by understanding that everything is related to everything else. Perhaps the greatest irony is that Sky itself has shown the government the way to go on this by subsidising the football costs not covered by the income garnered from it, from elsewhere in the Sky family.

But lord, it is very easy to imagine the outcry if the state spent a few billion on football rights, there would be all sorts of moaning and groaning about it of the "Why should I pay for football when I don't even like football?" variety. So we need politicians who aren't stupid, bigoted or evil to do this and to be able to articulate the case, and given we are currently cursed with uniquely hapless, deluded and often grotesque stupids in the House of Commons, that does worry me. The inability of politicians to look beyond their short-term narrow party interests, often because of the general public's equal inability to do likewise, is the reason we're sitting on the verge of climate emergency.

The British government declaring football to have listed status, buying reduced-value broadcast rights and making them free to air on BBC and ITV isn't a crazy idea from any perspective other than the one we've got so used to being the norm. I know it does sound extreme in one way, but that's only because the middle ground looks a long way away when you're inhabiting the extreme place that we currently are.

I put this idea to Niall Sloane, Head of ITV Sport, who responded,

"I understand the argument but I am not sure it has a viable chance of success. There are an abundance of free-to-air platforms who would welcome the opportunity to show some form of football. But I think the pay TV operators would protest quickly to government of any hue about the damage to their businesses, the general TV ecology, and how grassroots will be denied funds. I do not think that most governments would want to take this on despite it being an obviously popular move. They will file under Too Difficult."

I feel Niall is wrong about the government position because different days are coming. The old orthodoxies are breaking down. The old certainties are evaporating. A new generation isn't buying the old deals or old thinking any more. Also, I don't believe this argument has been made properly to the right people, if at all. Then again, it's not Niall's job to be a weird hippie thinker, though if ITV sport want to employ me as exactly that, I'm up for the gig.

I can see Niall's point of view but all of these protests can be dealt with. We will have rejected en masse paywall TV at this point, so that's just not viable any more. The reduced expenditure of this more sane financial world will free up plenty of money for grassroots, and there's the crucial health angle to approach this from. Contrary to what Niall says, I actually think it wouldn't be too difficult; rather it'd be filed under 'Populist'. Maybe it is hard to see the logic of it all from where we are now. That's why lunatics like me exist. Let's never forget using our consumer and political power, we can create any future we want to create. As Jim Morrison once said, "They've got the guns but we've got the numbers."

It is important to state that no-one has a god-given right to exploit football for profit. Why does everything have to be for sale to the highest bidder? Why can't we think differently? Life doesn't have to be totally about being a bread head. For any country to have a sense of its own nationhood, it needs things it can come together over. Has that been lost, perhaps especially in England? I think it has.

One of the reasons I live in Scotland is because it still does have a sense of itself. For all its problems, which I wouldn't seek to wash over, there is some palpable sense that being Scottish or living as part of Scotland triumphs over localism in a way that it doesn't in England. For all the problems of sectarianism, there is some sense of national identity. I find it a really positive part of everyday life and I miss it when I go south of the border.

But when you sell the notion of the primacy of the individual and of materialism over the collective and spirituality, this is what happens. When we're all just thought of as customers we all become mere cold units of production and consumption. But life is so much more than that. Coming together as a community over freely available football isn't some weird communist idea. It's just thinking of what we can achieve together, rather than being greedy and obsessed with some notional self-aggrandisement at the expense of others. It is all about the helping hand and not the iron fist. It is about the warmth of Us.

I do need to point out once more that our current situation with global communications companies having exclusive rights to show league football is not normal, is not somehow natural or clever or inevitable. We are living in an age of an extreme economic culture and beliefs, which seeks and succeeds in exploiting absolutely everything in order to create profits for a tiny amount of people. It has made us ill. It has ruined our health mentally and physically. The figures about this don't lie. We're being poisoned by this bitter harvest. But the good news is that we can begin to cure ourselves by unticking that direct debit box.

So what will be the consequences of our dissolving the Premier League? Well, all of them are healthy, sane and liberating. All will make us feel better about the football. All of us will have our sense of cynicism and unease removed.

We will stop saying, "It's all about money these days." This isn't fantasy, we can make this the new matrix.

As all these media changes happen, many other things will fall into place. The huge drop in income to clubs from the broadcast rights, will inevitably mean all the contracts clubs have with players will have to be scaled back massively over time.

With so much less turnover, the £220K per year salary cap will not seem so radical any more. Still a lot of cash, of course, but not enough to make us angry. And more emblematically, it removes the ecologically destructive imperative to be massively rich and push so much more carbon into the atmosphere in the name of material wealth. And that is more important than any other single part of this revolution. It really is. This is part of a huge shift in how we think about living on the earth.

We need role models for this new age of reduced materialism. All this sounds a bit hair shirt but it would be nothing of the sort. Only our conditioning to think four grand a week is paltry money for a human to earn doing anything is standing in the way. And when we consider being anti-materialistic, it doesn't mean living on solid air in a bare room. It's just pulling back to what we might have thought normal perhaps 40 years ago. Still plenty of everything, but this time, for everyone.

We've had a go at the buying-stuff philosophy of existence now and it's not made life substantially better in the way that was promised to us. It has made us a little more comfortable but choice has not freed us, rather it has oppressed us and made us less happy. We don't need everything, we just need enough. As for more than enough - well, that's more than enough.

We can travel all around the world and still stay where we are. We can stare into the sun and still not see the light. Life is lived in the mind, not in the wallet. Distracting ourselves from our own mortality by endlessly acquiring more things isn't fooling anyone, least of all us. It's time to be more at ease with a life without these dazzle ships taking us away from some of the greater, eternal truths.

And all these positive changes to life can start any time we want, and all we have to do to make all this happen is to stop that direct debit. One box to untick on your account. That is all. And just look at how it will change football and then change life. And let's face it. How much are we really missing by not seeing the Premier League while the revolution kicks in? Not much. Not really. And the commentaries are still on the radio and highlights will still be on Match of the Day, so we'll all be able to keep up to speed with things while the changes happen. That's plenty. Not having everything is not having nothing, and let's face it, this is zero change in the football lives for the vast majority of football fans anyway.

All so far, so good. However, we still have a big problem to overcome - the disparity of wealth among club owners which has led to what is sometimes called financial doping. In other words, the likes of Roman Abramovich et al. can pour a billion of their own money into a club and make them hard to compete with if your owner can only pour 100 million in. Can you believe these numbers? It's real money, y'know. It's actual money which could be spent on something positive and life-affirming, as opposed to paying a footballer a lot of money for not even playing much football. I'm sorry. I know I keep banging that drum but that's how I keep seeing this and it is the truth.

This is how mad the whole thing has got and I know it troubles so many of us and those it doesn't trouble have probably just made a decision to not think about it because it's all too big, other and beyond. These huge investment numbers are why many people question how good a coach Pep Guardiola is, even though that would appear to be madness. Oh, you've won the league by having the biggest budget and the most expensive squad, have you? Well done, they say, voice dripping with sarcasm. Whether this is a fair judgement or not, it is widespread expression of the financial imbalance in the league and how it sours achievements for many fans. I've no doubt Guardiola is brilliant. None at all. And it should be said managing the huge resources at your disposal is an art in itself, and we've seen some unable to be successful no matter how much money is spent. But it would be fun to see Pep working on a tighter budget. I suspect he'd be great at it because he seems to be able to make any player much better.

Looking at it dispassionately, it is manifestly unfair for the spending power of some clubs to be so very much greater than others, thanks to whoever owns the club. All Financial Fair Play has done is cement privilege by ensuring no club can spend more on wages than it turns over.

It's also worth mentioning how many fans feel they have to hold their noses when talking about their club's owners and where they get their money from. I'm sure many of us would rather clubs be owned, as Middlesbrough FC is, by someone like Steve Gibson, who is a local fella who made his money in the area and understands the nature of the club, rather than some distant sports investment conglomerate. We've even had people accused of human rights crimes at the helm of clubs, which is bound to trouble many. I'm sure if we looked into the business dealings of many clubs in the top flight, we'd find things that we don't like or are morally opposed to. This becomes a complex issue because fans get wrapped up in the defence on their club and almost incidentally end up defending that which they wouldn't defend in any other context, simply because it is their club.

The salary cap neutralises the power of an owner's wealth in the league, but we have to be vigilant. There'd need to be a ban on rewarding players in non-monetary ways. So an owner can't entice a player to join the club by buying them a massive house, for example. Draconian punishments up to a life ban from playing professional football would be needed to enforce it. We know all the ruses likely to be tried, the game just needs some sort of permanent investigative team to police it. Similarly, we need legislation to prevent rich owners signing up and hoarding all the best youth talent. But I'm sure this is not beyond the collective ability to sort out once we have agreed that we want to stop any sort of financial leverage by the wealthy.

But what about transfer fees? We have to solve the problem of rich owners using their money in the transfer market to hoover up the best talent. We need to neutralise that in order to keep the playing field level.

Transfer fees have been around forever. Boro paid Sunderland £1,000 for Alf Common in 1905 and everyone was rightly shocked at such largesse. The fee is to purchase the player's FA registration from the club that currently holds it. But I have to say, I've never, ever understood why they exist, or perhaps more pertinently, why have they been allowed to exist?

Why is money allowed to be paid, mid-contract, to extract someone from that contract?

By now you'd expect me to have an alternative idea and I have.

OK, let's remember all we want to do here is to maximise fairness, unpredictability and competition. So surely all we need to do is to outlaw transfer fees. It's that simple. You can't break your contract. You have to play for the club you've signed for until the contract ends. This would mean some players would have less interest in tying themselves to a club for say five years. One-year rolling contracts would allow you to move if you wanted to move at the end of every season and it would also allow the club to not renew if they felt you were not pulling your weight. OK, it means you don't have the same security of employment as a player, but actually, you will have more freedom to ply your trade wherever you want, and every year if you so wish. It means you can't coast and I think we see a lot of players growing rich by doing just that at the moment.

Think about it. No transfer fees. It does feel weird, doesn't it? We're so accustomed to the concept but familiarity is no reason to just keep accepting the notion. This would mean that no longer is the game all about who has the most money to spend on players. It would mean Manchester United would have no more financial leverage in the market than, say, Burnley. I can see why those losing their power wouldn't like this, but it would be for the greater good. There is no sporting virtue in money buying you success.

With the wage expenditure as a whole and per player capped, there will be far fewer players moving for a bigger pay day but players will be free to flit from club to club as they wish, as and when their contracts allow.

What is wrong with this? Nothing at all. It isn't some sort of denial of freedom to outlaw the fact that a player can be bought for £200 million. Yes, small clubs often rely on the income from sell-on fees when players go from club to club, but this is a different world now and I have a way to financially support such clubs in the future. I'll tell you about that soon.

Once the super rich understand that their money will not allow them to blow any other clubs out of the water, I doubt many will even be interested in investing in a club, but if they do then their wealth will be largely irrelevant. It is easier to negate them this way, rather than trying to decide who can or can't buy a club. That has proven so hard to do.

Making football unpredictable and competitive is the key to making it fun. By and large we do not want the same clubs inevitably dominating the league every year by virtue of greater cash resources. If no club can spend more than another on players either in fees or wages, then all the important things in football, such as coaching and training and youth development become the important thing. Now, I know what the argument against this is - that well-run clubs, or popular clubs cannot take advantage of that fact, attract more fans, build up turnover and be more successful. This is absolutely true. But this would be a different, better world where winning trophies and being successful will be achieved in a different way. In other words, the old idea of what progress is, will be no longer relevant.

A great coach will really make a huge difference. Last season Sean Dyche got Burnley to 7th on what must've been the smallest budget in the league. Of course the sides above them had invested hugely in their teams over the years and simply had a lot more players who were much better than Burnley's, attracted to the clubs for big wages and fees, neither of which the Lancastrian club could match. But in our Brave New World they would be able to. With a salary cap, there would be little or no financial advantage choosing to play for, say, Manchester United over Burnley. You'd choose who to play for on a different basis. Who inspired you as a manager would be important. And thus Burnley would have a far better chance of 7th not being their ceiling but pushing on and getting higher and higher. Surely that feels better for all of us?

This would be a totally new development for football because while in the past the gap between the wealth of clubs was far narrower, the clubs with the most money still used to have an advantage, though it could be more easily neutralised by a great manager or developing excellent young talent. This is a new future.

In my new far-out, love is all you need idyll, the pursuit of success via accruing ever more money is not the way to make life better, nor the way to make football better. Everyone should have enough to compete on a broadly equal basis. And what would be wrong with that? It is only so many decades of conditioning that makes us default to thinking that the route to success involves accruing ever larger amounts of money, to buy ever more expensive assets.

I do realise that this sort of talk is absolute heresy in the modern world of maximising revenue and profits, and I know it will sound shocking to some to assert that this is not the way forward, that this notion has had its day. But I will ask you this question: Has it given us, the football fans, more pleasure, more fun, more joy? Has Manchester United signing Alexis Sanchez and paying him £400,000 per week plus an additional £75,000 per appearance made your life better, or given you even a small drop of serotonin-induced joy? Or has it actually made you feel uncomfortable, angry or disgusted?

Has the fact that clubs have taken money from official coconut water partners improved the quality of your life? Has paying up to £500 (the price of some of the Champions League final tickets) for a ticket delivered anything to you that could not have been delivered on a more modest budget and without so much as a drop of coconut water passing your lips? I think we all know the answer to these and many more such questions.

We have irrefutable evidence that we, the public, will watch any football at any level in numbers that vastly exceed any other public event or gig. We are far less concerned with it featuring the finest of the finest - no matter how much they cost - and more concerned with just watching football per se.

There is one more problem to solve, however. A salary cap, maximum wage and abolition of transfer fees, even with vastly reduced TV rights income still mean grounds that hold over 60,000 can rake in three times the amount of matchday income than one which holds 20,000, and what becomes of all that income which is unable to be spent on players' wages and fees?

My first suggestion would be to use surplus income to pay staff much better. Instead of the thin gruel of the minimum or even the living wage, the business can properly remunerate those who make the whole place tick. They can be rewarded from being part of the success of the club in attracting paying punters. Spread the wealth around. Instead of paying £9.00 per hour, pay £18. Everyone deserves to benefit from the club being attractive to fans. This money would benefit the local economy significantly.

Given less need to maximise revenues in order to afford to pay players massive wages, ticket prices could be radically reduced in price. Perhaps there could be no ticket over £10.00 and the majority at £5.00 Do away with all those executive boxes and throw out all these revenue-raising privileges. Again, this makes football inclusive, available for all and not just a few and that spreads the love and reduces the hate.

Excess profits can also be ploughed into all those local sporting initiatives I talked about earlier, currently sponsored by McDonalds and the Premier League and other corporations as part of their marketing budget. Indeed, the income that the expenditure caps free up for a football club will allow it to be the vibrant fulcrum of the community, investing in all manner of local and international projects that often need micro investment to get them started.

In this way, rather than feeling our ticket money is just draining away into players' and their agents' pockets or being frittered away on transfer fees, we can begin to feel that football is a positive force in all of our lives. The possibilities are endless. The good all that money could do would be immense. And who could say it is a bad thing? Everyone is getting better paid. Players on their £220K are still rich by any normal standards and we still get to watch the game we love. All bitterness and resentment gone. Everything simply more human, more sane, more sporting.

But there will still be clubs that struggle financially. Some will lose income they once got from transfer fees. The infrastructure of football needs to be made safe and strong. Grounds need to be maintained and the motto of this new world is 'no-one left behind' so we still need to spread the wealth around a little bit more.

To this end every club should be paying a set percentage of their turnover into what I'd like to call a Football Sovereign Wealth Fund. This would effectively be a piggy bank for all football league clubs from the new Division One to the National League to pay a set percentage of turnover into. Funds can be withdrawn for development projects that a club cannot service from their own turnover. For example, say a small club like Crawley Town has a stand that needs developing but doesn't have the turnover to pay for it, that's where the FSWF comes in. The club applies to it in order to get funding to pay for the improvements.

Say a newly promoted club needs investment to develop its training facilities, the FSWF helps out. As it stands, when a club is promoted to the Premier League it's often said how the additional money, if well invested, helps upgrade much of the club. And that is often true. The new wealth fund would be a way to make sure that continues in the new world order. The development of facilities behind the scenes would also benefit the local community. Schools could take advantage of training complexes, for example. Again, we're looking to spread the money around, spread the love around. When you feel your ticket money or merchandise money is going to pay for such things, things that your own children, friends and family might benefit from, that is such a positive emotion, binding fan to club. And let's not forget the health knock-ons of better local sporting facilities and how that saves the state so much money. We're all about creating self-feeding virtuous circles now, not hiving off money for tiny cliques to the disadvantage of so many.

No longer would the wealth generated at any one club be used solely and exclusively for that club. The Football Sovereign Wealth Fund would be a mandated redistribution of wealth to ensure the health of the game from top to bottom. The lower reaches of the league have been starved of cash ever since the inception of the Premier League reduced the income share and we've seen clubs going to the wall, or not be able to pay players. Often this is due to the financial mismanagement of clubs, often in the Championship, often by owners who overspend desperately trying to get into the cash-rich Premier League - another unintended consequence of the massive disparity in wealth between divisions. The carrot is so big, club owners have broken the bank to try and grab it, and have failed, crashed and burned. But no more. With spending caps in place, this is far less likely to happen, though I suppose there is no legislating for total idiocy and mismanagement at any level.

The Football Sovereign Wealth Fund is a simple way of football saving for a rainy day to make sure the whole family is financially healthy and not just a rich elite. Who would argue against that? No-one with an ounce of soul. Only the most extreme and greedy political philosophy would oppose such a notion. We're all in life together, we're all on this planet together, we all rely on the earth together and we're all in football together, so why not come together to help each other? Isn't that actually really beautiful? Isn't it actually the only way we have any future at all on this beautiful blue marble spinning in space?

...AND IN THE END

So there you have it. That is my blueprint as to why and how to break the Premier League, dissolve the divisive model upon which it is has been built and replace it with a league, a game and a culture which are inclusive, positive, financially sane and both morally and economically sustainable.

The ideas I've expressed in this book need to become familiar and commonplace so they no longer seem as strange or odd as they might do right now from our position at the outer limits of an extreme political and financial orthodoxy.

The great thing about this revolution is that we have to do so little. All we have to do is withdraw our consent for the status quo, sit back and let it all crumble. We just need to come together with a unity of purpose after that fact. Remember, all of this isn't just selfishness or self-indulgence, it is a movement for the greater good of us all, for our children and their children too. We stand to lose nothing and gain so much health, wealth, happiness and love. Because, at the end of the day, the love we take is equal to the love we make, Jeff.

While I do not believe anyone reading this thinks it sounds awful, a lot of you will be thinking this all sounds like fantasy. I know, I know. I can feel the vibes. And it absolutely is.

Of course it is.

This will never happen.

That is absolutely what the league, Sky, digital broadcasters, the clubs, the players and a lot of other vested interests want us to think. They'll laugh at all of these ideas and at best pay lip service to them as ideals but not workable in reality and paint them as out of touch with How Things Are. I mean, football is Big Business and it will not surrender to this hairy old dreamer's portfolio of notions and ideas. Look at all the money, the power and influence the clubs and their owners and players have. One silly-headed writer's ideas are easily dismissed as nonsense. I know, I know.

But the fact we all are thinking it is fantasy right now - including me and I'm writing the bloody thing and even though I have thought about these issues for years - is just their propaganda software kicking in, software that each and everyone of us has had installed into our psyche. That's how it works. It keeps us subservient and pliant and runs in the background all the time like a virus checker, plucking out and deleting any challenges to its orthodoxy. Given this, it should not be a surprise that we feel at least an element of disbelief at this vision for a far better world.

They do not under any circumstances want us to take collective action to undermine everything that benefits them so much. Why would they? But I suggest stopping for a moment to think about why we all feel this is a dreamworld. Why does everything being nicer, more fair, more inclusive, seem so weird? What have we had put into us that makes us laugh and think, "Yeah, nice idea but it'll never happen, mate"?

We have been made to be harsh to each other, we have been divided and made to feel like we must fight for ourselves and not for each other. We all feel powerless in the shadow of such huge financial dominance. We all feel like those with money and power are the boss of us and that there's nothing we can do about it.

But here's the thing, right? Remember what I said at the outset of this book. Football is ours, it is not theirs. It is not for them to dictate to us what we will or won't do. They need us. Without us they have no product to sell and no living to make. So it's all about us, right? If you take only one thing away from this book, take this: We are in charge. What we say, goes. Do not let them divide and rule us. On our own we are weak, but together, sisters and brothers and others, we are stronger than we know.

If we do not like how things are, and I would suggest, given everything I have documented, few can feel good about how things are, then we can - we absolutely can - change it. And if we do not change the whole thing, or at least some things, then the blame will lie with us for not coming together to properly exercise our consumer power. I have cut a pathway through the overgrown woodland of propaganda to lead us to the lush upland pastures of a better, more fair, more responsible, more fun game. I'm sure it is not the only route and that other more advanced minds can come up with other alternatives to deliver a more fair future. We can choose to walk these paths or to reject where they are going, but if we do reject them, then we can never again complain about how modern football is.

There is a way out of all of this. It will take time and doubtless there will be many twists and unexpected turns along the way. But it is down to us. We will have nothing given to us, nothing at all. Those with money and power will forever cling to it, will try to turn us against ourselves to preserve their hegemony. And yet and yet and yet, the extremely awkward fact for them is that all their money and power is derived from us and relies on us as customers. Never, ever forget that. They want us to feel cowed and intimidated, of course they do - they know if we're not, then they're in trouble. We have nothing to lose and everything to gain. So untick that Direct Debit box and let the revolution begin. Let it be a revolution not just of football, but of the mind and a revolution of how we live with each other on this planet.

Because at the end of the day, the space between us all, leaves room for you and I to grow (I told you about the Rush lyrics thing, didn't I?) and never, ever forget that the grass is so green because of all the shite that's been on it over the years. These truths we hold to be self-evident. Power to the people, right on.

PART THREE:
MAYBE I'M A DREAMER,
BUT I'M NOT THE ONLY ONE

OTHER VOICES

I am aware that what you've been reading might sound like the ramblings of a deranged man and that I seem out on a limb with absolutely no support or sympathy for how I see the Premier League and football more broadly. So instead of just relying on the strange kind of magic inside my own head, I asked people in the football media to tell me where they thought the game was going. I also talked to an actual top-flight footballer and others who work in the business of football and found, in some cases, I was pushing at an open door.

Some understandably wanted to remain anonymous because they're so integrally involved in the game, relying on it for their living and not wanting to upset current or future employers or colleagues. So that's how it had to be.

First up to the plate is someone prominently involved in broadcasting live football on television in the UK.

"The cost of buying football rights are clearly prohibitive for terrestrial television. I can't see the Premier League or Champion League ever moving away from subscription services. However, there is a bubble and there's a danger it could burst.

"Big corporations are now increasingly trying to work out what returns they are getting from the massive fees they are paying out, and it's very hard to quantify whether or not they actually do provide any returns at all.

"With the emergence of Amazon in the marketplace - and the looming possibility of other monolith organisations like Netflix, Twitter or Facebook getting involved - it's clear there is scope for further upward growth in the price of rights. However, if these companies do get involved and don't see any clear gains in profitability then they'll pull out after one cycle and thereafter rights values could be forced down.

"Furthermore, if several Premier League packages (for example) did go to Amazon in the future then the nature of the broadcast may change. Perhaps we'll see multiple games being available simultaneously, at the click of a button on the app, giving subscribers more choice. This is a model Amazon will explore from December [2019] onwards in the rights they have already picked up. If it works, you wonder if they'll push for that style of broadcast option in the next auction. That would get us closer to an on-demand system of viewing, similar to what you get on services like MLB.tv. You'd log-in, pick your game and pay a small additional fee to watch your team. Clubs may not like this because they'll argue it could affect attendances, but if the price is right I don't think they'll argue for long.

"On-demand may also mean less studio analysis and fewer presentations. In this system your Live feed would begin a few minutes prior to the game starting.

"So we may see a change in what's on offer for viewers, but the truth is some of the monster businesses now in the football marketplace (or threatening to come in) don't really need football at all. Amazon certainly don't, the same goes with Netflix and the rest. They will make money regardless in the current model. They may test the water and see if football adds to their overall service, but if it costs them billions and they see little competitive advantage they'll pull out without hesitation. That would leave us back in a position of having only domestic broadcasters like Sky and BT Sport - but will they really fight against each other forever if they're the last two standing? In this situation, they may agree to cap spending."

I think this person has some very interesting points of view and raises some crucial points, especially that broadcasters are now questioning the profitability of buying the rights to show football. As I've discussed, it seems clear to me that it absolutely is not profitable at all and is at best a loss leader, subsidised by profits from other arms of the company. This just shows how financially vulnerable the Premier League actually is if all conclude that it is simply too expensive. Of course, I'm advocating we shut them down by simply by refusing to buy paywall TV and by the government mandating it as a 'listed' sport, but I do think this broadcast industry insider's points show exactly how easy it would be to break the model by abstaining from it. However it works out, it shows one thing very well: We're the boss here. We can break this model with our collective actions and by doing so can change everything.

The next insight is from someone who works in sports for a TV broadcaster. They remain anonymous because, as they told me, "I'd get the sack for what I'm about to tell you. But it needs saying." We talked for a long time and collaborated on this to keep it as anonymous as possible as they were so worried that it might be obvious to someone in the business who they were.

"What people don't understand is that when you work for a company such as the one I work for, you are in a constant state of paranoia. Or I am, anyway. You have no honest idea if what you're doing even has an audience. I do not believe any of the viewing figures we are told. I think basically, they're made up or at least heavily manipulated. I sometimes wonder if it is like website traffic. You can say you get a million hits but if 999,999 of them last less than

10 seconds, then they're not really interested in what you're doing, but you can still say you've got a million visitors, nonetheless.

"The waters are muddied by adding in podcast numbers, adding various bits of clipped content that are sold on as content to other outlets, catch-up numbers, various other player and device numbers and before you know it you're as popular as Eastenders! But the numbers are impossible to get hold of accurately - podcasts especially so - and it allows anyone to dress up unpopular programmes as far more popular than they are. That's my view, anyway. When viewing numbers have been raised, the bosses have always adopted that overly-relaxed mode which tells you they're trying to play down something embarrassing which might prove they're doing a shit job. I think they get that software uploaded to them when they get the job. They all have it. Sometimes they say the numbers we see are not the final numbers and there are other factors to consider. I think it's bollocks. If they got huge numbers they'd be shouting about it.

"The programme I work on at the moment...well...[laughs] Honestly? I am certain almost no-one watches it. I was told by a now-departed executive that they only put such shows on to make it look like they are an important part of the football business. It's all for image. It's all window dressing but behind it there is no-one in the shop. I don't know how it all financially works, I really don't. Every week I expect to get laid off because the money has run out. How can they pay for all this broadcasting which no-one is interested in? Moreover, right, what is the point? One day, when it has all fallen apart, you'll hear some incredible stories from inside the football broadcast world. It's not an original thought, but it really is the Emperor's New Clothes."

This is quite a glimpse behind the lighted stage. Of course, when people won't go on the record, you don't know if they're just a disgruntled employee, which is probably what the defence against these words would be. And we do have to bear that in mind at all times.

John Roder, the excellent long-serving commentator for the BBC and other broadcasters, got in touch to give me his perspective on what the future holds for football on TV as someone who has been in the industry for a long time.

"There's no turning back to what some see as the golden days of football on TV. A live match every so often, highlights of a couple of matches each weekend on BBC or ITV, and commentators that we all knew in John Motson, David Coleman, Barry Davies and Brian Moore.

"Nowadays you can see a compendium of all the Premier League goals of any of the players who have reached the milestone of a century or more.

Compare that with the scarcity of footage of goals scored by the incomparable George Best, only a few were captured on film, which is why you always seem to see the same action in any programme about the player who for me was a childhood idol.

" 'You've never had it so good' is a phrase applied to many things, and certainly in terms of the amount of football shown on the TV at the moment there has never been more, and yet I watch less complete matches on the TV than I ever did. It's like being trapped inside Willy Wonka's chocolate factory, able to scoff as much as you wish every day, and yet you just don't want/can't face anything to eat.

"How will football coverage on TV evolve over the next 20 years or so? Turn the clock back two decades and see the changes since then, or even from one World Cup to the next, and take it that a similar progression will be made. Technology is moving so fast, but some so-called innovations are gimmicks (cameras in corner flag posts), some are hugely subjective in their impact (spidercam), some are divisive (cameras in dressing rooms).

"To cover a football match to a sufficient standard used to be a six-camera operation. Now there can be as many as you like, pretty much where you like. Does this fascination with going 'behind the scenes' make football more like a computer game than a live sporting event, and is this the way we are heading?

"Covering live sport on the TV is the longest unscripted drama there is. Or of course there may be no drama at all. You can't predict what is going to happen, that's the beauty of it. Read Paul Armstrong's excellent book Why Are We Always on Last? which chronicles his career in television at the BBC, culminating in 15 years editing Match of the Day. The chapter dealing with the 2006 FA Cup Final is a lesson in how the unpredictability of live sport flummoxes and mystifies those for whom ensuring Doctor Who gets on air at its scheduled time is a priority, rather than the fact that Steven Gerrard's magnificent late strike has sent a superb Cup final into extra time.

"The most recent revolution has been/will be/is the way that football is delivered to the watching audience. Is traditional TV on the way out, losing to streaming services as people watch the action on a variety of devices in any location capable of receiving a decent signal? Possibly, but not yet, or not until the reliability of delivery can be guaranteed. Look at the problems Optus Sport had in Australia during the 2018 World Cup, which culminated in them having to allow SBS to show all the matches as well. Look at Eleven Sports in the UK, and their struggle to build a viable business model on the back of signing deals to show La Liga and Serie A. Look at Amazon and how they're going to cover the Premier League matches they have the rights to from the

2019/20 season. Actually we don't know anything about that yet, but is the Amazon way of delivery one which will become the norm in future years?

"The Premier League has been very, very clever in selling their product (horrible word) both at home and abroad, but I do wonder whether the time will come when they take complete ownership of it. So instead of selling live rights to BT, Sky, NBC in America, BeIn Sports in the Middle East etc. etc., they sell direct to the public right around the globe, using streaming technology. People have already used the phrase 'Netflix of Sport' which always seems to assume that a third party will sell it on behalf of the rights holders. Why shouldn't the rights holders go and sell it themselves, having thoroughly tested the technology needed through maybe a period of selling it through a company like Amazon or Netflix?

"You can picture the scene at the meeting of the Premier League clubs. 'OK, let's agree to cut out the salesman and keep all the profits for ourselves, that'll do nicely, and while we're at it, let's banish relegation as well, after all, we don't want any of those EFL clubs able to have a slice of our cash, do we?' What a horrendous thought, yet it's not that distant from reality is it?

"All of this assumes an audience that will gorge itself on what is being handed out. There is a growing movement here in the UK and in Germany that want to reclaim football from being totally dictated to by the TV companies. Monday night matches are hugely unpopular in the Bundesliga, and La Liga in Spain has said that it won't be carrying on with Monday evening games.

"Yet that totally ignores the audience around the world, for whom Premier League football is like an invitation to dive into Mr Wonka's chocolate pool. Get into a taxi in India or many other countries and the driver, upon knowing you're from England, will tell you all about his/her favourite team in the Premier League and where they are going right and wrong, who they should sign etc. The clubs know this, which is why their pre-season tours are no longer to Austria and Ireland, but instead to Australia and China, and the USA.

"And what about the EFL? It's actually a popular league around the world, but very much the poor relation to the PL, despite many of the matches being a good deal more entertaining. The EFL will surely become Oliver Twist, holding out a bowl to the gargantuan PL and asking for some more.

"From a personal work point of view the fact that more football is shown on TV has allowed me to make a living, and hopefully that will continue for a while for me. In a way I was quite fortunate, as due to my age I was able to take advantage of the introduction of satellite TV to go and carve out a niche for myself before joining the Match of the Day commentary team in 2004.

"In the future we will surely be able to choose from a selection of commentators, or even no commentary at all, for as Barry Davies said, one person's favourite commentator is another's pain in the backside. There are ex pros in the co-commentary role, but none (yet) in the role of main commentator, whereas in cricket on Sky you almost need to be a former England captain simply to be on air. So will we ever hear a former Premier League footballer as the successor to Martin Tyler. Probably not, although if someone is really looking for an unusual angle to launch a media career after their playing days have ended that is the one to go for. Although it requires a lot of hard work, discipline, plenty of research, and an intimate knowledge of the motorway system, particularly in relation to where the next M&S service station is. Probably easier to get driven to a stadium/studio and sit on a sofa."

A wonderfully comprehensive and wide-ranging contribution from John, and one that raises many of the issues and possibilities that I've talked about throughout the book, not least the clubs' desire to pump their own games direct to the public. While I've highlighted the problems with that as an idea, not least that it isn't allowed under the Premier League's founding agreement, in strictly business terms, it does make sense for some clubs. The most direct route from producer to punter is always the most profitable, all things being equal. The fewer people taking a slice of the pie, the better. This was the reason I founded my own publishing company in order to bring my books to the market. When I was writing for the nice people at Biteback - they published the first edition of We Ate All The Pies - I got a royalty which amounted to little more than 50p per sale. This is because so many people need to take a cut of that sale, namely the publisher, the wholesaler, the distributor and the retailer. Now, given that there is no money for any of them if the writer does not produce the book in the first place, you'd think that the writer would get the biggest cut, but no. The retailer gets the most money. It didn't seem fair to me that I got less than anyone else, so I set up Head Publishing and now I make over £5 per paperback sale from the website and about £2.50 for each sold to a store, instead of 50p. So, in the same way, if clubs can sell direct to the public, it offers a much better chance of a much better income.

However, once again, we know paywalls per se put off the vast majority and again, if we simply won't buy it from the clubs then their ownership of the rights will generate little or nothing anyway. Once again, it illustrates that we are the boss here, not the broadcasters, not the clubs. Us.

My next contributor, 5live's excellent sports presenter Steve Crossman, a man who hails from the glorious lands around the Tees, told me how he sees things developing on TV in the future.

"Discussing what football on television will look like in the future is a little bit like trying to work out what post-Brexit Britain will look like (unless you're reading this from a spaceship built by future industry leader Farage Tech in 2042, in which case you already know).

"I say this because the smart money is on a massive shake up, likely to happen soon and nobody knows what the fallout will be. The only thing that can stop this is sending Arnold Schwarzenegger back to 1992, not to smash Skynet, but to destroy Sky itself.

"So in many ways, it's the worst possible time to be writing about this, because I could be proved wrong, and that could well happen very soon.

"Why is (the) Sky falling? It's falling because so few people watch a product that costs so much, it's that simple. Major broadcasters get money from advertising and the advertisers will pay based on your audience. If you spend more and more and more on TV rights for football, you need that package to add more viewers so that next time you can say, 'Look we now have THIS many people watching, give us MORE money to show your adverts'. But that last bit isn't happening, broadcasters are paying vast sums, sums which will surely top out soon, but they're not covering that by increasing their audience.

"Also, there's now a lot more competition, which means bidding wars. If you've ever tried to buy a house and it's gone to 'sealed bids', you'll know what I mean. The price of that delicious three-bed semi in Stoke Newington gets higher and higher and eventually it gets so high that the valuation gets knocked back and the deal collapses, [and] that's what will happen to football.

"Nobody had heard of Eleven Sports before last summer and their demise is a case in point. They spent a lot of money securing rights to La Liga and Serie A, all they needed was loads of subscribers, but they didn't get them. They won't be the first or last to come out of nowhere with a far post run only to discover they're trying to get on the end of a cross that was whipped in, in 1992.

"I'm not trying to have a go at Sky, I watch their games and their coverage is excellent and the great players we watch, week in, week out, wouldn't be here if not for them. Though, to my shame, I also watch the most recent example of their dynasty - midweek red button Championship matches. I've seen some done as single camera jobs (no close-ups or replays), which offer nothing of the superb punditry and presentation they deliver for their Premier League and first choice Football League matches. It's no wonder that EFL clubs are furious and Sky's subscribers should be aghast too. Even then, plenty of people will stay at home rather than go to the game.

"'But you don't have to watch it', I hear, 'go to the game instead!' I would, if the bloody ticket prices weren't so high...if only one could work out who/what is responsible for that.

"The greed in the game will soon result in such frantic feasting that its head will swell and pop like the bloke at the end of Big Trouble in Little China. Sorry, showing my age now. Google it. I'll go back to Terminator references.

"Recent events do offer renewed hope. (I was going to write A New Hope but I really must stick to just one science fiction metaphor). ITV salvaging La Liga rights from the wreckage of Eleven Sports has shown that terrestrial television can still ride in to the rescue.

"It's my genuine hope that - if you are reading this in 2042 - it's after watching a free-to-air Premier League game, not cycling through the 193 different apps you've downloaded, because they all have one game a season, and they cost 10 billion crypto quid a piece to watch. If football on television is allowed to shatter into as many pieces as a T1000, it won't have the liquid structure required to pull itself back together.

"In short, wind your neck in football and come with me...if you want to live."

A brilliant and very amusing summation of where we are. Football is eating itself in an orgy of financial gorging. But we, the punters, have gained nothing from this. They may well think they'll be forever frotting themselves in a never-ending cash-soaked wet dream but we are reaching the end game. The fees are too high, the profits non-existent...so now what? That's why this was the right time to write this book. We are approaching the moment of maximum flux and if change is to happen, now is the time to put our shoulders to the wheel to make it what we want it to be.

Next I'm turning to another of our excellent and best commentators.

"If I could change one thing with a magic wand then I would strip TV of its power. The power that dictates when and where PL games are played and now its influence has crept into the Championship and beyond. Look at the final weekend of the Football League. Staggered kick offs with League 1 at 5.30 and the Championship all played on a Sunday lunchtime. All designed around the armchair fan rather than the paying punter.

"I accept it's the TV money that has seen the PL explode into this global brand and enables clubs to attract the star players but it's to the detriment of the game [and] I fear there is no way back.

"The lack of regard for the paying fan and often the travelling supporter when kick off times are changed with just 4 weeks notice is annoying. The scheduling around the festive period for example, is a joke.

"The arrogance of TV [is] that football is their product. Such arrogance means the majority of people who work on TV have an inflated, misplaced ego that they ARE the game. There are exceptions such as Kelly Cates. There are many, whether it be presenters, touchline reporters or commentators, strutting around preening themselves thinking they are gods gift and it's about them.

"There is an insatiable hunger/desire from TV executives which I think will only see an increase in even more games.

"When pay per view was introduced it was Sat, Sun and Mon...now it's almost every day of the week and often 3 or 4 games shown on Sat or Sun. Even Europe has staggered kick offs purely for TV. They will maximise every slot.

"TV calls the tune and the clubs are reliant on the money. They said the bubble will burst yet it continues to grow but the money is obscene.

"The appeal of TV has opened the eyes of the marketing men at clubs with their own channels. Once again the basic economics of supply and demand translates into advertising = money.

"With that in mind, Richard Scudamore was very savvy to lose sponsorship and base the PL as a stand-alone brand. Compare the Barclays Premier League previously to now the Premier League in association with Budweiser say on NBC in the states. His decision enables every foreign TV company to tout for their own advertising in their respective countries which in turn will boost revenues for future overseas rights.

"The PL has broadcast managers who organise the various interviews with managers/players for pre- and post-match. There's only one show in town as far as the Premier League is concerned and TV is their priority because money talks.

"The women's game will be next. At the moment, they need the exposure so it suits the BBC to promote their game. However, there will come a time when ££ signs will start to dominate their decision making and greed will be the primary focus rather than the good of the game. That means the power won't be shifting because terrestrial TV can't compete regardless of gender."

There's much truth in this, I think. Television is at the core of so many issues I've discussed here and given how the money from the rights has transformed everything, it is easy to see why those who work in the industry might sometimes think it really is all about them. And in a way, they're right. It is. Because without the aggrandised contribution of TV, the financial situation would be far, far different and the whole landscape changed.

However, I do think where this commentator is unduly cynical is in feeling this will only get worse. I am an eternal optimist and while I can see how it could all easily walk further down the wrong road, it absolutely need not be the case and if they do, it is always rescuable as soon as we act collectively. The absolute fact that TV needs an audience remains unchanged. If we deny them of that, they have no reason to be there.

My next contributor is John Murray, who is regularly voted the best commentator on radio. He's certainly someone I listen to pretty much every week of the season and have always thought brilliant. When I asked him for his views of where we are right now, he had some very interesting things to say. He's really on the frontline of the game in terms of radio broadcasting, seeing at least three games every week as well as interviewing the main protagonists on 5live. He's been doing the job for nearly 30 years and has travelled all over the globe to commentate on the game, so he's very much worth your attention.

"Maybe I have been too close to the game for too long because for me, to a large extent the extreme numbers (wages, fees, etc.) involved have been normalised. I strongly feel it's up to the individual to set their own values in life. Yes, it's absurd that a footballer earns so much more than a nurse/teacher... but I suspect that I as a sports broadcaster also earn significantly more than most people in those occupations and is that acceptable and right?

"Yes, the exorbitant amounts of money in the game are mind-boggling - grotesque you call it (a word I'd used in my message to John) - but we are talking about a very lucky minority who have won the golden ticket in life and to an extent it comes down to old-fashioned market forces. They earn what football clubs are prepared to pay them.

"Put it this way; in how many other professions is an individual's wage broken down into how much they earn per week? How does a top footballer's wage match up in those terms to City fat-cats, business high fliers, Hollywood stars? I see the Premier League/Champions League being shown on television wherever I go in the world. They are global entertainers and the best-paid players these days do entertain and their talent helps to make countless millions of people's lives a little more enjoyable. When such riches exist in the game, is it not right they should get their share?

"For me the down-side of all of this is less the players and more the people connected to the game who are after an easy buck. There is sooo much money in the game and it seems anyone who can talk their way into a position of influence can get a share and here I am thinking specifically of agents, but also some fairly moderate administrators and club officials. I am yet to receive a satisfactory explanation about what it is an agent does that justifies the astronomical fees some of them take out of the game.

"The whip-round for Richard Scudamore (a brilliant football administrator, by the way) for his 'retirement present' is probably the best example of the question you're asking because I got the impression that those close to the decision simply did not get why there should be any public outrage at all about it. That speaks volumes.

"Personally, I think more now than ever before there is a resentment and anger in society from many of those who have been lucky in life rather than accepting their lot. It's similar to the general lack of respect that exists for anyone in authority. That's a different story but not completely unconnected, I feel.

"One thing I would say is that for the whole time I have worked as a commentator - almost 30 years - the footballers I've worked alongside over that time have almost all expressed the feeling of 'if only I'd been born 10 years later'. That, I suspect, will continue to be the case for as long as I do this job.

"To paraphrase something Gareth Southgate said a little while back - I still love the game but the financial side of football is very easy to dislike. Fortunately, I find there will always be a great match or a great player to richly entertain us around the corner that helps the former to outweigh the latter."

John's a thoughtful chap and he brings some important points into focus. I share his bewilderment at what agents do for their money. I've had it explained to me many times and it amounts to going, "My client wants this, you've offered him that, why don't we split the difference?" Which is fair enough but not a massive job worthy of such riches. And many of the agencies are huge and seem to act as some sort of elaborate concierge service as much as anything. All of which seems very immature. As one ex-player once told me, "Agents are just gobshites for money."

But I also think John makes some classic errors. In rhetorically asking if it's fair that he earns more than a nurse, that's just the sort of cul-de-sac of debate that the monied and powerful want us to have. I feel this is how we get divided and ruled. Whether one of us earns 50 or 100 grand more than another per year is but chicken feed in this context. My point isn't that top footballers shouldn't earn big wages but that they should be big by our normal standards, not by football's weirdly inflated levels.

I also don't think that, as John says, they've won 'the golden ticket', simply because I don't consider this level of money per year 'golden' - I think it is immoral. It is wrong. It's a very normal position to adopt to think they're lucky, but I'm not here to think normally. The normal we have assumed to be normal isn't normal. It is merely one choice, one point of view, one way to think about what money is, what it's for and how desirable it is when you look at the whole picture.

I think it's an illusion that being very, very rich is great, or at least a version of one peculiar reality that the rich and powerful people have always sold us, largely to keep us down and to justify the model which they have so benefitted from, but which hasn't delivered for the rest of us.

They know that if you hypnotise people with a dream, no matter how unlikely it is to become a reality, you keep the people pliant, controllable and exploitable. Surely we need to think differently about life than this? Surely we need to realise that even if you are the 'lucky' one, you have to live in the society that your 'luck' begets. And who wants to step over a beggar while wearing gold shoes? And let us never forget that no amount of money will prevent you from suffering the consequences of a climate meltdown and biodiversity holocaust coming down the pipeline, that you and your gross consumption habits have contributed to.

It's my firm belief that when such discussions are removed from a societal and environmental context and discussed in the abstract, they lose their power and become so much debate about numbers. However, when you stand one decent person living a decent, valuable life next to another and one is on £27,000 per year and the other £475,000 per week, the grotesque disparity simply feels wrong. Because it is. And we shouldn't ignore that simple engagement of our humanity. I do understand that we cannot right all of the wrongs in the world. We can't easily make a list of jobs in some sort of notional order of importance and devise a pay scale to accommodate each one. But we can damn well do a better job than we do now. £475K per week vs £27K per year? C'mon. To paraphrase Chris Sutton, "We're better than that."

I do sense some in the industry of football, be it media people or pundits, are actually quite defensive on behalf of the players because players suffer so much horrible abuse. Again, I understand that, as they probably establish relationships with some and many are clearly very decent, intelligent people. But my criticisms are not of them personally but for the accident of history that has seen them at the epicentre of such wealth. Nor is it a decrying of their talent. This is not a situation they have engineered. Nor would I expect them to be some sort of financial freedom fighters, taking it on their own shoulders to overthrow the largesse of the system and of its political and economic norms. They're just there to play football. My critique is of the system and economics which made it happen and those who promulgate them.

I also maintain that being super super rich is not a blessing and that Chris Sutton's question, "How much money do you need?" is more than valid and needs answering at every instance. At the very least it needs thinking about seriously. For too long there has been a non-questioning of the acquisition of money and possessions, as though it is an almost holy pursuit in and of itself and look where it has led us: doped up on antidepressants and narcotics, over-eating and over-drinking, staggering blindly towards the brink of a climate and biodiversity disaster. None of that is happening for no reason.

I don't disagree with John that everyone has to set their own values in life, but where the rubber meets the road is when we consider what this means for the whole of society, what it means for the earth. None of us are islands unto ourselves. The values we have set for ourselves have an impact on everyone else and what if that impact is very negative, is destructive and discriminatory? Then what? As you know already, it is my belief that such thinking leads directly to the primacy of the individual over that of the community and that is at the core of so many problems that we have to overcome. We need to come together to pursue strategies for the common good, not merely what is good for us as individuals.

The point John makes about there being resentment and anger towards those who have been 'lucky in life' being connected to a general air of anti-authoritarianism, is well worth discussing too. I'm all for disrespecting that which is oppressive and challenging any and all authorities where and when necessary. Given the track record of those in authority, that seems only sensible. I'd rather it was focused and not just witless abuse, obviously, but I think this is what happens in societies which are viciously unequal and when any area of society becomes viewed through the prism of money, the way football has. At root I simply don't think we should put up with being put down by those with money and power. That is not a good night I am prepared to go gently into. But it has to be focused and not just manifest in bad manners and vulgarity.

The reason newspapers run stories about footballers buying flash houses or cars is because they know it hits two audiences square in the face: the envious and the disgusted. Both emotions are great drivers for sales and clicks. People feel oppressed. They see people with so much and they have so little, so is it any surprise people get stroppy? It's not personal in some ways. It's just a reaction to the insult of opulence in the face of deprivation and it is ruthlessly exploited by some in the press.

I've had the point made to me many times that if there's a lot of money in football then they'd rather young working-class blokes got it rather than anyone else. Again, I know where that is coming from but such thinking just doesn't get us anywhere. OK. Yes. And now what? It offers no gateway to change. Rather, it seems like a shrug and a 'what can you do?' sort of statement. The problem is not ameliorated by it being men from deprived backgrounds who are rich rather than the middle class.

My next big giant football brain belongs to someone who works in the business side of the game. Sorry I can't say who it is, nor specifically what they do, as they wanted to remain anonymous in order to keep their job. Which is fair enough!

"I meet footballers all the time and with only a couple of exceptions, they're decent lads, some are very special men who have greater issues on their minds than just football. Some want to use their money and status to improve people's lives and future people's opportunities. I admire them and there are more than you might imagine, often doing things on the quiet or anonymously.

"The fact is they've got so much money, you can hardly get your head around it. Some understandably don't have a clue what to do with it. Once they've bought themselves and their parents a house, and a car, beyond that, they simply don't know what to do with it all. Mostly they just bank it. Some of them put it into various schemes recommended to them by accountants. Some are super smart and have investment portfolios. The good agents protect them from the worst rip-off merchants, the worst agents are the rip-off merchants.

"This idea you've been writing about - shaking up the levels of money in the league - well, more than once, I've had lads tell me that if they were paid 100 grand a year and not per week, they'd be just as happy. No word of a lie. They're simple kids with simple tastes, mostly. Often from really deprived backgrounds and certainly usually from the working class, they're not going to start collecting art or stamps. They buy the expensive clothes and such but that makes little dent in their income. I spoke to a lad today whose summer holiday is costing him £75,000 for two weeks. In those two weeks he'll have earned over £200 grand from the club alone, that's aside from other lucrative sponsorship deals. Like I say, they can't spend it all. It's so much cash. Even they think it is ludicrous. An international player even told me that he is embarrassed by it and doesn't even ask for a wage increase any more because he's already got more money than he'll ever spend but his agent demands one anyway when negotiating his new contract.

"A philosophical player told me that until he was obscenely rich he hadn't realised that happiness wasn't connected to wealth at all. He drops rolls of £20 notes into beggars' cups on the street because he feels so guilty about it. I've heard that happens quite a bit, one way or another. It is mad. Totally mad. And I agree with you, it needs sorting out. It's insane and unsustainable.

"If someone turned round to them and said, 'Sorry mate, [your] wages are being cut by 90 per cent', the majority would just shrug and keep playing. I know it sounds crazy to say this, but in my experience, most of them are not that bothered about money. They're surrounded by people who are, by hangers on who siphon it off them one way or another, but I'll tell you this for nothing, right, the majority are not greedy in the slightest. They think it's funny that they get all this money and get everything done for them by the clubs, as though they are little children.

"A couple of years ago, one player's agent got him a £30,000 per week increase in his wages taking him over £150,000 per week, right, and you know what he said to me? You know what he said? He said, 'What am I going to do with another 30 grand?' It was almost as if it was becoming a burden to him. He'd got a rise per week that was more than what normal people earn in a year. He wanted to keep it quiet because he thought it made him look greedy. I suspect he'll just give it away.

"Some get a bit paranoid that people are ripping them off. Getting ever more money doesn't make them happier. I swear it doesn't. They worry that their girlfriends are only with them for the money. That's a common one, actually. That famous Peter Crouch quote - 'What would you have been if you weren't a footballer - a virgin' - that is so true for so many of them. I don't know this particular player but a teammate of his told me that he once said, 'I'm an ugly fucker, why have I got this beautiful wife? Money. That's why.' And that blew my mind. We don't think about that, do we? It must do your head in. You don't love me, but you do love my money. That's no life. OK you're shagging a gorgeous woman but the thrill would go away after a while. One lad told me, after his second divorce, that in both marriages it was like being married to a hooker. Will fuck for money, y'know? I can't remember exactly what he said now but it was something like, when he was humping her, she's just looking at the 20K watch he's bought for her, hoping it'll be over soon so she can go shopping again. That's how he told it anyway. He was very bitter.

"So what I'm saying to you is, if all the big money went away tomorrow because the TV deals evaporated, 99 per cent of them would play on. They don't play football to earn big money, that's just happened by accident. But if you listen to their agents, you'd think they're all money mad. It's in their interests to make us think that. I actually think some would be glad to play for £100 or £200 grand a year. I really do."

This is a fascinating insight into the modern game, isn't it? It shows just how insane the money culture in football at this level is. The whole supply and demand argument is so bogus when you have footballers who would play for a tenth of what they get now. In no other business, or at least, no other sane business, does the company insist on paying its workers vastly more than they would be happy to work for. Imagine if you were on £30K per year and happy enough and then the company said actually you can have three million. You don't have to do anything else, just take it. As is so often the case, it is only when that which is normal in football is set into an everyday context that the ludicrous nature of it shines most brightly.

Now, I thought it would be really interesting to get a current Premier League player to talk to me about all of these issues but obviously this wasn't going to be easy because my name hardly commands any weight or heft in the football world; I couldn't offer any money and what would anyone have to gain by spilling their guts to me? Nothing. So I hit a blank for many months until, as is the way of these things, someone heard from someone else that someone they knew, knew someone who knew me and knew I was writing a book about how mad the league is and all the rest of it. Eventually, he got in touch. He wanted to stay totally anonymous simply because he's worried his life would be made hell by what he called "agents, greedy bastards and other assorted cunts." So that was fine with me. What he had to say was shocking and heart-warming in equal measure. We talked for some time. I got straight to the heart of the matter and began by asking him how much he earned.

"I'm earning less than some in the first-team squad but a lot more than the youngest players. I know some of the lads talk a lot about their wages with each other but I don't and I never have. I wasn't brought up that way. But also because I really don't think I deserve the money. People might think that's just me being...what's the word...false bragging [he meant false modesty]. But it isn't. I kick a ball around and that's it. It's not a special talent. I know not many can play as consistently as I can but so what? It's just football. Football isn't important. It's not like I'm curing cancer. Do you get me? Yeah I'm a good footballer and, like, OK pay me as someone who is really good at his job. But it has got totally out of hand.

"I hear people outside the game defending us. Saying that we've got to have incredible dedication and there's so many pressures and how we deserve every penny we get like, but that is...it's crap, isn't it? OK OK, it might be true for Cristiano Ronaldo or a few of the top top players, but for people like me, workhorses who play, if we're lucky, 35-40 games a season, it simply is not true. I just don't believe it is. So how much do I get? OK, well, I'm not showing off, right? That's not me.

"So, I get into my account every month, just over £200,000. It works out with win bonuses that I got paid over 2.5 million across the last 12 months. It is fucking insane, isn't it? And I'm quite low paid at this level. In the last 5 years I've earned at least 10 million. Across my whole career by the time I retire it'll end up around 18 or even 20 million. And c'mon, you and I both know, I'm a decent player, I'm a hard grafter, I do a job and I don't give managers any shit, but I am not worth £20 million of anyone's money. I don't think anybody is. But there are boys on 10 and 15 mill per year now. It's mental."

I asked him about his tax arrangements on this huge money. Did he have offshore investments and the like?

"No. I'm a working-class boy from a council estate. I don't want anything to do with that shit. I don't even understand it. I've got an accountant that a friend recommended. He thinks I'm insane because I insist on paying all the tax straight off the top. I don't understand it all, he fills out all the forms but basically I pay, I think, is it 45 per cent of it in tax? I don't even know. So I'm left with a little more than half of that total. How do I survive?! [laughs loudly]

"My dad was a union man, he told me straight from the day I signed professional forms, you pay what you owe and if you cheat on your tax you're cheating the working class out of their money and I still believe that. It's right, isn't it? When you hear that there's no money for kids and schools and everything, that's because people like me haven't been paying into the pot. That's what dad told me years ago. The bottom line, and this is why I wanted to speak to you, the bottom line is that I don't need all that money. None of the boys do. I live a nice life, I've got some saved for when I stop playing. I mean, like my dad says, 'How many dinners can you eat?' do you know what I mean? But if I told some of the boys this, they'd think I was a real prick. To some of them, you get as much as you can, for as long as you can. They're not bad lads. Well, some are twats, but no more so than in any walk of life."

"Are you very much the exception then?" I asked.

"I'm in a minority, yeah. But some lads do things on the quiet, giving money and that. Some of them are really keen on giving back. They are. Footballers are all tarred with the 'thicko' brush, aren't they? But loads of us aren't thick, we've just not gone to college or we speak like working-class boys so that's why people think you're thick. But if I sat down and explained this to some of the lads, they'd understand because a lot of us are from similar working-class backgrounds. But they're told from day one by their agents that they've got to earn the maximum all the time and if you don't take it someone else will. Some lads go, 'Well if he's getting 100 grand I want 110', and they're all crazy about it being disrespectful to them if a player they think is worse gets more money than them. I used to think that when I first got in the first team but my dad put me right and I'm glad he did because, and this was another reason I wanted to talk to someone who might understand this, and you've been saying about the money and how it's wrong and I agree, because it doesn't make the boys any happier. What I'm saying is the money doesn't do anything for you. Do you understand me? Everyone wants money money money, wants this and that, but that's because they don't have it. When you get it, you sit there with a few million in the bank, have a cup of tea, take a shit, go and train, come home, have some chicken, watch the TV, just like any normal guy. So what the fuck do I need all that money for? It's a waste. I've had everything I need for fucking years. I don't want anything more. That's what I think. What I also really hate is these people in the media, on TV and that, who are always going on about how we deserve it. We fucking don't deserve it. Why won't anyone ever say that? I drives me mad."

"So do you give money away then?"

"That's hard to talk about in public."

"Yeah, but you're anonymous in this so you won't be in public."

"Well, you feel like a bit of a cunt if you say I gave this and that money to whoever. It's not in my nature. Again...my father, y'know. I mean, I've had sponsorship things from sports companies, fuck knows why - who would want to play in the boots I'm wearing - but they'll give you thousands of pounds just to use your name. And I've given all of that to charities that I support. I don't want to say which ones because it might trace back to me. I've given handfuls of notes to homeless people, I do that all the time. A lot of the boys do, actually. But that shouldn't be my job. It shouldn't be down to me or one of the boys to make sure someone gets a bed for the night or enough food to eat, know what I mean? Like, it's hard to explain but it feels dead wrong to me. I don't know what to do about it though. And I don't know how to change it. It feels like it's out of control. Like, I'm not political, left or right wing, I don't know about any of that but it can't be right that I can drop £500 like it's litter and not notice it and there are people who are working their arses off for a week to earn that and are doing something important for it. Do y'see? It doesn't sit right with me."

"So how much do you think you should be getting? What would be plenty for you?"

"I was thinking about that today. Don't get me wrong, I don't want to be poor. I'm not mad. I want to be comfortable, nice house and car and everything. I want to make sure the kids are well looked after, just like every dad does. But they go to the local school. Not fucking Eton or that shit. I know plenty that do fine on 35 grand a year and they're not less happy than me. But I reckon if I played football, got £100 grand a year because I'm good at it, a few extra perks here and there, that would be plenty of money. Plenty. Nobody I grew up around earned that sort of money, nothing near it and would never have been able to. Maybe I'm daft in the head for saying that, but if it all went away tomorrow - and it will go away at some point - it wouldn't bother me in the slightest."

"What will you do when you retire?"

"I've got lots of things planned. I want to live my life. Football robs so much away from you. It's all you think about. I plan on earning a living, I'm not just going to live off my money. My main interest is in coaching kids. I always fancied being a PE teacher actually. What do you get for that as a wage?"

"I dunno. Probably about 30 grand after a few years."

"There you go then, that'll do me. The wife earns 27, so we'd have about 60 grand a year. Who wouldn't want to live off that, especially when you've paid for your house? Piece of piss. And I'd be doing something useful and not just being called a cunt by fans. Mind you, the kids might call me a cunt mightn't they! Ha ha."

We talked for ages and I couldn't help feeling he was really unusual in his outlook on life; a one-off perhaps but he insisted that he wasn't and that teammates probably felt the same underneath or at least just felt they'd got lucky so if the money disappeared, they'd just be thankful for what they'd had.

"There are some really greedy bastards out there though. I could give you a list of names, you'd be amazed at how obsessed they are with milking money out of the club and out of everyone in fact. Some lads are like that because they're from some really deprived country and about 200 fucking people live off what he sends back. That's terrible, that is. You can see the pressure on them lads. Everyone is relying on him. But there's one boy I know who is the worst of the worst. You'll hear him talk and basically the only thing that matters to him is money. When he hears players going to China for 600 grand a week he's fucking consumed with jealousy. He was half decent 10 years ago but he's shite now but he'll probably end up there aged 45. I hate the cunt. He gets us all a bad name. Plays up to the stereotype. Spends like 50 grand on a watch. It's not necessary, is it?"

"Does your wife agree with you on these things?"

"Yeah. She grew up on an estate like me. She hates the whole footballers' wives thing. WAGS and that bollocks. Stays away from it all. We've got the same values. When she sees one of the boys has bought some massive fuck-off car, she just calls them a wanker, not to their face though. But like me, she says, 'All that money and there are people who can't feed their kids'. She actually says that, you can print it. And I bet ordinary people all over would say the exact same thing. But some of the boys never hear it. They've just got yes men, tarts and hangers on, always in their ears. Footballers are treated like babies. I mean, man up."

"Speaking of that, I was just listening to the Peter Crouch podcast and he said he's always had his underpants provided by the kitman on match and training day. I was amazed. Why can't you provide your own underpants?"

"[Laughing] It's true. You don't know the half of it. That podcast is funny but it's funny because it puts what is normal to footballers into the real world and in the real world it's all just totally mental. And I don't know why it is like that. But it just is."

I explained all my ideas to him and asked him if it had a chance of working. I expected him to say no.

"To be honest mate, I'm amazed this hasn't happened yet."

"Really?"

"Yeah. You can't tell me Sky and BT are making any money. You tell me its nine million per game, they paid. Mental. Absolutely mental. It's stupid money. People are skint out there and we're swanning around in massive cars like proper cunts just because a TV company has overpaid. That can't last. People get pissed off at other rich people like bankers and politicians but somehow we get away with it. I don't know how to express it really but as you said to me earlier everything just feels wrong about football. You know what I mean? It just feels wrong."

"That was exactly my feelings as well. I've felt like that for a long time now. But you're right it is hard to pin that feeling down exactly."

"So what is it? It's the money isn't it? That's really behind everything."

"The money, the people who come with the money, the agents and dodgy owners…"

"It's all of those things and loads of other things as well. Like, for example, when I've played Manchester City, there was so little chance of my team winning that we might as well have not bothered. The gap between the top sides and the rest is huge. Bigger than I ever remember it. But it's always going to be that way when they've got so much money. They just buy all the best players. It's no more complicated than that. For anyone else to get a look in, a big side has to really have a bad day. Well, that's not what sport is supposed to be. You wouldn't put a lightweight in the ring with a heavyweight, but that's what is happening now in football. It all makes me feel like it's not our game anymore. It's still a great game, obviously, but everything that goes with it is now shit. I mean, right, this coming season there will be at least 12 maybe 14 clubs that won't even take a point off City and will probably get beaten 4 and 5. It does make you wonder what the point is."

"That's why I wanted to write this book, just to try and break this horrible feeling open and find out what it's all about and hopefully suggest ways to make things feel good and increase competitiveness."

"Your problem though isn't to get the players on board with massively changing the situation, right? We're just prawns [sic] in the game, it's all the other people - agents, club chairman, owners, TV companies. They'd kick up a stink, y'know? The way to fuck everything up is to stop paying for it on Sky and BT. I know you've said it isn't even that popular, but that's where all the money comes from basically; alright there are rich owners like Abramovitch and the royal family bloke at City and the rest of them, but if you kill it on

TV, that'd make everyone shit themselves. That could be the spark that sets it all alight. And what are they going to do? They can't make people pay for it, can they? That email you sent me with all the points in it laid out, that made sense to me, but nothing will happen until the TV deals end. I'd love it. It'd be brilliant. Cut everyone's money if that's what it takes. That'd sort the men from the boys. I mean, right, my dad only has Sky and BT because I pay his bills. He couldn't afford it if I didn't. Any government would be stupid if they couldn't see how popular that'd be as a policy.

"Honest, it's a great idea and since no-one knows who I am, I'll say this, right? I think another big problem you've got with making this happen is that a lot of people are thick as shit. And the ones that aren't thick are lazy twats and would rather moan than do anything. But, right, if a few high-profile players backed the idea, then they'd all fall in line right away. They would. If I did that, no fucker would care. I've got no name, have I? People would go - 'I thought he'd retired!' [laughs] People are like sheep and football fans more than most. Tell some of them to jump off a cliff and they'd do it. The tribal warriors at clubs are all gullible twats, everyone knows that. The club knows that those fucking idiots will turn up and pay money they can't afford to watch their team no matter what. They say they respect the fans but that's shit. They take the piss if you ask me. I look at some of the fans and I wonder what the fuck they think they're doing. Especially on Twitter. When you see them swallowing the PR shit from the club and fighting with other fans about it, honest, they're pathetic jokers. Big club fans are the worst. I hate them and I'm not the only one. Obviously, you're never allowed to slag off fans, it's rule number one, but to be honest, there are too many cunts at games of football. Sorry, I've gone off on one there - winds me up, though - I won't miss tribal football fans when I retire, put it that way."

"Well, I think a lot of fans feel the exact same way. Writers do, too. Those one-eyed fans make all our lives worse. But just to move it back to what we were talking about. Are you saying that if a popular footballer went on TV and said I support the movement to make football free on TV, it would swing everyone in behind it?"

"Definitely. But your problem is the agents will be in the lads' ears saying this will lead to their wages being massively cut and like I said, a lot of them can only ever see more and more money as a good thing. That's what they've been told since they were young. Most people just want more money even when they've got loads."

"Yeah, I can see that."

"But then, if everyone stops paying, not even the agents could stop it. I just think that no-one has ever thought of doing it, not, like, as one big group. I talked to dad about this, this morning actually."

"Oh aye, what did he say? You said he's a union man."

"He is. He'd tell you he's proud to be a socialist though I don't think he really knows what that means and I certainly don't. I told him like and he was a bit, 'Well, that'll knacker your money, son', but I was saying fuck it, why do we have to earn so much more than we can ever spend and dad agreed and he did say it's obscene."

"He used that word?"

"Yeah. And 'disgusting'. But I can't see Sky and them lot just rolling over without trying to fight back. And as for the government making it a special case, they're the shittest ever. Haven't a fucking clue. So good luck with that. Anyway, I hope what you're doing with the book has some effect. Wouldn't surprise me if it had none at all, but wouldn't surprise me if it kicked something off either. You never know until you try, do you? Something needs doing, though. The way things are in top football is wrong. End of."

I thanked him for his time and promised to respect his anonymity. It got me wondering how many others in the game there are like him, that share his point of view. The idea that anyone might say "No thanks" to a shitload of money is not something ever considered possible. But he definitely would and that in itself is a revolutionary act. He was very intelligent, self-effacing and quite the opposite of what is commonly thought of as a typical footballer. He was also quite insecure talking about all of this but it was obviously something he'd thought a lot about. And by the sound of it, he's not the only one to have done so.

Back to writers. One of my favourites and a real thinker about the game, the journalist Paddy Barclay, gave me some of his views on the future of the game.

"I don't believe everything about the Premier League is bad - I know quite a few of the staff, and they are mad-keen football fans in the main - but I do think the club owners have set some terrible standards of governance. The best example of this - and the worst thing about the League - is the influence of, and therefore cost of, agents and other intermediaries. This could easily be addressed with help from the FA and FIFA. Instead the multi-million-pound siphoning away of money that could be used for good purposes becomes more and more scandalous with every season that passes.

"In my ideal world, football - by which I mean football as entertainment - would be a mixed and planned economy rather than capitalism gone mad. It would make a lot of money but instead of handing it straight to the players - Alan Sugar was right about prune-juice economics - and their agents there would be a top-slicing of say 50 per cent of every television deal that would be used to finance improved stadiums and facilities at every level, other community projects and charities and campaigns such as one against child obesity. Also there could be subsidised tickets and travel for fans. By regulation this vast sum could not be touched by the players and this would naturally produce a 50 per cent reduction in wages. The percentage could be even higher - but it would certainly never be lower."

I do like Paddy's thinking here. His 'mixed economy' is an eminently sensible way to go. Again, in a world gone mad, it probably seems like extremist nonsense, but by now we should be able to take a more sane outlook on things.

Jonathan Northcroft is another writer I admire tremendously, so I asked him where he thought football was going and he responded with some typically thoughtful, profound and imaginative words.

"As a young football writer, working for Scotland on Sunday, I did a piece asking what football's future would look like. A sports marketing guru suggested the following scenario. Football, he said, would become ever more a television show existing for the screen consumer and not the fan at the ground - in fact, 'fans at the ground' could well start becoming scarce as habits of football consumption changed.

"You know, he added, the audience in Top of the Pops (now that dates the discussion), how they're not 'real' people-at-a-disco but handpicked by the producers? That will be the future football crowd. First clubs will start letting folk in for free, to fill stadiums because empty seats look bad on TV. And eventually they'll have to get actors in to fill the stands. Even a hologram crowd. One step further: hologram players as well.

"This was circa 1997 and it was one of those conversations that sticks with you. I often think of the vision he outlined and as time goes on it feels ever less unlikely. When I go back to Scotland, I don't see a game that has changed too much in the last 22 years (except for being, sadly, of lower quality) but the football I report on in England and in club and national competition abroad, is not the football I grew up with. Not at all.

"Many of the differences are good - better playing surfaces, higher technical quality, ramped-up fitness makes the best Premier League games astonishing. But many do not feel beneficial. Money, elitism, manipulation of the sport, the distancing of clubs and players from their localities - these are negative developments. They stem from that fundamental change of 'screen entertainment' replacing 'live entertainment' as football's main purpose and are trends that seem very likely to continue.

"Money: domestic TV rights may well have peaked, but international rights appear to have big scope to keep growing and the Premier League to stretch away from every other domestic league in earnings. Pretty much every troubling development of the last two decades stems from TV income: mega transfer fees, exorbitant player wages, increased commercialisation, kick-off times that are all over the place, higher ticket prices (to help pay for the wage/transfer inflation that TV started). Not to mention the rise of the super rich, disconnected (from the club's locality), profiteering owner - and/or owner who wants to exploit all that TV power, that global reach, for propaganda.

"Because TV's funding and hold upon the sport will continue to increase - at least for a decade until, perhaps, international rights values plateau too - there's no reason to imagine an end to the pattern of inflation, community-distancing, commerce and nefarious PR. It's clear, within Britain, we're moving towards a two-track game: the Premier League and all the other leagues/clubs, English and Scottish.

"Within the Premier League there's the 'Big Six' but another tier is emerging, that of 'establishment clubs' - those who have stayed in the top flight long enough to grow wealthy enough for relegation to become an increasingly remote prospect. Four years in the top flight is now worth at least £500m of guaranteed TV income - at that point only mismanagement is going to get you the drop.

"Logically, the constituency of 'unrelegatable perennials' - the Burnleys, Watfords, Palaces, Bournemouths - could keep increasing until there are 15, 16 of them and at that point the Premier League edges towards franchise territory.

"Of course franchise territory is where a number of the top European clubs want to be in, vis a vis the Champions League. They see turning it into a European Super League with guaranteed spots the only way to increase their own TV income to compete with the 'EPL'. In a sort of reverse Brexit scenario, however, the Europeans can only quit their home terrain if the English help them - by agreeing to this kind of Champions League revamp. And the English, the Premier League clubs, are not currently minded to - why would they, when it would only potentially harm their own cash cow?

"A prediction? The Premier League becomes the 'world league of football', like the NFL or NBA, with all other competitions subservient. Yay for Bournemouth. Not yay for romantics who rather like the different flavours of Borussia, Dortmund or Betis being strong.

"Players? Harder to relate to than they were, living different lives to the average person - yes, and increasingly so. Add in the academy system and all that sport science and, money aside, you are talking about lads entering the system at seven, eight years of age (or even younger) and being taken out of school teams, then out of school classes and finally out of normal schools. Gym work and nutrition will be shaping their physiology from early life. They'll have PR training, social media training, agents, entourages from adolescence.

"So players and 'the rest of us' are being stratified, too. Though I reckon it must be as confusing (and perhaps unwelcome) for them as it is for us - for it continues to be my experience as a football reporter, even in this lunatic era where £250,000 per week is a normalised top wage, that footballers are just people, just lads, and not necessarily 'out of touch with reality'. I actually think many would accept a game with lower wages, if someone could only show us all how to get there.

"Worst thing about modern football? The manipulation of it. By brands. By governing bodies. By media. By venture capitalists. By - biggest wrong of all - loathsome regimes or individuals to sports-wash their sins. But this will continue, even increase, the more football becomes that global television show. Release the holograms."

Jonny's deep thinking here chimes with much of my own but I think, once again, he illustrates how the future of football, footballers and everything that goes with it, while it seems to be owned by rich owners and clubs, is in fact within our control. As Jonny says, almost every reprehensible aspect of modern football comes down to one thing: money. And the money is sourced entirely through the sale of broadcast rights to digital paywall broadcasters. Turn off that tap, or elect a government that will effectively do that by 'listing' live football, and it all returns to a more familiar reality in the long term. Similarly, as people who go to games, we can use that power to force clubs to do what we want. By emptying grounds we ruin both the club and the TV product because, as I've said before, no-one is paying to watch football played to empty grounds. I know the arguments as to why this doesn't happen, but the fact remains if we do not use our consumer power to affect change, we are destined to be mere moaners and not revolutionaries.

So while I think Jonathan is on the money with how football could develop if there is no radical alteration of our attitude and economic choices towards it, and I'm sure it will be every bit the heinous dystopia he paints, I have great faith in the power of the people to exert and force change. And don't forget, we can do that at any point in time. There's no deadline we have to meet. At any point when we feel en masse, we've just had enough, we can withdraw our money and support and break the whole thing open right there and right then.

And we shouldn't think that we are alone in this, that we are outsiders barking at the moon. This next interview had to be anonymous and you'll soon see the reason why. He makes some great points and very forcefully. By 'forcefully', I mean by swearing a lot. Just thought I'd give you a heads up on that. I could've sanitised it, but I thought it was best to quote him verbatim. He has worked in various jobs, at various clubs, over the last four decades. That's as much as I can tell you. He got in touch with me when he heard via someone else that I was writing this book, because he was so disgruntled with the Premier League and how it has changed football. We talked for over two hours and I condensed our conversation into one long diatribe to try and convey the frustration and fury he felt at how the big TV money has changed the game he loves so much. Strap in.

"When someone told me you were writing this book I thought well I've got a lot to fucking say about that. Too fucking right I have. I've got plenty to say. Oh fucking yes. But obviously, I've asked you to keep me anonymous because you don't want there to be anything out there that anyone can hold against you, do you? It's a small world is football and all of what I'm about to tell you would bring me big trouble and shut a lot of doors. I'll try and explain why as we go along.

"See, the idea that the Premier League is this premium product is bullshit: total bullshit. Mind, I've said the exact opposite in public. You've got to, or it's like slagging off your boss to his face, you see what I mean? What sort of league is it when the chances of beating one of the top six are so low? It's not a proper competition any more. Yeah yeah people say Leicester did it but to me, that just proves how fucked it all is. That was a freak result. Everyone knows that. We all know there can be freak results in any walk of life and in any game, but what you want is it to not be a freak. Will they win it this year? Of course not. Not a fucking chance. And call me old fashioned but I don't think we should be getting excited by the idea of a side like them or Everton maybe aiming at sixth like it's a big thing. That's pathetic. The league should be way more competitive but it can't be now when you've got these billionaires owning clubs.

"The best league in England is the Championship. Absolutely no doubt about that. Ask anyone in football who isn't a bloody fool and they'll tell you the same. It's the most competitive football. And it still looks like football, you get me? You don't know who is going to win any game, or win the league at the start of every season. you just don't. That's how it should be. The top flight is 75 per cent dross. The great games are fucking great, yeah, but most of it is very fucking average and predictable. Well, you know that, don't you? We all do. You just have to fucking watch it. But in the business we've got to pay lip service to it, haven't we? Oooh, the Premier League is where we all want to be. Fuck off. That's what we say, but it's shit. It's all to do with money and fuck all else. That's the truth. Anyone who says different is a liar. If you want competitive, unpredictable, honest football, don't watch the Premier fucking League, watch any other league instead.

"OK, here's something that no-one will say in public about what all the money that has poured into the game has done. Some players in the top flight, especially young players, are now egotistical nightmares. Some, not all. But I bet you've talked to agents or players who say they're not. But they fucking are. It is all about money for them. It's not their fault that that's the case, I know. This is the world now. But it makes some of them absolute pricks. God help us, it would've made me the same when I was their age.

"Yeah, yeah, some of them are fine, I have to say that. Some are right good lads. They are. They handle the money well. But a load of them - dear me - they are not fucking fine at all. You can't even have a go at them or they'll run home and tell their mother, or should I say, agent. The little pissy fucking darlings. Dear me. This is usually the lads who are under 21. They're the worst. They've been brought up with this sense of entitlement for years. They think they're the dogs bollocks. Been in a top club for 10 years, some are 19 or 20 and are on 20 grand a week and they've not even played a first-team game. That can't be right. So they're not even bothered about playing first-team football, some of them. Some of them are already millionaires. And because they're kids and this is all they've known, they think it'll always be fucking like this. But at some point they'll get let go, no fucker will take them on big money and then what are they going to do? But they can't see it. The money has, in a way, ruined them because talented kids fritter it all away and just don't put the effort in to become a top player. Happens all the time. That's just one of the things the big money has done to football culture. And even some lads who work hard and make it because they're really talented, they get to the first team or get a move to a big club and after a year their form drops off. They'll have got some fashion label deal, be doing adverts for some clothing brand. They're worshipped on social media, which is often encouraged by the club by the way, John, and he gets a big head, or just gets distracted and that's why you see it time and again. Great players who just don't fulfill their potential because they get obsessed with their star status and earning even more money off the back of it.

"And what's more, what really gets my goat is a lot of players who get paid this big money are no better than some of the best League One players, really, and I'm serious about that. They're not. But the money has meant that top flight clubs rarely even look down there. It isn't sexy enough. I know that's a cliche now, but it is the truth. For some managers and especially execs there's more kudos to be got from buying a player from Belgium than from Birmingham. It's just as narrow-minded as the chippy Little Englander mentality.

There are whole armies at clubs who have huge detailed spreadsheets on every player. They have all their stats. Some of them don't even watch football, it's just a stat breakdown for them. If you say to them that there's only so much you can learn from stats, they look at you and you know they're thinking, 'What a fucking old fart we've got here'. But I'll tell you this. When you see a transfer fail badly, chances are it'll be one whose data looked good but in reality he was not right for the team, or was at least far less effective than the numbers would make you believe. Happens all the time. Now, the whole stats thing is also a product of the money. They waste it on what they think is science, do you get me? It's like the money has puffed the whole business up. But it's just fucking football. It's not quantum fucking physics. I'm not against the stats at all. But it dominates far too much. It's information but it's not knowledge. You get me?

"But here's my point - do they think no-one signed a good player before Opta and them lot existed? Before all this Moneyball bollocks, managers put together brilliant teams. Look at Bayern in the 70s, Ajax, Inter in the 80s, Forest in the late 70s, Liverpool in the 80s for god's sake. They played brilliant football that would piss all over many teams today. All done without the statistical analysis. Even Ferguson in the 90s. All of them did it the way it had always been done. They didn't have a bunch of twats looking at computers. They sent out people who could spot a player. It is all bullshit to think you can do it from statistical analysis. You can argue all day long about it but it is still bollocks. What the fuck do I care if a player has run 15 kilometres and another has done 12? What the fuck has he done? Tell me that. You can tell a lazy player by scouting them. By watching them - if you're any good you don't need the stats to tell you much. They mostly just reveal what you can already see.

"Now, the fucking stupid thing about this is I can't say this in public now. I'd never get work. I'd be thought of as a dinosaur. But look, there are just as many bad transfers now as there ever was, probably a lot more. So what has been achieved by all this Opta shite? The square root of fuck all. But the game is addicted to it. I'll give you, occasionally, it is useful, very occasionally but the past isn't always a good predictor of the future anyway. There are so many variables. Them what tell you otherwise are up their own arses. But it's the money that's done this. It was a sport but now it's something else.

"Listen, John, listen. You can see a good striker in a poor team who you know will be a better striker in a really strong side. But his numbers will be crappy because he doesn't get the service, but that doesn't make him a bad player - you get me? You can see he's got it. Now, you can't fucking tell that from any amount of statistics. You have to go and see the player a few times. You have to find out what sort of lad he is. And obviously, some clubs still do that, fair enough - so what exactly is the point of this huge industry of statistics? What's it all about? It's fucking ridiculous. Like I said, it's football, not fucking physics. But now there's so much money involved, they use that as an excuse to try and ramp up all this crap. It's because football is now a business, not a sport. But even now, I bet you anything even the top managers who get all the data from their fitness teams telling him how off peak condition a player is will sometimes overrule it and still say, 'He looks up for it to me'.

"And don't get me fucking started on fucking V A fucking R. It makes me so angry that they are fucking with football in this way. It's the same wankers to blame. The same shitheads who want everything measured and everything just so and if it isn't they think something is wrong or throw their fucking skirts over their head and whine about big money being at stake here. They're arseholes and fucking dipshits and they need a fucking good slap. [laughs] I'm sorry but it gets my blood boiling, John. They're ruining the game at the top end. You don't even fucking know if you've scored now! They have messed with the single most important moment in the game. That's unforgivable for me.

"I don't fucking care if his fucking toe was offside. Fuck off. That isn't football. Football was meant to be played to spectators in the ground not wankers watching television in high definition in slow cunting motion. And it's not my age, loads of young people fucking hate V bastard A R. It's not age, it's the sort of people they are. Them what have never been to a game in their lives are the ones bitching about this and that and wanting to get decisions right at all costs. Fuck them. They won't be happy until they've turned it into a fucking computer game and I've been replaced by software. I know all the arguments for it, most of them are to do with money. Everything is to do with money. That's where we are now.

"People get hypnotised by the new technology but there are values in football that you can't learn in any other way than watching a lot of football in real time in the stadium. You look at a lad and you know, you just know, if he's got the stones in him for the battle. I can't prove that to you with an algo-pissing-rhithm but it is true and it is as true now as it ever was. Yes the game is a bit faster and pitches better. Yes the players are more athletic and much more fit - though I could argue to the cows come home about that as well - after all John, it's football, it isn't middle-distance running. It's about skill and vision and power at the end of the day. And it is nowhere near as physical as it was - and actually, you might think I'd wish it was, that it was still full of dirty bastards, but actually I don't. I never liked seeing men get hurt. But even though it's not the violent battle it once was, you still need the stones, the guts, the balls for the fight, for the competition and no stats on earth will ever reveal that. It is about understanding a human being. You get me? But it seems like that's been outlawed by cold numbers. At a time when we are so focused on player's psychological welfare and mental health, and rightly so, by the way, football was way behind the curve on that side of things. But right when we're all about looking after their brains as well as their bones, it's fucking ironic that understanding the man and his character has been buried under a tsunami of data.

"I know you invented the Proper Football Man thing and I totally get why. I'm totally with you on it. I hate the Old Boys Club as much as anyone. The way they blow smoke up each other annoys the fuck out of me. All those chippy idiots who think they're being kept out of their jobs by foreign coaches make themselves look stupid. Fuck off abroad and coach if you can't get a job here, y'know?

"Owners or CEOs or whoever the fuck makes the decisions - you never know half the time - you sit in front of a prick in an expensive suit and he's just a puppet for some other prick in an expensive suit, who is a puppet for an even bigger prick in an even more expensive suit, who has all the money. Anyway, don't get me started on that. But the fact is, they look at you and if I say certain things in a certain way and don't use the modern jargon they use, or think I should use, even though they only use it as a substitute for actual fucking knowledge, they'll think I'm one of your PFMs who thinks a white board is fucking high tech, eating pasta is modern and I'll play old school long ball 4-4-2. Seriously. If I went for a job and said we'll play 4-4-2, these planks just think you're a neanderthal, even though plenty of the best teams around play 4-4-2. It's like a toxic brand or something to these people.

"Like if I think xG is fucking ridiculous, which actually, I don't, it's one of the more useful ideas actually, much more useful than measuring how far some poor cunt has run, or his percentage of sideways passes, but say I didn't, then I'd be judged harshly in the business basically for doubting any statistical development. It's like you'd be wearing unfashionable clothes. It's gotten out of hand. But that's all the money for you. All these people who don't understand football have come into football and started to tell us what to do. Well, fuck 'em.

"It makes me laugh that we have all these old ex-players in the media making a living out of saying that the Premier League is all top top players and it's 'The Best League In The World' and all of that. They're propagandizers - is that a word? - you know what I mean - they're just pushing the brand. Shut the fuck up, you gobshite. That's what I yell at the TV.

"I'll tell you this, John, I want nothing more than for the whole thing to get binned.[laughs] How it has become does not serve the game well and it takes the piss out of the real fans who've seen everything get a lot more fucking expensive. It used to be a game for the working class who had little money. Now it's not. The game needs money, of course it does, plenty of it, but 100 to 150 million per year to every top-flight club is mental, totally mental. No, hang on, no, it's not mental...well, it is...but more than that...it's just wrong and that was what you said to me when you first rang me. You said you thought it was wrong and that's when I twigged that we had like minds. It is fucking wrong on every level. Who does it suit? No fucker, no fucker except agents and players and all they do is buy cars, phones and shit houses. Fuck them. Football isn't that. You get me? Where is it going to end?

"The more you look at it, the more it's obvious it is the money that has fucked football. It has directly led to some of the biggest bastards coming into football, greasy agents rubbing their hands together who earn millions for doing hardly anything. All these owners who are in it for god knows what reasons. 'Sports washing' is a word now, isn't it? I've no fucking idea what it really means but I bet it's not a fucking good thing y'know, John.

"I bloody well hope your book helps break the Premier League or the model its based on or just pisses them bastards off, I really do. It needs breaking. But no-one in football will speak on the record against it because it's got us all locked into it for a living. We're all its bitches. Even if you want to get a job lower down, if you are known as vehemently anti-Premier League, you'd never get that job. Owners would think you were a weirdo. They're hypnotised by cash. That's why they're so in debt. Everything is fucked, so, so fucked - look at the Championship finances! They all owe millions. And the thing that annoys the hell out of me is this: everyone knows it. I don't know if you've talked to a lot of people in the business but anyone who has got a brain knows it's fucked. Do you know TV are paying nine million to show every game?!!! Idiots. Idiots. I mean, who signed off on that? If that doesn't show how fucking stupid the people involved in the TV game are then nothing will.

"Here's what it's like now because of the big money giving the players all the power. If the manager wants a player to do something he doesn't want to do, he just goes into a sulk and rings up his agent who then starts to agitate for a move. Happens frequently. A gaffer is saying to an absolute twat of a striker that he's got to drop back and work as a shielding midfielder when they've not got the ball, basic stuff really. But he's not having it, week after week. So eventually everyone is glad when the twat is transferred. You want rid of the sulky prick, so you lie to the acquiring club that he's a top top lad who just doesn't fit into our system.

"What galls me is that if you could've got a kid out of the 3rd tier for no money at all, he'd give you so much more and you could shape and educate him. But no, because clubs have got all this money to spend they scour the world for players to waste it on. And you know why, John? It's because if they go and buy an 18-year-old for 500 grand from, let's just say Gillingham, people at the Premier League club would think it looked bad on social media. Yeah, really!! They'd think it looked cheapo. They think it shows lack of ambition because you've not bought someone from Sporting Lisbon for 30 million. It's nothing to do with how good they are, not really. And the more stupid fans agree with them. They actually want to show off about spending money in the Premier League. It has become equated with looking successful, but look at how many players are bought for 15 to 50 million, play like crap, get dropped and the next time you hear about them is when they're on their sodding bike. And they're no better than any fucking number of kids I could go and show you right now playing further down the leagues. Some in the game will tell you all top clubs want to find players in the lower leagues, but they don't. A lot just don't. Same with Scotland. Fact is, loads of clubs barely even scout north of the border. They'll scout Belgium or Austria though. Oh yeah. If clubs didn't have all the fucking TV money to waste then they'd have to go and look at those kids and take them on and train them up. What's wrong with that as an idea? The money isn't needed. It just puts the prices of everything up. It's created this horrible short-term culture. You're in a job for 18 months at most before everyone gets sick of you. An old manager said to me recently that too many clubs have forgotten that it's the meat and potatoes keeps you alive and if you just eat sweets you'll get sick, do you get me? I thought that was a good way of saying it. They live off sweets.

"Sky is the worst thing that has happened to football. It was Sky who changed it all. OK, it wasn't perfect before, we all know that. But we've lost so much in return for the money and it's made football into something it never used to be and never should've fucking become. When I heard about this book of yours I wanted to let your readers know that a lot in the game hate the same things you hate, but we just can't say so. They just can't. I know a great bloke...you've met him as well, you said, I'd better not say what he does... but all your readers will know him. He feels just like you and me. But you'd never know it from his work.

"You don't work for a paper or a TV company, John, you work for yourself, so you are an independent voice but the football media world all pisses inside the same tent and it all relies on each other for a living. You never know when anything negative you say will come back to bite you. So we all smile and pretend it's all brilliant and everyone is great. Plenty think it's a total shitshow but pretend otherwise to make sure they keep their jobs. That's what I do. Everything I've told you today, I'd probably say the opposite if I was on TV. You've got to. You become very good at lying.

"And when it comes to owners, fuck me, it's like you're living in a circus. I'm a normal working-class man who knows what real life is like, right? I do. But when you've got a billionaire owner from god knows where in the world, they swan into the club every now and again, like they have any clue at all. Here he comes, the silly fuck. Everyone is his play things. It's pointless to pretend otherwise. He put the money in and so he owns everyone. The silly fucking prick. Time was clubs were owned by a man in the town who'd made a few bob. Fair enough. Mind, some of them were idiots and bastards by the way. But you knew where you were with them. You could have it out with them. These days if the owners are going to be at the game, everyone runs around them like silly cunts just so they feel wanted. Twat has got his money from some terrible fucking place, y'know. Exploiting people. Being a twat to everyone. Human rights shit and all that? Doesn't matter. Doesn't matter in football. Fucking Hitler would pass the fucking fit and proper person test. 'Yeah, come on in Adolf, bring fucking Rommel with you. How much have you got to spend?' Seriously.

"I think the only way any of this will change is by everyone stopping buying it on TV. That's the start to it. I know that's what you're writing about. Kill subscription TV and all the worst excesses will go. We can all earn a bloody good living playing and coaching the game we all love and we always fucking have. People love football and they always will as long as it doesn't get fucked with. Even decades ago, the best players were earning great money. I knew lads earning 40 grand a year in the early 80s and that was probably four or five times more than the typical fan. OK, fine. But now they're earning £400,000 per week when the fans are on £400. Mental.

"The silly sods that say it is like show business these days. I think they're out of their minds, me, I really do. Show business is the movies, Hollywood and all that. It isn't watching 22 men running around some grass whilst sitting on a plastic seat in the north of England, with a cold wind blowing and rain coming in off the moors. It's football. Get me? It's football. It's not Tom fucking Cruise on a zip wire in Mission Impossible. Do you know what I mean? People who say it's show business need their heads examined. They don't understand that fans go to games not to have the time of their lives, you know this John, they go to be part of something.

"It doesn't even have to be great entertainment all the time. What sort of show business is that? All this exaggeration is just to try and justify the huge wages. And don't get me started on transfer fees.

"So what do we do about it? The problem we've got now is if you're 35 or under, this is all you've known. They think those of us who are older are just old men shouting about the good old days. That's bollocks of course, but they're all hypnotised by their fucking phones and porn aren't they, so what would they even know? [laughs]

"Ultimately it is about money. The rest of it can get sorted out - who puts it on TV, what wages are paid, fees, all of that would settle down once there was no big TV money coming in. Oh, and for what it's worth, I know Amazon are doing this one-day showing all the games but that's all bollocks. If you want my opinion, right, none of them big companies will touch football long term. They can't make big money, that's why. They're huge companies them, but football clubs are not big business. They go on like they are, but they fucking aren't. What's Man United worth? They turned over about £600 million the other year. That's not big. Someone told me Facebook turned over $55 billion!! Yeah fuck you United. How do you like that? You know what I mean? You think they need football? Fuck off. Forget it. We're a piss in their ocean. Sky has been bought out last year. I reckon they're almost done. BT is fucked. No-one watches it whichever channel it's on. Them numbers you gave me proves it, but I've always thought that.

"The whole fucking thing is a con trick if you ask me. When you work in the business it all feels massive. It does. You think you're involved in the most popular thing on earth but it fucking isn't. You get me? When you come out of the bubble, you realise that. Yeah, you can get a cab in Hong Kong and the driver will say he's an Arsenal fan but millions and millions of people don't give a fuck about football.

"People in most countries are just not obsessed with the Premier League the way we're told they are. Some might be, but most still care more about their local team or their local league than watching fucking Burnley or fucking Watford or fucking Bourne-fucking-mouth. Of course they are. And that's how it should be.

"So there you have it, John. I've been in the game, one way or another, all my life. I've seen it all and I know what I'm talking about. That's not me being arrogant, it's just the truth. I don't want football to be like it was - it was fucking brutal and the violence around it was sick. But I don't like the top-flight game as it is now with average players earning more in one week than my house is worth. That's fucking stupid. Money has changed the game massively and not for the good. I think it has ruined much of the top flight game.

"I don't know if it's possible to somehow stop all the money coming into the game, but if it is - and I think chucking the subscriptions in the bin is as good a start as any I can think of - it'll get rid of some of the biggest twats and I think that can only be a good thing, me. And fair play to you for having a go at writing this book, but I've got to say, I'm a cynical old bastard and I doubt it'll make any fucking difference to anything. You should still write it, mind, but one lone voice will do nothing. Now, if you got millions on your side, that'd be totally different. Things need to change. I hope this helps you, anyway, John. And if you ever tell anyone that I said all this you do know I'll rip your fucking lungs out, don't you? Right? Good."

Well, what about that? I hope his spoken passion came across powerfully. As we talked I realised something - football had been his whole life. It wasn't just a career or a job, it is who he is. So his belief in it and his commitment to it has been total and whole, so no wonder that when people whose commitment hasn't been so profound come into the game and see it as a project or as just another job, he feels personally insulted and angered by them, as anyone would in any profession they'd invested their whole working lives in. He feels he's having that which makes him who he is taken away by bean counters and TV executives, and who can blame him for being pissed off?

And finally, to close this book, I went to Anthony Vickers, a fine, creative writer and journalist from Teesside who works for the Teesside (formerly Evening) Gazette and is the go-to man to cast the runes on the fortunes of Middlesbrough FC. As such his perspective on the daily world of football is one based in the Championship League and how in thrall to the Premier behemoth it has become.

"For Championship clubs, the Premier League is a pernicious black hole, a singularity sucking in cash, players and ambition. It sucks in talent, fans, pocket money, sponsorship, column inches, screen time, pixels and the precious oxygen of publicity, leaving a league of proud and famous second-string clubs flailing in its orbit. The juggernaut gravitational pull is dangerously distorting the once-stable financial and cultural universe of the second tier creating an existential crisis and undermining the historical integrity and structure of the national game. Ambitious clubs who aim to gatecrash the gravy train are driven to the limits of sanity - and beyond - to fuel the dream. Burning banknotes in a bid to reach escape velocity is juddering a once strong and stable chassis. Championship clubs have a collective debt of half a billion pounds. Half a billion. That's crazy.

"Most of that deficit is mounting at the top end of the table as high-risk hopefuls bid to bridge the gap to the big league. It is unsustainable. And as the financial framework judders a host of clubs are braced for pain. It is not just Bolton in trouble. And not just them up for sale. Owners are increasingly feeling the crushing pressure from above. Running a Championship club is becoming hard enough. To harbour ambition [is] a natural instinct but one with a sting.

"The explosion of TV money from new Premier League broadcast deals has largely been poured into the mink-lined pockets of players and agents. Wages and fees have soared. Average players earn eye-watering sums. There are millionaires who switch between a fleet of swanky sports cars in colours that match their trainers but who have yet to play a first-team game. There are fringe players and young hopefuls confined to early-round cup cameos who are bloated beyond belief. And these are the players that the Championship dream-chasers have traditionally tried to sign: under-used hot prospects who need pitchtime to hone their skills and seasoned pros who can still do a job. But now those go-to players capable of bridging the chasm are almost unaffordable.

"The scales have shifted decisively. Last summer Middlesbrough were deep in talks with Yannick Bolasie, a spare part and available on a loan. He was on a reported £70,000 a week package and Everton wanted it paid in full while the winger also asked for a seven-figure promotion bonus. His agent wanted a fee too. That would be the thick end of £5 million. Total income through the gate at Boro is around £7 million. That scenario is played out at every club across the Championship as the eye-watering wages filter down. And fees. There was a time when Steve Gibson could put £10 million on the table and it would fund two or three top-quality game changers. Now the same sum would barely buy a top-flight reserve left-back and cover the wages and agents' fees.

"The fundamental dynamic relationship between the top two divisions has been changed. What was once a fluid environment with teams moving between the divisions as part of a healthy life cycle has now become far more problematic. Relegation can sound a death knell. More teams struggle to adjust on the second shelf and slip down to the third than bounce back with ease. The drop is a financial toxic shock. A failed promotion push can be just as costly as debts mount up, barged teams through the FFP ceiling and face a double-or-quits dilemma, to go again and risk all on success or opt for a slash-and-burn spell of cost-cutting and retreat. It is Russian roulette. Yet at many club's fans demand clubs load the bullet and spin the barrel despite knowing the risks.

"But the Premier League Black Hole has not just distorted the political economy of the Championship. It is buckling the cultural foundations of proud and famous institutions, undermining a century of solidity. The hungry vortex is sucking in money, not just the TV cash but also advertising revenue and pocket money. There was a time when small to medium employers with an eye to their profile in the business community may have sponsored the shirt of their local team, putting in vital life-blood investment. Now they get more bang for their PR buck schmoozing would-be clients in a season-ticket three course and wine list hospitality box. Even 'the likes of' Huddersfield or Burnley or Sheffield United get to host the big six to impress suits with little interest but [with] cogs to oil.

"The Premier League is sucking in the passive support that non-sexy parochial clubs depend on. Every fledgling playground fan that pledges allegiance to one of the big boys, who buys a heartbreaking alien kit, who learns to sneer at their local side as losers and talks about a team 300 miles away as 'we' and sees football as a small-screen hobby, is one fewer thick and thin loyalist chanting 'We support our local team' in the rain, one fewer casual fan to have their latent affections ignited by a cup run or a promotion push. The Premier League is sucking in media attention, relegating the match reports of great institutions who have served their time in football history to two paragraphs below the betting adverts. It has shunted their highlights off into a digital ghetto, a blur of blink-and-you've-missed-them goals and the analysis as clipped and vague as a fortune cookie.

"A big six-centric press view everything through the prism of the lucre-bloated battle for fourth and degrade even the Premier League pack to the bit part role of cannon fodder or curio. Beyond that, the cold dark wastelands of the Championship - the most crazy, compelling competitive league in Europe - are all but ignored. Sometimes a narrative arc is fashioned into a patronising noose for a contractual obligation cup clash. Sometimes the cheerleaders for the cartel urge the elite to pillage the provinces for a rising star to be stockpiled, transfer cash thrown down brusquely with the disdain of a braying Bullingdon club bully squaring up after smashing up a bistro.

"Only rarely do the national media descend to the second tier, and then en masse when they believe a sacking is imminent, shark scribes scenting blood. The all-powerful Premier League has sucked the money, the life blood and the prestige out of the Championship. And now it is starting to pop the cultural rivets that hold it together."

Isn't that brilliant?
So good that I wish I'd asked Anthony to write this whole book!

And it all goes to prove that if you want the truth - well, you ask a Teessider, don't you?
Now, let's go and make a better world.

PART FOUR:
THE MANIFESTO

WHAT DO WE WANT?

1. End paywall TV via a collective boycott, leading to massively diminished value in rights fees, thus undermining the entire monetary basis the Premier League is predicated on.

2. Rights fees acquired by the state for the good of the nation's health and societal cohesion coupled with proper substantial long-term government investment in sport.

3. Live football to be 'listed' so it has to be broadcast free-to-air to 95 per cent of the population to prevent it ever being sold behind a paywall again.

4. All games on BBC One, ITV1 and a jointly operated specialist channel.

5. Premier League abolished as a concept to be replaced by Divisions One to Four.

6. Maximum player wage 220k per year.

7. Overall wage bills capped at the same total for every top-flight club set at the poorest club's affordability level.

8. A long-term outlawing of gambling sponsorship, and other negative partnerships and advertising.

9. Draconian policing by an independent body of non-monetary rewards to players.

10. Transfer fees and transfer windows abolished. Players and clubs have more freedom of movement via rolling contracts.

11. All staff at all clubs, contracted or employed, to be paid the Living Wage as a minimum.

12. Establishment of a Football Sovereign Wealth Fund to redistribute some of the wealth of the biggest clubs to smaller, less well-off clubs, to raise standards of facilities, training and staff remuneration throughout the leagues.

WHY DO WE WANT IT?

1. To maximise TV audience and make televised football an inclusive community experience which does not exclude anyone on economic grounds.

2. To improve public health, inspiring better, more active lifestyle choices for children and adults, thus reducing lifestyle-based illnesses such as Type 2 diabetes and ending social isolation.

3. To make top-flight football more competitive, unpredictable and sustainable by ending the financial hegemony of some clubs. More clubs will have a chance of winning something as it will be almost impossible for clubs to exercise wealth to buy success, thus encouraging success to be achieved through development and training. Coaching becomes all important.

4. To help stop escalating gambling addiction and related suicides, help people enjoy the game once again without gambling, save the public's money and encourage less destructive lifestyle choices.

5. To place footballers' wages in line with the rest of society and end the pointless and grotesque wealth of a small elite and in doing so tackling a root cause of the abuse culture.

6. To emblematically inspire an understanding that the orthodoxy of infinite consumption on a planet of finite resources, via the pursuit of enormous wealth, is unsustainable and is killing the planet.

7. To stop lower-league clubs bankrupting themselves in pursuit of the Premier League wealth.

8. To help financially support, via the Football Sovereign Wealth Fund, the whole of the football pyramid of clubs and redistribute wealth for the greater good so that facilities, training and grounds are kept in good order and ensuring a consistent supply of youth academy players to first teams.

9. By killing off the potential for financial leverage and returning the league to being unpredictable and highly competitive, it will dissuade morally dubious billionaires from buying clubs for sports washing, for soft power adventures, for money laundering, or simply to acquire a profit-generating asset for their global corporation.

10. To return fans to being the most important element in the game, not TV broadcasters, because without fans there is no game. The game is played for us, so our considerations should have primacy.